From Your Friends At **The MAILBOX®** Magazine

Big Collection
Of Teacher Tips

BOOK 1

W9-AXF-249

Editors:
Lynn Bemer Coble
Marcia Harmon

Artists:
Betty Askew
Marilynn Barr
Teresa Davidson
Carol Eldridge
Virginia Lundy

Miss Katie Shrigley

©1987 by THE EDUCATION CENTER, INC.
All rights reserved except as here noted.
ISBN# 1-56234-008-5

Manufactured in the United States
10 9 8 7 6 5 4

Big Collection Of Teacher Tips

About This Book

In this volume, we have compiled many of the best teacher-tested ideas published in *The Mailbox®* magazine. These ideas were sent to The Education Center, Inc., by elementary teachers from all over the country. We have selected ideas from two regularly featured sections of the magazine, "Our Readers Write" and "Management Tips" (now called "Lifesavers").

The Mailbox® is now available in four separate editions:
Preschool
Kindergarten
Primary (Grades 1–3)
Intermediate (Grades 4–6)

How To Use This Book

We are pleased to offer these tips again in one convenient collection. The ideas are arranged so you can refer to them quickly and choose just the idea you need to make your job easier. In each section, you'll find creative ways to teach a skill, management tips, or activities to fill in a few extra minutes. Many of the ideas may be adapted to any grade level.

You may want to look in several sections for tips to suit your needs. For example, if you are looking for a game idea for a classroom birthday party, be sure to look in both games and the birthday sections. We're sure that you'll find many new ideas in these pages to add to your teaching success!

Table of Contents

Testimonial Writing

At the beginning of school, each child writes his/her name on a piece of paper. These are put in a can. A name is picked from the can weekly. The teacher's, principal's, and aides' names can be added to allow for a person for each week of school. The class tells of positive things about the person. One by one, the students state attributes and favorites of the chosen one. The story is written on large chart paper. The entire class signs the writing, and the honored subject takes the story home after it has been displayed. The procedure not only enhances a positive self-image, but it gives the class experience in writing and expressing thoughts.

Cathy K. Schreiber
Redondo Beach, CA

Magic Numbers

As each child enters my class for the first time, he is given a "magic number." This number is used when textbooks are issued and throughout the year on permission slips, report cards, and other papers that must be returned. A quick check of papers will tell the teacher which ones are missing. It is easy to check papers, record grades, and file tests because the papers are always in order. We even play games, line up, and move to centers using magic numbers.

Arlene Johnston
Bradenton, FL

Classmate Concentration

I always take photographs of my students to break the ice on the first day of school. Later, I glue each photo on a cut-out card. I label another set of cards with student names. Students can use the cards to play a game of Classmate Concentration. I also include photos of important school personnel—principal, secretary, janitor, music teacher, etc.

LaDonna Hauser
Wilmington, NC

Back-To-School Headbands

Have students play this "get to know you" game. Students write their names on construction paper headbands or visors. Collect all headbands in a box. One child chooses a headband and puts it on without reading the name. He sits in front of the class and asks questions answerable by "yes" or "no" until he guesses his classmate's identity. It's fun for the teacher to take a turn too!

Sr. Ann Claire Rhoads
Emmitsburg, MD

Time Capsules

Use this activity to help you get acquainted with your students. Students fill in the first column of blanks on the survey the first day of school. Then seal them away in a potato chip can until it's time to "break the seal" on the last day of school. It's fun for students to see how much they have changed in one school year.

Tanya Wilder
Broken Arrow, OK

My Time Capsule

Name _____ Date _____

A time capsule is a container that holds historical records and information. This is a survey about you. Fill in the first blank of each item. You will fill in the second blank on the last day of this school year.

AGE: _____ _____
MY BEST FRIEND: _____ _____
MY FAVORITE FOOD: _____ _____
MY FAVORITE SINGER: _____ _____
MY FAVORITE COLOR: _____ _____
MY FAVORITE TV SHOW: _____ _____
MY FAVORITE GAME: _____ _____
MY FAVORITE SPORT: _____ _____
MY BEST SUBJECT IN SCHOOL: _____ _____
MY NEWEST FRIEND: _____ _____
THE THING I LIKE BEST ABOUT SCHOOL: _____ _____
THE THING I WANT MOST: _____ _____

A New Slant On Penmanship

Children sometimes have difficulty slanting their papers correctly for good penmanship. Solve this problem by taping the outline of a correctly slanted paper on the child's desktop.

Jo Farrimond
Broken Arrow, OK

Right Handed Child

Left Handed Child

Signature Tic-Tac-Toe

To help students learn names at the beginning of the year, run off copies of a blank tic-tac-toe grid containing as many boxes as you have students. Students collect signatures in the blank boxes. Then, as names are called at random, children mark their boards, trying to be the first to complete a row in any direction.

Eleanor Messner
Dalton, PA

	Billy Richardson	
Adam Vurnabee	Mary Smith	Jason Barr
	Michael Day	

Positive Apple

Start the school year with a positive approach. Cut out a large apple from construction paper for each child, and add stems and a leaf on each. Each day or two, write something positive about the child on his/her apple. At the end of September, the child takes the good apple home. This results in an eager child!

Helen Peaslee
Keene, NH

MICHELE

Beautiful Smile
Sept. 26 Good Sentence
Nice Writing
Kind to Others
Careful Worker
Good Listener

Colored Bus Tickets

BUS #6
BUS #14
BUS #498

Use a colored-ticket system to alleviate first-week fear of getting on the wrong bus. Assign each bus driver a different color, and place matching colored circles on bus doors. Pass out the correct, colored ticket to each child to give to the driver when boarding. Children soon learn to recognize their bus drivers and lose school bus jitters.

Nancy Greeley
Hopkins, MO

Gingerbread Boy Shows The Way

Use this adventure early in the year to orient students to the layout of the school building. After reading *The Gingerbread Boy*, bring out a tray of unbaked gingerbread cookies for the class to decorate. Have students take them down to the cafeteria to bake. Upon returning to the cafeteria to pick up the baked cookies, you and your students find only note #1 on the oven door. Follow the directions on that note and on the others until you wind up back in your room, where the cookies are waiting.

4
Dear Boys and Girls,
This adventure has been fun.
But back to our classroom I must run.
Come as quietly and quickly as you can.
You can't catch me,
I'm the Gingerbread Man.

3
Dear Boys and Girls,
I've gone to the office on my next caper
To get a movie, book, or paper.
Come as quietly and quickly as you can.
But you can't catch me,
I'm the Gingerbread Man.

2
Dear Boys and Girls,
Up the stairs you must look.
I've gone to the library to borrow a book.
Come as quietly and quickly as you can.
But you can't catch me,
I'm the Gingerbread Man.

1
Dear Boys and Girls,
To the nurse's office I must go.
Someone stepped upon my toe.
Come as quietly and quickly as you can.
But you can't catch me,
I'm the Gingerbread Man.

Carol Lambert
Slippery Rock, PA

Share Table

Our faculty uses a table in our teachers' lounge to display any math sheets, magazines, or art ideas teachers wish to share. We also have a "Help Yourself" table of wallpaper samples, leftover skill sheets, or anything else fellow workers might want to use.

Arlene Frost
Morgan City, LA

Getting To Know You

Have children in each reading group learn to write the name of one person in the group each week. Before long, they will know how to spell all their friends' names.

Ann Geils
Frostproof, FL

Let's Get Acquainted

To get children to learn more about each other, have them come to the front of the class or stand whenever they fit a description:

1. Kid who has a turtle
2. Kid who likes spinach
3. Kid who is left-handed
4. Kid who plays the piano
5. Kid who is on a soccer team
6. Kid who likes to draw
7. Kid who went camping this summer
8. Kid who wanted to come back to school
9. Kid who is wearing orange
10. Kid who has a younger brother

I tried this activity on the first day of school and had a lot of success. Usually more than one kid fits the description, and each gives his name when coming to the front.

Rebecca Webster Graves
Burlington, NC

Information Sheets

Give students practice in learning important information. Label manila folders and cut windows under the labels. Students insert paper and fill in each section. You might provide a laminated copy of this student information for easy checking.

Karyn Heichel
Lancaster, PA

Class Movie

At the beginning of the school year, I use the school's video recorder/player to start our own class movie. During the year, I tape different activities (book reports, parties, plays, songs). At the end of the school year, we have 2 hours of video memories to enjoy.

Helene Sparaco
Middleburg, NY

Paper Headings

Like your papers labeled just so? Make a large chart that resembles notebook paper, and label it with headings. This is a good reminder for forgetful students!

Elizabeth Cole
Annapolis, MD

O	Name	Date
	Subject	

Audio Math Problems

I make word problems more intriguing by having my husband or a friend record them on a tape recorder. Each year I invent a character who discusses his math problems on the tape with my class. (Bo was his name this year.) For example, Bo had ten problems when planning to attend Michael Jackson's concert this year. He had to calculate money for tickets, programs, T-shirts, refreshments, and new clothes.

Marlene Rubin
Blackwood, NJ

Walk To The Library

TREASURE ISLAND BY ROBERT LOUIS STEVENSON 10-27-86 JASON BARR

JESSIKA HORTON THE GHOST OF DIBBLE HOLLOW BY MAY WALLACE 10-30-86

Encourage reading by starting a trail of class footprints to the library. After each child reads a book, he puts his name, the title of the book, and the author on a cut-out footprint. I put the footprints on the walls in the hall. We try to get all the way to the library and back by the end of the year. Your class could race another class to the library. Be sure to set rules for verifying books read.

Valerie Hornbaker
Hutchinson, KS

Test Treat

Try giving students a treat during a test. I provide popcorn for each child. It soothes nervousness and makes the situation more relaxed. Pop the corn, and fill a bag for inexpensive, nutritional fun!

Sr. Ann Claire Rhoads
Emmitsburg, MD

Puzzle Message

Greet each child on the first day of school with an envelope of puzzle pieces to assemble for a sunny message from you. As they enter the room, sit down, and work the puzzle, students forget their nervousness.

Darlene Shelton
Memphis, TN

WE COME TO MY CLASS

Welcome Mat

Welcome your students back to school with a personalized mat. On top of a rectangular, foam pad, place a poster board labeled with students' names. Cover it with clear contact paper, or laminate it.

Lisa Waters
Philadelphia, PA

WELCOME

JASON EVA TERESA BETTY APRIL BRYAN DERRICK BECKY GENE JENNIFER RODNEY MIKE

Beat The Clock

For those children having trouble organizing bookbags and desks first thing in the morning, I play "Beat The Clock." The first week students have 5 minutes to get organized; the second, 4 minutes; the third, 3 minutes; the fourth, 2 minutes. Individual records are kept on index cards. Each day, I punch the cards of students who beat the clock. Awards are given on Friday. By the end of one month, my students are ready to start class on time.

Mary Anne Haffner
Waynesboro, PA

David's "Beat The Clock Card"

A Time To Bloom

During the first week of school, I have my students make a very special bulletin board. I ask the children to draw a self-portrait on a precut piece of oval paper. I supply a mirror or two for each table and get a chance to see how my students handle sharing. When all the pictures are completed, we have a guessing game as I try to match students and portraits. These pictures are then put on a board, and we read *Leo the Late Bloomer*.

Jane Cuba
Redford, MI

BETH ALBERT ALICE

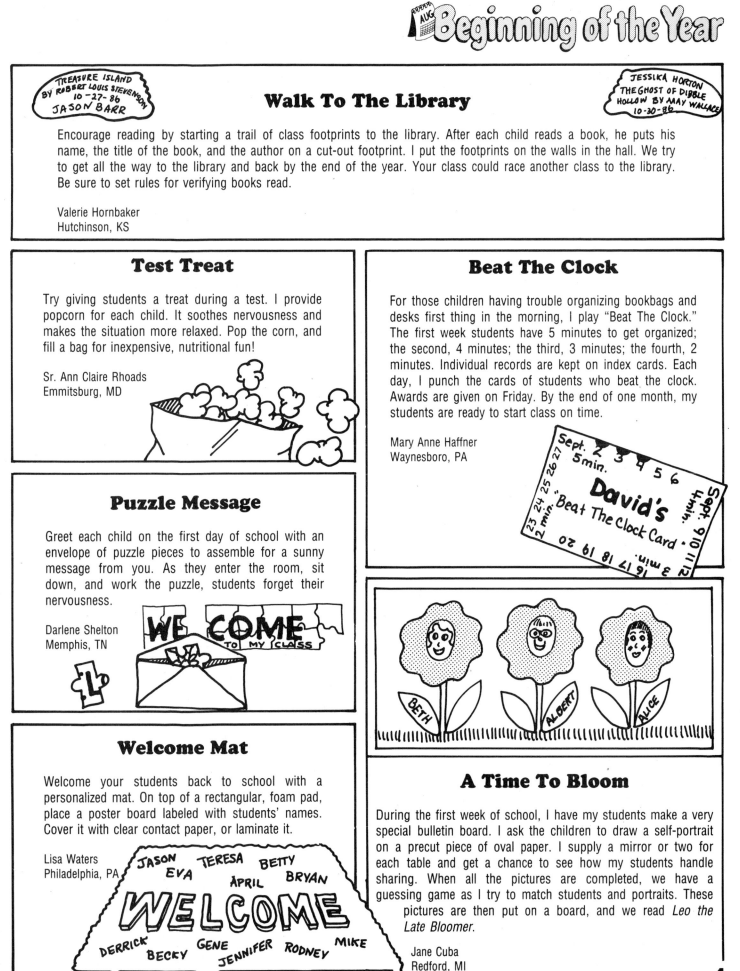

License Plate Name Tags

Make personalized license plate name tags, using a pattern duplicated on colored construction paper. Fill in appropriate information for each student to aid recognition and spelling of the school, your name, and student names, as well as the grade and year.

Shari Strode
Bowling Green, KY

Train Engines

At the beginning of the school year, make each child a paper train engine. (Ask mothers to color the train cars—they love to help!) For each page of vocabulary words correctly read, add a train car to the engine. Display the trains until the year's end, when children take them home.

Sheila Underwood
Stanford, KY

You're My Teacher

Here's a warm, inviting way for a class to feel comfortable with a new teacher. I ask students to draw a picture of me, to describe me with words, and to guess my age, favorite color, hobbies, car, etc. The children are always thrilled to discover how many of them guessed correctly.

Pat Shulman
Englewood, CO

Art Treasure Hunt

Conduct an all-year scavenger hunt to collect scrap materials for art projects. At the beginning of the year, make a list of all items needed for art, with a point value written next to each. Use team competition to encourage students to win points while adding to the stockpile of art "treasures."

Sandra Reynolds
Hixson, TN

Art Treasure Hunt
paper towel tube—5
soup can—5
bottle cap—5
coffee can—2

Fruit Salad

Sharing a meal with your class soon after school starts will help lay the groundwork for a good year. Have students bring their favorite fruits. Prepare the fruits together, mix in marshmallows, then eat. Show the children a piece of spoiled fruit, and explain that a complainer, tattler, or show-off can spoil the class, just as the bad fruit can ruin the salad. The students can then easily see how good behavior will help the class work as a team.

Diana West
Big Horn, WY

Class Time Line

One of the best ways to teach children about a time line is to make one for class events. Beginning with the first day of school, record events on adding machine tape. For convenience, roll up as the tape is used. Unroll and enjoy on the last day of school!

Rebecca Graves
Burlington, NC

Scratch-'N'-Sniff

Use a new sensation to teach the alphabet! Write letters with glue on paper, then sprinkle with Jell-O. Makes a super scratch-'n' sniff.

Jo Farrimond
Broken Arrow, OK

Spelling Trip

Use this classroom idea all year to practice rounding numbers to ten and to motivate good spelling. String a clothesline across the room, attaching clothespin markers at equal intervals. Each clothespin designates a ten-mile distance. After a spelling test, have the class round the number of A's to the nearest ten. (Keep track in your record book of the total number of A's.) Attach a cardboard car to the correct ten-mile clothespin marker. After the next spelling test, add the actual number of A's to last week's total, then round to the nearest ten. Move the car to the new ten-mile marker. When the car has traveled 100 miles, treat the entire class to popcorn. The following week, start a new car, bus, or truck across the string. See how many vehicles are parked at the 100-mile marker by the end of the year!

Elaine Trexler
Coopersburg, PA

Name Tag Puzzle

To break the ice on the first day of school, make a name tag puzzle for each child. On a piece of poster board, 3" x 6" or larger, write a child's name with a broad-tipped marker. You may also add other decorations to the card— flowers, kites, balloons, etc. Laminate the card. With scissors, cut the card into several pieces, depending on the level of your students. Keep the puzzle in an envelope with the child's name on it. On the first day of school, put each envelope on the desk where you want the child to sit. As the children come in, they can amuse themselves by working their own puzzles. Later you can let them trade and work each others' puzzles. Ultimately, they can be taken home.

Barbara Dixon
Loveland, OH

Handwriting Paper

At the beginning of the school year, my first graders often can't tell the top of the paper from the bottom. I cut out a border of black and white characters and paste them in a line that will fit at the top of our handwriting paper. I make a ditto master of the border and run a ream of paper at a time. I change the border with the season. No more upside-down papers—and children love it!

Roberta Brankman
Hoosick Falls, NY

Pronunciation Keys

Instead of posting a large dictionary pronunciation key in your room this year, provide students with their own individual pronunciation "keys." Label small cut-out keys with pronunciation symbols and key words. Place each set of keys on a key ring or tie together with a piece of yarn. Give each student his own set of keys to help him pronounce words he looks up in the dictionary.

Janet Sheppard
Paragon, IN

Hide The Alarm Clock

Play "Hide The Alarm Clock" to help children realize the importance of listening, their sense of hearing, and sitting quietly. After one student leaves the room, hide a ticking clock or cooking timer. The child returns, listens, and tries to find the clock before the bell rings. All others remain still with occasional hints of "warm," "hot," or "cold."

Missy Ruggles
Minerva, OH

Meet Your Classmates

Here is a proven way to learn a bit about your students and their writing abilities. At the beginning of the school year, I have every student in my fifth-grade language arts classes make a page for a booklet called "Meet Your Classmates." The students are instructed to write at least a short paragraph that tells me something about themselves, their families, their hobbies, their likes, etc. I have them include either a drawing or a design to decorate the page. Plain white paper is good to use for this activity. The pages are put into a laminated, construction paper booklet that is placed in my reading corner to be enjoyed by the students whenever they have spare moments to read!

Kathy M. Peterson
Alpha, IL

Personal Dictionaries

I list and alphabetize all the reading words my first-grade students will encounter during the year. Then I type stencils for the letters of the alphabet and include the vocabulary words on them. From these, I make individual dictionaries for the children. When a new word is introduced, the children must find it in their dictionaries and circle it. They are learning dictionary skills as well as the rules of alphabetizing.

Kathy Duxbury
Rapid City, SD

Dudley, Dog Detective

Let Dudley, Dog Detective, introduce school workers and new school areas to your students. Make a puppet and flannel-board characters who "investigate" workers and make daily reports to the class. This is super for lower-grade students who need to become familiar with their school.

Barbara Blackburn
Boiling Springs, NC

Suggestion Apples

Give each student an "apple sheet" the first day of school. Let them write a letter to you suggesting projects, discipline, seating arrangements, and any ideas that might make the year interesting. Then use the letters to help plan the year!

Kathy Leggett
Pascagoula, MS

Dear Teacher,

Dear Teacher,
I would like to take a field trip to the zoo and to the mint. I would like to sit close to the board so I can see.
Yours truly,
Ginny

Roll Call

Avoid the monotony of checking classroom attendance, and make it a learning experience at the same time. Instead of answering "here" or "present," have students answer with their birthdate, address, or phone number. Be sure and have the information handy to help children with their answers. This adds a little variety, and it's an excellent way for children to review important information.

Linda Tankersley
San Antonio, TX

Reflections

Early in the year, I challenge my students to think about their goals and what they hope to accomplish during the year. We discuss the meanings of *reflect* and *reflection*. Children decorate paper-doll books to resemble themselves and write their reflections inside. Reflection books are mounted on a foil-covered board.

Sheila Baird
Stone Mountain, GA

School Bus Recognition

Cut out school bus shapes from yellow posterboard and laminate. With a nonpermanent marker, write the bus number and riders on each. Line up buses above the chalkboard. At the end of the school year, wipe off and be ready to start fresh the next September!

Jane Smith
New Haven, NY

Weird Portraits

To practice following oral directions, have students place a pencil, point down, in the center of a scrap piece of paper. Instruct them to close their eyes and keep them closed while they draw as you give the following directions:

Draw a circle.
Put eyes in it.
Put ears on it.
Add a mouth.
Add eyebrows.
Draw a nose.
Add hair.

Those children who followed the directions will have less-than-perfect results, while those who peeked will have drawn everything in the right place.

Sharon Gullett
Tyler, TX

Freckles Frog

This class mascot encourages children to learn to write their names! Cut double frog pieces from green material. Stitch around, leaving an opening. Add a red tongue and large wiggle eyes. When a child learns to write his name, he writes it on Freckles with a marker. Let children stuff the frog, and sew him up. The helper for the day keeps the mascot at his or her desk.

Retha Mancil
Ozark, AL

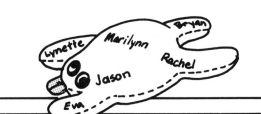

Initial It!

To record students' independent reading, have each child make an initial key ring out of poster board. Laminate for durability. Run off copies of keys on heavy paper and label with titles of books read. The children love tying new keys onto their key rings with string.

Sue Miller
Eagleville, PA

Weekly Student Schedule Sheet

Help your students get organized by giving them a weekly schedule sheet. Fill in all group and independent work, leaving space for students to add in any extra assignments. Students check off each job as it is completed. I give them a new message and picture each week.

Bonnie Pinkerton
Bowling Green, KY

Pencil Holder

Team up with Velcro tape to end the constant ping of pencils dropping. Attach a piece of Velcro to each desk, and wrap another around a pencil for each child.

Paula Noga
Ayer, MA

Fire Drill Class Lists

When the fire drill alarm rings, I am unwilling to take valuable time to locate my attendance book to carry with me. However, I need an accurate list of my class so I can take attendance and be sure no one is overlooked. At the beginning of the school year, I make class lists of all classes that meet in my room. I mark them Fire Drill Class Lists and tape them to my doorway. When the fire alarm rings, I take them down and carry them along.

Peggy Neubauer
Parma, OH

Party Committees

At the first of the year, I determine the number of parties we'll have, usually Halloween, Christmas, and Valentine's Day. Students write their names on paper slips and place them in a bowl. I draw the names out, assigning the first ⅓ to the Halloween committee, the next ⅓ to Christmas, and the last ⅓ to Valentine's Day. Children on each committee are responsible for planning the party, games, refreshments, etc.

Barbara Ihnen
Silver Lake, IN

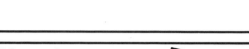

Parent Newsletter

Many parents ask, "How can I help my child learn at home?" To answer this question, compile and duplicate a monthly newsletter full of easy-to-do learning activities that can be worked at home.

Connie Connely
Catoosa, OK

Adopt A Tree

The first week of school, let students pick a tree to watch throughout the year. As a seasonal art project, draw sketches that can be kept until the end of the year. These will serve as a record of the tree's changes. In science, study the plant and animal life around it. In language, use it as an inspiration for poetry writing. By the year's end, the children will really feel like the tree is theirs.

Roberta Miller
Lombard, IL

L Is For Left

"Lefty" is a great aid for teaching youngsters to work left to right. Draw a left-hand outline (placing the thumb at a 45° angle), and add facial features. Children place Lefty on the left side of their papers so they'll know where to start and in which direction to work. If placed on the wrong side, Lefty can't see!

L. E. Putnam
Miami, FL

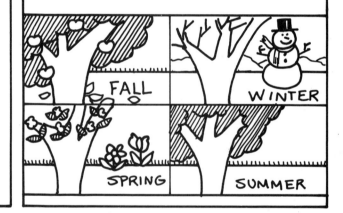

Teacher's Pet

At the beginning of the year, assign each student a week to be teacher's pet. For that week, put his desk beside the teacher, and place a Teacher's Pet sign on it. Various duties can be chosen for this student. The teacher avoids picking favorites and gets to know students better by sitting next to each one.

Rita Peat
Elkhart, IN

Partner Reading

Each week, my students enjoy reading to each other. On Thursday, I introduce a story to my reading groups, and they read it silently. I assign each student a partner. On Friday, we all go outside, find comfortable spots, and take turns reading a page to our partners. If a student has a problem pronouncing words, his partner helps out. At the end of each page, the listener asks the reader questions about what he has read. Partners give each other praise and develop better attitudes toward their own reading.

Caroline Carter
Leesburg, FL

Permanent Name Tags

For name tags that will last all year, I use name tags made of contact paper in a children's design. I put these on the front of desks so substitutes and visitors can easily call everyone by name.

Fran Petersen
N. Tonawanda, NJ

Get Acquainted Curtains

Make simple curtains for your classroom, and let each student draw on them with crayons (iron the wax out later), permanent markers, or fabric markers. This activity helps students get acquainted with their new surroundings and promotes a sense of classroom pride.

Cynthia Galloway
Conway, SC

First Day Blues Cure

To start the year off with a bang, cut out a strip of paper for each student, and on it write a stunt. Blow up balloons, placing a strip in each one. Students choose a balloon, pop it, and perform the stunt for a real icebreaker!

Judy Brisbine
Wessington, SD

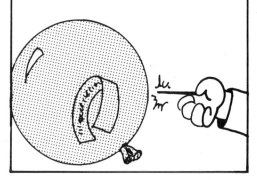

House Address Match

To help students learn visual discrimination as well as their addresses, have them draw their homes and match the pictures to correctly addressed envelopes. Pictures can be placed on a pegboard divider, where students hang the envelopes, or they can be used as a floor matching game since there will be as many houses as students.

Barbara McCool
Beaver Dam, KY

Welcome Puzzle

Help your students learn their classmates' names with this word search puzzle. Draw a large numeral to represent the grade and inside it list all students' names, hidden among other letters. Keeps the students working while you're busy with first-day paperwork.

Grace Conway
Hillside, NJ

Back-To-School Stands

On the first day of school, get acquainted by playing Take a Stand. Ask the class a question. Students stand whenever the question applies to them. Helps you and your students get to know each other better.

Sample Questions:
Do you play the guitar?
Are you wearing red shoes?
Do you like pizza?
Can you program a computer?

Rebecca Webster Graves
Burlington, NC

G A M E S & LEARNING ACTIVITIES

Dare To Care

Involve your students in current social issues and motivate writing at the same time! Pick an issue (whales, seals, polluted rivers, etc.) and request information by writing letters to the state or federal government or "action" groups. The kids will get tons of pictures, pamphlets, and postcards and will feel like they're really helping the world. It's a wonderful feeling to know that hard work and caring may have made a difference. Most of all, students learn to exercise their freedom of speech. Even lower grade children can draw pictures and have their teacher record their thoughts.

Diane West
Big Horn, WY

Practical Averages

An excellent way to teach averaging is to let students keep daily records of their own grades and average them weekly. Students can also learn to round off fractions to the nearest number or to add fractions in columns before dividing. This practical experience helps children develop responsibility and an awareness of their individual progress.

Rebecca Graves
Burlington, NC

Banking And Business

This project helped our students become aware of the services a bank provides the community.

Introduction:
1. Bring a tied quilt to school and display it.
2. Talk about the materials needed to make the quilt.
3. Discuss the cost of the materials.
4. Ask where money could be obtained.
5. Tell students you are going to make a quilt in school.
6. Discuss the bank and the services it gives to the community.

Mrs. Rada Hutchinson
Story City, IA

Activities:
1. Take a field trip to the bank and tour the facilities.
2. Borrow enough money to purchase the materials needed.
3. Go to the store and purchase the materials.
4. Put the quilt together and tie it with yarn in school.
5. Display it at the bank and sell it by sealed bid, or sell chances on it if permitted in your community.
6. Go back to the bank, pay off the loan, and deposit the profit into a savings account.
7. Later in the year, use the money for a special project for the whole school or for the purchase of school equipment.

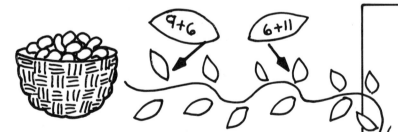

Jack And The Beanstalk

Children who climb this beanstalk will be rewarded with golden praise. Tape large, laminated paper leaves to the floor in a beanstalk pattern. Write a problem on each leaf. Children must give the correct answer to step on a leaf. Those who climb to the top get paper eggs labeled with words of praise or jelly beans from the goose's nest.

Cathie Weaver
Springfield, GA

Balance Beams

Create balance beams by using masking tape on the floor. Place the tape in the shape of squares, rectangles, or circles. Children follow the lines as they would on a balance beam. This activity takes up no extra space, and the tape can be easily removed after the exercise.

Pauline Wallace
Bayville, NJ

Tic-Tac-Toe

I made a giant tic-tac-toe game by using an old rug and 2″-wide masking tape. The tape wears well and can be removed when soiled. Large, colorful **X** and **O** cards are perfect for the children to use when reviewing computation skills. The children must say the answer to a flash card correctly before they can put a card down.

Glenda Robinson
Augusta, GA

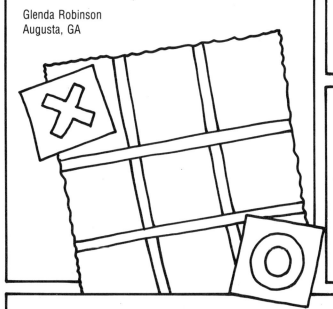

House Address

Duplicate a house shape and label each shape with a child's name and address for a learning tool. For a letter-writing unit, children can trade houses to write to friends in the class. At the end of the year, children may take their address houses home. I always write each one a little good-bye note on the back.

Claudia Wilcox
Vernon, CT

Number Concept Chains

To reinforce number concepts, place a number at the end of a paper strip. Let the student use a hole puncher to punch that number of holes on the strip. After the student completes strips for all numbers, allow him to link them together forming a chain.

Connie Connely
Catoosa, OK

Got A Minute?

I like to teach students to do math problems without paper. I tell them a number, then follow with directions to add, multiply, divide, or subtract other numbers from the first one. All work is done in their heads. Example: Start with 7, add 2, divide by 3, and subtract 3; the answer is . . . 0.

Susan Risius
Bagley, IA

Wanted: A New Teacher

I ask children to write an advertisement for a new teacher. They include everything they've ever wanted in a teacher in terms of physical appearance, conduct, and attitude toward homework. It really gets kids writing!

Kym Byrd
Wyoming, MI

Hidden Spelling Words

Have each student make a word search with the week's spelling list on one-inch graph paper. Children may write words horizontally, vertically, or diagonally. After their papers are checked for accuracy, they fill in the empty squares with extra letters. Staple a copy of the list to each word search. Exchange for a class word find. When all words are found, reward the class.

Paige Grabau
Marshall, MN

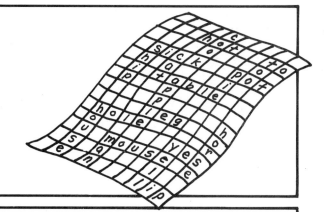

Understanding Tens And Ones

Children often have difficulty understanding how sets of ten can be converted back to ones. A foolproof method is to put ten Cheerios on a pipe cleaner for each set of ten. Children can hold each pipe cleaner, seeing it as one unit or one ten. Then they can take the cereal off and count each one individually.

Barbara Hosek
Canoga Park, CA

"TROYOPOLY"

I use a game in math called Troyopoly. It is set up like Monopoly except I have changed all the property to the names of streets in our town. I use it for work in subtraction, addition, and money. By giving a different job to each student—bankers, deed people, players—I am able to involve all my students each time we play. The game is large enough so that the students are able to walk around the gameboard and become completely involved.

William J. O'Connell
Troy, NH

Cursive Practice

Bring in a bottle of ink and a few feather pens. Give a few instructions on the proper handling of a feather pen and have your students take turns practicing cursive writing. A fun incentive!

Brenda McGee
Burlington, NC

Yes And No Cards

When children finish a reading lesson, I have them take out their yes and no cards. I ask questions about the material read, and children hold up either "yes" or "no" to show the correct answer. Each child gets involved rather than waiting to be called on. I also use vowel cards for drill on long and short vowels.

Nancy Simmons
Whittier, CA

Crazy Libs

I use a "Mad Libs" book for vocabulary word practice. I prepare word cards, labeling them noun, verb, adjective, or adverb on the backs. Cards are placed in piles on the table. I read until reaching a blank, and tell what part of speech is needed. Students take turns drawing cards from appropriate piles and read the words. Most often the reading turns out to be hilarious. We thoroughly enjoy it.

Carol Gillespie
Chambersburg, PA

Calling all cars... calling all cars! Be on the lookout for a ___(noun)___. He is wearing a ___(adjective)___ suit, a gray ___(noun)___, and is carrying a ___(noun)___.

Council Meeting

Pattern your classroom after a city government for an exercise in politics. This is particularly effective following a social studies unit on government. First discuss the role of the mayor and of the city council in making laws and ordinances for the city. Then elect a mayor and council members. Once a month, have the mayor call the class to a meeting and begin the session with his gavel. Class members submit written problems, and the council acts on them following a discussion of each one. The council votes to approve laws and ordinances to meet class needs. You may want to follow up with a second election to get more students involved.

Claudia Nisbett
Greenville, MS

Fun With Sequencing

My fifth graders were losing interest in sequencing activities because the stories and phrases were not interesting. I make sequencing more exciting by writing nursery rhymes and jokes out of order. Students then number the phrases in order or rewrite them correctly.

Rebecca Graves
Burlington, NC

Math Of Old

While studying colonization in American history, blend math with social studies by making up word problems using information about the period.

Rebecca Graves
Burlington, NC

Examples: 20 colonial students are celebrating the last day of school. Elizabeth is making spoon bread. Each pan holds enough to serve 10. How many pans does she need so each child will have 2 servings?

Place Value Jackets

After discussing safety precautions concerning plastic bags, my third graders have fun in math class wearing tall kitchen garbage bags as jackets. A slit is made at the top so the bag can be slipped over the student's head. Each bag has a digit, 0-9, written on the front with magic marker. Two sets of jackets make possible a greater variety of number combinations for studying place value.

I call a number, and students wearing jackets must arrange themselves in the proper order. They may also rearrange their order to form the smallest or largest number possible with those digits. Alphabet jackets have great potential for teaching alphabetical order too.

Donna Lea
Fisher, IL

Checkbook Magic

Create classroom checkbooks for student practice in addition and subtraction. Give each student the same amount in his account, and pay bonus dollars for accurate and prompt homework, books read, or good behavior. Students add these deposits to their accounts in anticipation of shopping day. Price objects around the room for sale. Students make a shopping list, write out a check for the total, and balance their checkbooks. Exchange bank statements to check calculations.

Paula K. Holdren
Louisville, KY

Find Out Fast

On Monday, I place five questions on the board. They vary, including topics like "How is cheese made?", "Who is __?" (someone in the news, sports, etc.), "How long do turtles live?", and any questions I can create. Some are hard, some easy, and some silly. On Friday morning, students turn in their answers. Sources for answers *must* be given, with only one allowed from "my folks or a neighbor." The rest must come from a book, news report, magazine, etc. Whoever gets the most correct in a month helps me do the questions for the coming month. If there's a tie, we all work together. Both the kids and I learn new things. They've even found answers to questions I couldn't answer, like "How many pennies are minted per minute?"

Diana West
Big Horn, WY

Plastic Bread Tags

Durable, colorful game pieces can be made from plastic tags found in supermarket produce sections or on bread bags. They can be cut in interesting geometric shapes. The edges of the pieces can be smoothed with an emery board or sandpaper. These are ideal for The Education Center's Pocket Pals and other gameboards.

Jean Youngsteadt
Springfield, MO

Backward Spelling Bee

Hold a spelling bee in which children spell each word called out backward. It's fun and challenging, because kids have to think as they learn to visualize each word.

Rebecca Webster Graves
Burlington, NC

Group Happigrams

For an activity which offers a change of pace and produces a worthwhile product, let your students work together to write group "happigrams." Brainstorm with students about the good qualities of a chosen classmate, allowing only positive comments. When the session is over, the entire happigram can be written out or tape recorded for writing down at a later time. Children will be especially excited about taking home happigrams written by their fellow classmates!

Carolyn Wilhelm
Maple Grove, MN

To: Bobby
From: The Class

Bobby is fun to be around. He likes to laugh. He always shares.

Stump The Teacher!

Play "Stump the Teacher!" Students read an assignment in the text and supplementary materials, then prepare questions to stump the teacher. The teacher cannot refer to the text during the game. Each student, in turn, asks the teacher a question. If he/she stumps the teacher, he receives a reward of the teacher's choice, such as a sticker. This is a fun way to cover basic science and social studies information.

Melissa Noonkester
Blacksburg, VA

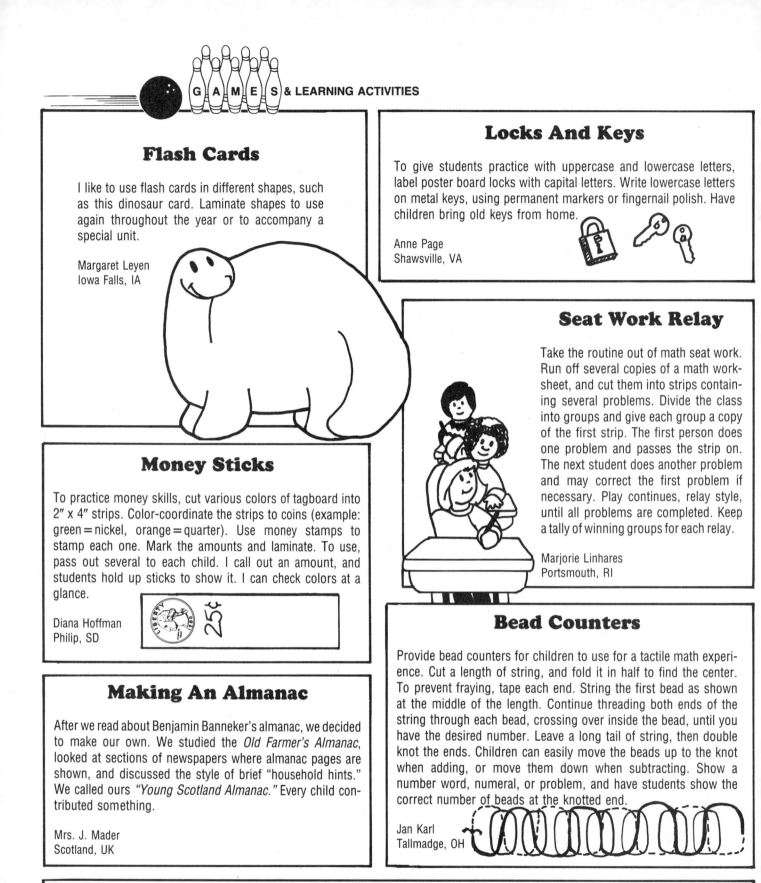

Flash Cards

I like to use flash cards in different shapes, such as this dinosaur card. Laminate shapes to use again throughout the year or to accompany a special unit.

Margaret Leyen
Iowa Falls, IA

Locks And Keys

To give students practice with uppercase and lowercase letters, label poster board locks with capital letters. Write lowercase letters on metal keys, using permanent markers or fingernail polish. Have children bring old keys from home.

Anne Page
Shawsville, VA

Money Sticks

To practice money skills, cut various colors of tagboard into 2″ x 4″ strips. Color-coordinate the strips to coins (example: green = nickel, orange = quarter). Use money stamps to stamp each one. Mark the amounts and laminate. To use, pass out several to each child. I call out an amount, and students hold up sticks to show it. I can check colors at a glance.

Diana Hoffman
Philip, SD

Seat Work Relay

Take the routine out of math seat work. Run off several copies of a math worksheet, and cut them into strips containing several problems. Divide the class into groups and give each group a copy of the first strip. The first person does one problem and passes the strip on. The next student does another problem and may correct the first problem if necessary. Play continues, relay style, until all problems are completed. Keep a tally of winning groups for each relay.

Marjorie Linhares
Portsmouth, RI

Bead Counters

Provide bead counters for children to use for a tactile math experience. Cut a length of string, and fold it in half to find the center. To prevent fraying, tape each end. String the first bead as shown at the middle of the length. Continue threading both ends of the string through each bead, crossing over inside the bead, until you have the desired number. Leave a long tail of string, then double knot the ends. Children can easily move the beads up to the knot when adding, or move them down when subtracting. Show a number word, numeral, or problem, and have students show the correct number of beads at the knotted end.

Jan Karl
Tallmadge, OH

Making An Almanac

After we read about Benjamin Banneker's almanac, we decided to make our own. We studied the *Old Farmer's Almanac*, looked at sections of newspapers where almanac pages are shown, and discussed the style of brief "household hints." We called ours *"Young Scotland Almanac."* Every child contributed something.

Mrs. J. Mader
Scotland, UK

Domino Or Dice Addition

Let children create their own addition problems with dominoes or dice. Each student turns a domino faceup, counts the dots on each half, and records the two numbers to make an addition problem. For dice addition, each student rolls two dice and counts the dots on each to make a problem. Use a worksheet with empty boxes to help them write the problems.

Sue Krul
Aliquippa, PA

Creative Writing

When working on a newspaper unit, the students enjoy writing their own comic strips. We cut out the comic strips from several Sunday papers and white out the captions using white correction fluid.

The students write their own creative captions to the comics, and the finished products are shared with the class. The result can be very humorous, and this is one activity everyone wants to participate in.

Tanya Wilder
Broken Arrow, OK

Tune In To Phonics

Students love to have you read to them. Why not make this a fun phonics drill at the same time? Choose a good book. Then choose a vowel sound, consonant sound, or consonant blend for which students listen. After reading one or two pages, ask students for words they heard with the chosen sound. Another approach is to say words from pages you read and ask for the sound.

Terry Clem
New Albany, IN

State Flashes

Flash cards can help students learn the states quickly. I duplicate outlines, code the backs, then laminate and cut them apart. The cards will hold up through a great deal of practice.

Teresa Starnes
Raleigh, NC

Math Super Stars

Use interclass competition to spark interest in math practice. Our second grade teachers give their classes a weekly math quiz. Students with all correct answers have laminated stars with their names put on a bulletin board. Each class has its own color, so students can tell at a glance which class is the weekly winner.

Marjorie S. Martin
Elyria, OH

Egg-Cup Concentration

The game of Concentration takes on a new look with cups cut from egg cartons. Number them inside, and place cups upside down. Students try to find different number combinations.

Karen Billings
Atlanta, GA

Word For The Day

To help increase vocabulary painlessly, introduce each day a new word that the children are not likely to know or use. Write the word on the board, with its definition and a sample sentence. Have children say the word in their own sentences. Children retain a surprising amount and have fun using their new vocabulary words when speaking to each other.

Linda Rabinowitz
Atlanta, GA

"Car 54..?"

Use old license plates, newsprint, and crayons to practice number recognition. Have children put newsprint over a license plate and rub over it with a crayon. Students say each number as it "magically" appears, then remove the plate and complete the outline of the number.

Lynn Klomfar
Gulfport, FL

Printing Practice

To help my youngsters learn to print, I write their names, numbers, letters, etc. on tagboard strips, then cover each with clear acetate. Each child gets his own name strip and a plastic mark crayon to use in practicing. The crayons wipe off clean, ready to use again and again.

Joan Holesko
North Tonawanda, NY

Exercising Your Spelling Words

Combine spelling practice with an exercise session. Have your children spell their words in movement, using their various body parts. New words are practiced, and both the teacher and the student get a good workout!

Mary Dinneen
Bristol, CT

Versatile Place Mats

Plastic place mats can help children learn colors, shapes, and body parts. Cut out shapes, such as circles, triangles, and rectangles in a variety of colors. Pass out shapes for a game in which children must listen and follow directions such as "Put a red triangle on your head," or "Put your elbow on a green circle." Place mat shapes are very durable. Try a variation of the Twister game.

Debra Thorne
Gate, OK

Going Fishing

For sight word drill, my students go fishing. Make two fishing poles with a magnet at the end of each line. Label sets of construction paper fish with words color-coded as to difficulty. Attach a paper clip to each fish. Children fish in a fish pond formed by a ring of blue bulletin board border. They catch words and keep those they can say, throwing back any that are too difficult. At the end of an allotted time, students sort their fish by color and are awarded points for each level of difficulty. The winner has the biggest catch of points!

Valerie Hornbaker
Hutchinson, KS

Number Simon Says

Simon Says gets a new twist with a numbered headband for each child. Simon directs commands to certain numbers: "Simon says #17 stand; all odd numbers raise your hands; all prime numbers put fingers on noses."

Lynn Klomfar
Gulfport, FL

Stove Pads

Activities backed with magnetic tape from The Education Center will adhere to an inexpensive stove mat or pad. These can replace traditional flannelboard activities for practice in letter or number recognition and matching activities. The stove pad can also be used as a small write-on/wipe-off surface at a center. Provide different colors and sizes.

Denise Cox
Greenville, NC

Tactile Number Sticks

To make visual and tactile math aids, color white glue with food coloring and place glue drops on Popsicle sticks or tongue depressors. Children can see and touch the dots as they count.

Connie Connely
Catoosa, OK

Timed Gameboard Competition

To extend the use of gameboards from *The Mailbox*, try this variation. Place a gameboard which is already programmed with problems or questions in front of two to three students. On your signal, each player writes down the answers to the problems as quickly as possible. The first player to finish says, "Stop." Players then check their work with an answer key. The student with the most correct answers wins. The competition appeals to students and helps them prepare for other timed tests.

Susan Layne
Bedford, VA

Newspaper Graphs

Use newspapers to help students bone up on graph reading. Make a black-line copy of a graph from a current newspaper. Use it to make copies for your students and a thermofax for the overhead projector.

Ruby Pesek
Lake Jackson, TX

Sock Sorters

Looking for an economical source of playing pieces for your games? Sock sorters make great game markers. They are inexpensive and come in a variety of colors per box.
Bonnie Jo Kyles
Ennis, MT

License Plate Game

To improve visual memory, play this game with license plates made from cardboard. The children pretend to be policemen and write down the plate numbers of lawbreakers. Flash each license plate for a few seconds as the students write down the numbers. Progress from simple 2- and 3-digit numbers to combinations of numbers and letters.

Lynn Klomfar
Gulfport, FL

Sentence Contest

Add a new twist to penmanship practice with a sentence contest. Challenge students to write sentences that contain every letter of the alphabet. Award prizes in several categories: most humorous, longest, shortest, most syllables, least syllables. Not only will the students enjoy handwriting for a change, but you'll have a supply of sentences to file for future practice sessions.

Mary Anne Haffner
Waynesboro, PA

Wally Zebra very carefully did a quick jog with six merry partners.

Common Tools

A fun science unit enjoyed by my third graders involves the study of common tools. Have students bring old tools from home, or ask a hardware store or building supply house to loan you some tools. Students learn the names and uses of common tools and gain practical knowledge which can carry over to their adult lives.

Linda Zahm
Huntington, IN

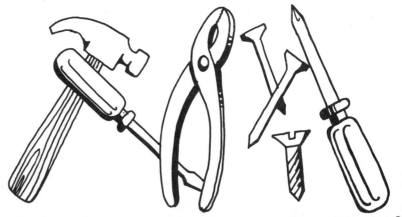

Poker Chips

I've found large-sized poker chips useful in teaching children the alphabet. Stick adhesive letters on the chips, or use Scotch Magic Transparent Tape to stick on the letters. Store the chips and answer key in a plastic butter container. Students place the letters in ABC order.

Reye Olsen
Winchester, KY

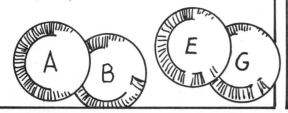

Common American Expressions

We often use expressions which describe people and events and things. These expressions often combine and use words in unusual ways. Try to picture these common expressions. Then discuss the meaning of the expression. (No specific answer key is given as there will be a wide variety of pictures and comments.)

He's in the doghouse.
You're behaving like a fish out of water.
Erik is a big frog in a little pond.
She thinks she's hot stuff.
He's all steamed up.
I'm sitting on pins and needles.
I'm all thumbs.
Kate spilled the beans.
Keep it under your hat.

Lois F. Roets
Madison, WI

Bounce The Ball

I write 10 words (or letters or numbers) on cards in red and the same 10 words in green. Each child hangs a card around his neck or pins it on a shirt where it is visible to everyone. All the reds get in line, while the greens form a line parallel to them about 5 feet away.

Each child has a turn to bounce a ball to his word partner in the other line. To make the game last longer, we then bounce the ball to someone whose word begins with the same letter or has the same number of letters, etc.

I vary this game from just matching letters or numbers to matching uppercase and lowercase letters, words, or easy math problems with answers. This is a greaty rainy day game!

Lynn Klomfar
Gulfport, FL

Plant Activity

For a plant unit activity, place carrot tops in a saucer of water and watch them grow. Students will eagerly check the carrots' daily growth, and it brightens the room in the dead of winter.

Jill Robbins
Ogden, IL

State Flash Cards

To make flash cards of states or foreign countries, run off copies of maps. Mount them on cardboard, and shade in a different state or country on each map. Answers can be written on the back, and cards can be laminated to make them more durable. Children love to test one another on these.

Barbara Clore
Clemmons, NC

Learning To Use Resource Materials

Divide the class into groups to research questions on a fact-finding page. Take questions from resource books including the dictionary, *Guinness Book of World Records*, atlas, almanac, and encyclopedia. Have all groups begin work at the same time. The first group to get all answers correct earns a special privilege.

Marilyn Sparks
Drumright, OK

Letter Puppets

Drill letter recognition using cardboard tissue tubes. Cut out letters from old greeting cards, and glue them on tubes to make letter puppets. Small fingers will fit right inside the tube.

Connie Connely
Catoosa, OK

Musical Alphabet

The sound of music may be just the trick for learning the alphabet. Tape a popular record while saying the alphabet to the beat. Your kids will love this method of memorizing and will learn the alphabet in no time. Great for rote counting, too!

Toni Johnson
Warren, AR

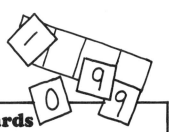

Place Value Cards

Have children make sets of number cards to reinforce the concept of place value. Each child needs four 1½″ x 1½″ cards for each numeral, zero through nine. Provide strips that measure 3″ x 1½″, 4½″ x 1½″, and 6″ x 1½″, and divide them into 1½″ squares. Students place their number cards on the digit squares to show place value, expand numbers, and practice regrouping.

Sheila Barid
Atlanta, GA

Mail Order Math

Start saving mail order catalogs now for lots of math practice later in the year. Give each student a catalog, making sure the original order form is enclosed. Students choose 3-5 items to purchase, then fill out the order form. Be sure each student includes the total cost, postage and handling, tax, and final total of the order. They then exchange catalogs to check each other's orders.

Jan Hicks
Sewickley, PA

Quiet Spelling

Team up to practice weekly spelling words. Let students choose a partner and silently pronounce, then write a word for their partner. The partner watches carefully and checks the students' spelling.

Kathy Leggett
Pascagoula, MS

Barter Day

To introduce a money unit, we have a barter day during math time. Several days before, we ask students to bring in items they no longer want or need to use for bartering. On the designated day, students put items in a circle on the floor and stand behind theirs. At a signal, they walk 2 times around the outside of the circle and return to their items. Then they barter. Set a time limit, or continue until all items are traded. The first time, some students may not bring an item to trade, but they won't want to be left out again. You may want to have a tape recorder or camera handy.

Pat B. Redgrave
Loughman, FL

Teach A Word

For vocabulary development, let each child pick a new word and teach it to the class. Encourage students to be creative. For example, if a child chooses the word "lavender," she might wear a lavender dress, pass a lavender sachet around for the class to smell, and write the word on the board with lavender chalk.

Isobel Livingstone
Rahway, NJ

Sponge Dice

Instead of using regular dice in your learning games, cut cubes out of sponges and label the sides with numbers or dots. Not only are sponge dice cheaper—they're quieter too!

Diane McGuckin
Kankakee, IL

A Visit To The Zoo

Cut shapes of animals found in a zoo from colored paper. The children then write stories about the zoo on the cut-out shape itself. When the stories are completed, they can be placed as a mural or as a border around the classroom. Additional ideas might include:

A Trip to the Airport
A Day at Santa Land

K. Sherman
Rochester, NY

Lollipop Letters

Make lollipops by gluing cardboard circles to tongue depressors. Label each lollipop with a letter of the alphabet written in uppercase and lowercase. Place these in a colorful container and pass them around the room. Each child picks a lollipop and is responsible for naming the letter and thinking of an object that begins (or ends) with that sound.

Joan Holesko
N. Tonawanda, NY

Mitten Find

Use a mitten to find the answer in the palm of your hand. Have each child trace and cut around a mitten pattern, then cut out a hole in the center. Laminating the mittens creates clear plastic windows. Duplicate number or sound grids. Say a word or math problem. Children place their mitten on the grid so that the answer shows in the hole.

Connie Harper
Parishville, NY

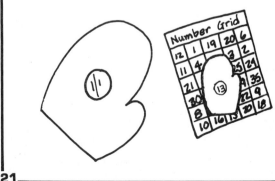

What Day Is It?

To help us learn our days of the week, I have small, stuffed animals with the names for the days of the week printed on them. In the morning when we discuss the day, date, weather, temperature, etc., the children take turns finding the correct animal. We put it on display for the day. This activity helps in learning the names for the days of the week, and we have fun learning them.

Joan Holesko
N. Tonawanda, NY

Take A Step

We play this game outside on our patio, but it could be played indoors too. I mark a chalk starting line and a finish line about 20 feet away. I put two or three sets of small cards (numbered 1–10) in an old hat.

The children line up on the starting line, and the first child picks a card from the hat. He reads the number aloud and takes that many steps forward. Then I pass the hat to the next child, and he does the same. We keep taking turns until someone reaches the finish.

Lynn Klomfar
Gulfport, FL

Stop And Go Cards

Add variety to an oral reading lesson by providing *stop* and *go* cards for your reading group. Cut out paper cards, or use a deck of blank game cards. Write the word *stop* on a few, and write *go* on the rest. When it's a child's turn to read, he draws a card and either reads or skips a turn according to the card.

Sara McCormick Davis
Oklahoma City, OK

The Learning Train

The children sit one behind the other and pretend to be on a train. Each child has a card with a number, letter, or word written on it. One child is the conductor and gets to wear a special hat.

The conductor walks down the row asking each child for his ticket. Each one shows the conductor his card, and if the conductor can read it, he goes on down the line. If he misses, he changes places with that child, and the new child becomes the conductor.

Lynn Klomfar
Gulfport, FL

Number Fun

I stick gummed circles on the back of each child's hand. Then I let the child choose a number from 1-10 to write on the circle. When everyone has their numbers, I say, "Everyone with a four hop to the door like frogs." "All sevens walk to the sink like Frankenstein." Continue to give directions until each one has a turn.

Lynn Klomfar
Gulfport, FL

The Human Alphabet Train

Kindergartners have fun lining up in an "alphabet train" which reinforces alphabetical order and upper/lowercase letters. As each child enters the room, I put a capital letter on his right hand and the matching lowercase letter on his left hand. All students take their seats. Later, I ask child *Aa* to stand, find child *Bb* and take his hand. Children continue, holding hands to form an alphabet train with their bodies.

Jane Martin
Savannah, TN

Tens By Toes

To reinforce basic numeration skills, borrow some popular phrases from a surfer's vocabulary. Using posterboard, make ten sets of surfers' feet "hanging ten" or "hanging five." Use these to help illustrate counting by fives and tens.

L.E. Putnam
Miami, FL

Paint With Water

Dip a paintbrush in water and paint a letter on the chalkboard. Have children think of words that begin with that letter. See how many words the class can name before the letter dries.

Isobel L. Livingstone
Rahway, NJ

Sorting Trays

Ask your local grocer or produce manager for the Styrofoam or pressed-paper dividers used when shipping apples in cases. Number each cup or indentation to use for sorting activities:
- Cut apart numerals from old calendars and have students sort them into the correct "dents."
- Have children count beans into the tray.
- Provide number words to match numerals.

Sue Guenther
Waterloo, IA

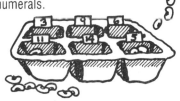

Culture Fair

To celebrate America's ethnic heritage, my fifth graders organized a culture fair. Booths made from refrigerator boxes were decorated with a country's flag, agricultural and industrial products, words from the native language, and other important information. After booths were completed, each student chose a booth to research further. Student teams studied the country's culture and presented their information to the class on culture day. Specially prepared dishes were also served. As a follow-up, students contacted older relatives to explore their family heritage.

Kathy Beard
Keystone Heights, FL

Punctuation Please!

Make a set of posterboard capital letters and punctuation marks. Attach a small piece of magnetic tape to the back of each letter and mark. Write several uncapitalized and unpunctuated sentences on the blackboard. Call on students to put the posterboard letters and marks in their proper places.

Marianne Armstrong
Urbana, IL

Cheerio Bingo

Here's a perfect way to solve a shortage of bingo chips. Use Cheerios instead of chips! When a student wins, everyone gets to eat the Cheerios on their boards.

Kathy Sopczneski
Bristol, CT

Spelling Box

A box full of spelling flash cards provides practice in types of sentences, writing skills, and oral reading, while keeping a running review of spelling words. Each day a child reaches into the box and pulls out two spelling flash cards. Students write one word in a statement and the other in a question on their papers. Then children read their sentences aloud and ask each other what punctuation mark should be used.

Connie Harper
Parishville, NY

Little Reminders

This masking tape reminder works better than a string tied to your finger. Write a number, phonics sound, letter, or word on a piece of masking tape, and adhere it to a child's hand. When teachers, parents, or classmates ask what is on his hand, the child answers. This provides frequent reinforcement and is a source of pride for new learning. Use the same technique to remind yourself of duties or appointments in a teacher's busy day.

Rhonda Thurman-Rice
Tulsa, OK

Sheet Gameboard

Try using an old sheet for an easy-to-store gameboard. Use permanent markers, and it will even be washable. Sheet games are especially good for flipping chips or tossing beanbags.

Sr. Annette Fiala
Waterloo, IA

Take A Chance

Save rejected duplicator sheets and extra activity sheets in a bag to play "Take A Chance." Each student pulls out a sheet without looking. If the paper is blank, he can draw, write, or cut it up. If half an activity is printed, he does the work, then whatever he wants on the other half. If he has already done the activity, he may return it for another "chance." It's a clever way to make use of school leftovers while getting in some review.

Beccy Baldwin
Hopkins, MO

Seat Work By Students

Seat work can take on a whole new dimension if students design their own papers. Even first graders can make up a simple math paper and illustrate it for interest. Filling in the blanks and matching activities are also possibilities.

My rules include: work must be neat, answers must be correct, the activity must be worthwhile, and paper must be put to good use (not two or three lines on one page).

If a paper is accepted, I transfer it to a ditto master. Older students could do this for themselves.

Reward: the student who authors the worksheet has the privilege of checking everyone's paper. This is very popular with younger students.

Fran Petersen
N. Tonawanda, NY

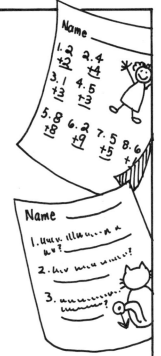

Sponge Letters

Use letters cut from sponges to "toss and call," "feel and name," and to print with paint on paper or with water on the chalkboard. Best of all, sponge letters are quiet!

Donna Rankin
Panama City, FL

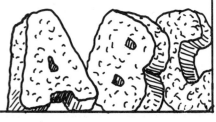

Independent Worksheets

To give your independent reading worksheets a personal touch, write stories with your students as the main characters. Include current vocabulary words and comprehension activities. Silly stories receive the most enthusiastic response.

Connie Connely
Tulsa, OK

Contraction Cards

Help your students visualize the contraction process. Write the words making up a contraction on a small card. Label a small flap with an apostrophe, and tape it to the card so that the apostrophe covers the contracted letter(s).

Mary Hood
Shevlin, MN

Good News

Tired of all the bad news, I wanted some good news! Now we have a weekly news report, sharing good news gathered by a class hot on the media's trail. We share reports that show how people care. If the heroes are local, we send cards thanking them for brightening our world.

Diane West
Big Horn, WY

Ping-Pong Math

Here's a way we sharpen our number skills and eye-hand coordination. I've gotten quite a few of those old-fashioned, paper egg trays. I fastened two together with yarn, so there is a top and a bottom that opens like a book.

I numbered each egg pocket (1-36) and each of the Ping-Pong balls (1-4). The children toss the balls into the egg pockets and add the number of the ball to the number of the pocket.

Early in the year, I use blank balls and the children must just identify the number of the egg pocket. I store the balls in the carton and use a yarn string to keep it closed.

Lynn Klomfar
Gulfport, FL

Super Heroes Knockdown

On sheets of construction paper, I draw the super heroes and laminate them. I glue each one onto a Pringles potato chip can and write a number on it.

The children set them up in a row and throw yarn pom-poms at them. At the beginning of the year, we just count how many cans were knocked down. Later on we add the numbers on the cans knocked over to see who gets the highest score.

Usually I make eight cans and put them in an eight-pack soft drink carrier with the pom-poms stored inside the cans.

Lynn Klomfar
Gulfport, FL

Red Light, Green Light

Try a new way to get your students to remember capital letters and punctuation by using green and red crayons or markers. Periodically when writing sentences, have students use a green crayon for capital letters and a red one for punctuation marks. This will help to make the students more aware of correct capitalization and punctuation.

Marie Schermetzler
Springfield, VA

Traveling Exhibits

On rolling carts, have students create exhibits to move from class to class for viewing. This gives kids an opportunity to organize an exhibit, show off their work, and possibly talk in front of a class. Exhibits could include your city or county, a country, plants grown in class, types of insects, or math in everyday life.

Rebecca Webster Graves
Burlington, NC

Helpers' Names

Liven up a mundane list of classroom helpers' titles with these. If you don't provide definitions, your students can get in some dictionary use also.

    plants—horticulturist
    aquarium—marine biologist
    hamsters, etc.—zoologist
    messenger—courier
    lunch money—financial assistant
    paper passer—distributor
    hall monitor—special investigator

You may want to tie in career awareness activities using these titles.

Debbie Leonard
Georgetown, KY

"Hot Rocks"

Playing "Hot Rocks" helps students learn their color words. Make an assortment of rock shapes out of tan or gray poster board, and write a color word on each with black ink. Laminate to prolong their usage. Place the rocks on the floor. The children take turns stepping from rock to rock, reading each color word correctly to avoid burning their feet because of errors. When the game is over, wipe off the rocks and put them away for another day.

Joan Holesko
N. Tonawanda, NY

Taste And See

Enlist the help of parents in your study of other cultures. In advance, send home a note asking parents if they would like to make a loaf of special bread or cookies that are eaten in a particular country.

The teacher then schedules the treats to come in on particular days. Before the date, the teacher locates the country on the globe or map and introduces the country. Language arts is also included when a thank you note is written to the parent.

While using this idea, we learned map study, foods of other countries, and appreciation of other people.

Isabel B. Rand
Hightstown, NJ

Story Day

Once a week, let students help you write a special story. Brainstorm together to come up with title, beginning, and ending. Then students dictate story events and details to you. Let each author sign the original, and provide duplicates for all. Students read to the class and draw pictures of the main idea to get more practice with new words, sequencing, sentence structure, and sharing.

Barbara Penn
Niles, MI

Tuning Fine Motor Skills

Place transparencies on the overhead projector. Have your students trace designs, shapes, and pictures on large sheets of newsprint. This activity is motivating, as well as beneficial in developing eye-hand coordination.

Nancy Scroggins
Bunker Hill, IL

Upset The Shoe Box!

Do your students have trouble grasping scientific classification? Use this simple activity as an illustration. Break the class into small groups, and ask each member to remove a shoe and place it in the middle of their circle. Group members then make a list of all possible ways of categorizing the shoes: left shoes, right shoes, tennis shoes, sandals, boots, etc. Discuss group lists with the entire class, and watch the light dawn.

Susan Servatius
Kenosha, WI

Multiplication Key Chain

Let students carry their own set of multiplication keys. Write the numbers 1 to 10 on a cut-out key labeled with a times table. Punch a hole beside each number, and write the answer on the back beside the hole. Students poke a pencil through the hole, say the fact, then turn the key over to check. Make a key for each table, and hold keys together with a plastic tie or small key chain.

Lisa Walker
Chocowinity, NC

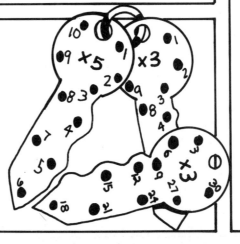

Time Buddy Booklets

Once my students have learned the basic concepts of time to the quarter hour, I have them make time booklets for buddies. Each child interviews a classmate and records the digital times for his friend's daily activities. Then he draws hands on a clock face to show the analog time on each page. Buddies love hearing about their days and taking their booklets home.

Lynne Kasparian
Bedford, NH

Autobiographies

To prepare for writing student autobiographies, have each child make a time line of his or her life. This helps to organize thoughts and put events in the right order before writing.

Bethany J. Porter
Flint, MI

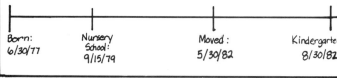

| Born: 6/30/77 | Nursery School: 9/15/79 | Moved: 5/30/82 | Kindergarten 8/30/82 |

Sentence Practice

To make spelling sentences more fun, I choose three students each day to make up a sentence using one of their spelling words. After sharing their sentence with me, the students dictate the sentence to the rest of the class for a quick practice session.

Melinda Smith
Owasso, OK

Oral Reading Game

To vary oral reading and improve listening skills in my class, I have one child read a paragraph or several sentences aloud. He may stop reading at any time and call "popcorn" and another student's name. That student then has to start reading where the first child left off. The children enjoy paying careful attention in order to play this game.

Julie Hagedorn
Sioux Falls, SD

Handwriting Practice

Get children involved in writing practice to liven up the class. Give each child a piece of paper. Call on one student to choose a letter to practice. Everyone writes a row of that letter. Continue to call on students one at a time to choose letters. Make sure everyone has a turn, because they look forward to participating.

Mary Jo Morrissey
Batavia, NY

Math Word Problems

Spark student interest in word problems by having each child compose his own problem. Rewrite problems on a ditto, or laminate them onto a file folder. Include the author's name. Students are excited to see their problems in print.

Diane Vogel
Chamblee, GA

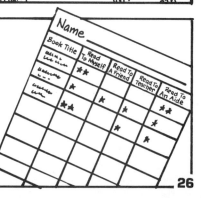

Julie had 3 Cabbage Patch dolls. Her mother bought her two more. How many does she have now? ☐
Written by:

Repeated Reading

I have children select books from a list of short paperbacks. They read the same books several times in different ways to different people. Each child records books as shown. He receives stars for books read, with a maximum of four stars per title. This improves fluency and self-confidence.

Anna Mae Kiatskie
Sunbury, PA

Games With Labels

Save those colorful and boldly lettered labels from canned goods to use in making reading games. Cut to uniform size and mount on cards. Collect identical pairs for Concentration and Go Fish games. Use to reinforce visual discrimination and memory, as well as reading skills.

Sylvia McFeaters
Slippery Rock, PA

Counting People

For a quick math lesson, first thing in the morning, I string a length of twine across the room with cut-out figures on it. When I call the roll, one student moves either a pink or blue figure for each child present. After roll call, we can count boys, girls, and the total class, and then we decide if more boys than girls are present or absent, etc.

Beverly Goodman
Silsbee, TX

Cookbook Adventure

Turn students' favorite recipes into a class cookbook. Expand into a real business venture by selling it to other teachers and friends. Students learn various aspects of business through the assembling, selling, and record keeping of the books. After the hard work, treat yourselves to lunch with the profits!

Barrie Faison
Seattle, WA

Daily Paragraph Writing

After working on topic sentences in paragraphs, I have each student write a topic sentence of his own on a piece of paper which I collect. Each day, I choose one topic sentence that becomes our topic sentence for the paragraph of the day. The child whose topic sentence is chosen doesn't have to write the paragraph on that day only. This creates enthusiasm as children eagerly await the selection of their own sentence and enjoy writing on subjects chosen by their peers. For added fun, read some paragraphs aloud the next day!

Jill McCormack Rutter
Tucson, AZ

The door to the spooky house was open.

Creative Writing

My class wrote some of the most imaginative stories of the year on a day that I was absent! I told them ahead of time where I was going, and asked them to imagine what would happen if I suddenly disappeared. The creative writing assignment made an easy-to-manage activity for the substitute and resulted in stories fun for us to read and share!

Gretchen Neilson
Marion, IN

Count A Meal

Make counting to 100 a fun experience! Duplicate a worksheet with an empty meal tray and menu for each child. Children build a burger meal by gluing a piece to their tray when they master counting to a certain number (see the menu). Duplicate the meal pieces and have children help with cutting them out.

Jackie Schultz
Great Bend, KS

Menu	
Tray	10
Bottom Bun	20
Hamburger	30
Cheese	40
Pickles	50
Top Bun	60
Fries	70
Pop	80
Straw	90
Prize	100

Nancy Smith

Odometer Place Value

To teach place value to hundred thousands, I help children visualize large numbers by having them imagine an odometer on a car. We talk about a new car on a lot that could have 000,001 on the odometer, compared to a one-year-old car which might have 015,798 miles. Then we imagine a very old car with 112,465 miles on it. Each time, we say the complete number aloud.

Mary Bonifay
Wetumpka, AL

Classroom Marble Game

Your students will assume more responsibility for homework with this game. Divide the class into two groups. Every day each group earns a marble if everyone in the group brings in all of their homework. The group that reaches twenty marbles first earns an award chosen by the teacher. Students remind each other about homework and rarely forget it.

Darlene Shelton
Memphis, TN

Calendar

When changing the monthly calendar in my Special Education classroom, I involve my children in a minilesson that can be adapted to benefit all. I ask them, for example, to remove two numbers with a sum of five, take down all even numbers, or remove a letter from their names. Do the reverse while children put up the new calendar for you.

Caroljean Kacho
Leesburg, VA

Alphabet Soup

Children will think this activity is "m-m-m-m good" for practicing alphabetical order. Ask students to bring in labels from soup cans and place them in ABC order.

Elizabeth Cole
Annapolis, MD

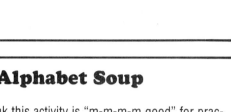

Colonial Correspondence

When working on a unit on the American Revolution, have students assume the identities of famous people and correspond with one another concerning the problems of the day. Add to the fun by using the language of the times and writing on onionskin paper with quills or fountain pens. Here are some examples:

- George Washington writes to Robert Morris concerning the lack of supplies at Valley Forge. Mr. Morris replies.

- Abigail Adams writes to her friend Martha Washington concerning what the ladies of Boston are doing to promote the cause of the Revolution. Martha responds.

Mary Anne Haffner
Waynesboro, PA

Japanese Kimonos

To help children get a real feeling for the Japanese culture, let them design their own kimonos. Purchase (or seek donations for) disposable surgical gowns from a local hospital supply company. Provide one kimono (gown) for each student. Students add their own Japanese design to the garments. Sashes can be made of fabric remnants, scarves, rope, etc. To culminate the study of Japan, children wear their kimonos at a Japanese tea party.

Jo Farrimond
Broken Arrow, OK

Easy Poke And Peeks

Cut out picture rows from old workbooks, and glue them to poster board. Punch a hole under each picture and stamp or draw a smiley face on the back over the correct answer holes. Good for rhyming, visual discrimination, etc.

Elaine Belscher
Spring Hill, FL

Coloring Book Sound Review

Coloring books make great tools for reviewing initial and final consonants. Give each child a sheet from a coloring book, with instructions to color things which begin with *s* red, things which begin with *m* blue, etc. Be sure there are several items on a sheet rather than just one large figure.

Isabel Moon
Englewood, FL

Class Response Strips

Cut card stock or poster board into 2″ x 8″ strips, then fasten 5 strips together at one end with a brad. Write vowels on one side of the strips, and number them 1-5 on the backs. To use in lessons for auditory training, children hold up the letters for the vowel sounds they hear. They can also show the numbers for syllables heard. Numbers can also be used in response to addition and subtraction problems. Sometimes print shops will donate old card stock, which makes this a quick and economical teaching aid.

Fran Cress
Jacksonville, NC

"Secret"

"Secret" is a favorite reading group game of my students. On the blackboard, I list some of their reading vocabulary words. One child secretly chooses a word and whispers it to me. He calls on other children to take turns guessing the word. They must come up, point to a word, and read it. The correct guesser gets to have the next secret. Once the students are familiar with the game, they take turns being the "teacher" who listens to the words.

Nancy Johnson
Greensboro, NC

Class Newspaper

After students have discussed recent community, national, or world events, produce a newspaper. Appoint a staff which includes an editor, a business manager, artists, and reporters. The production can help children understand different writing styles, while learning how to work together.

C. Heltler
Brooklyn, NY

What's The Order?

Use a card system for a change of pace in choosing student reading order. Label cards with students' names. Also include cards with directions such as: person on your left reads, skip 2 cards, read again, choose a boy, teacher's turn, free choice, etc. After each child reads, he picks up a card to determine the next reader.

Jeane Cowin
Elmore, MN

Times Tables Tapes

Pick up the beat in math drill with these "awesome" multiplication tapes. Choose a popular song on the radio that has acceptable lyrics. Then use it as a background as you record yourself saying the times tables facts to the rhythm of the song. Go through the times tables once in order, followed by reciting facts with pauses before the answers. You can say one times table about 5 times before the end of the song. Challenge students to say, think, or write the answers before they hear them.

Kathy Beard
Keystone Heights, FL

Beat The Teacher

An exciting way to review multiplication facts is to play Beat the Teacher. Duplicate practice sheets for a timed contest. (Work the problems once yourself to set a time.) Then students who beat your time with 100% accuracy win "I Beat the Teacher" buttons and a certificate. You might expand the contest to see who can beat the principal!

Charlene Wroblewski
South Bend, IN

Handwriting Game

Add excitement to handwriting practice for young students. After students do a practice row of one letter, tell them to write six more of the same letter in their best handwriting as you think of a "magic" number from one to six. When all are finished, say the magic number, and students circle that letter. For instance, if the letter is *d* and the magic number is *3*, students would circle the third *d* in the row. Check the circled letters. If "letter-perfect," the child gets a point. Count points at the end of the session.

Sr. Annette Fiala
Denver, CO

Using Quotation Marks

I use newspaper comic strips to help teach quotation marks. Students read a comic strip and discuss the use of "balloons" to indicate speech. They also discuss the action, setting, and characters' emotions. Students then use this information to write the comic as a story, placing the characters' words in quotation marks and adding tag words, such as "Dennis replied." This activity gives practice in using quotation marks, writing paragraphs, descriptive writing, and narration, and it is more fun than correcting sentences on a worksheet.

Karen Spunaugle
Tulsa, OK

Matching With Stickers

For an attractive, fine motor/visual discrimination activity, purchase a package containing multiple sticker designs. Place matching stickers in two columns on a piece of construction paper. Trim to fit inside a Zip-Loc bag, or laminate. Students draw lines to match pictures with a wipe-off pencil.

Denise Cox
Greenville, NC

Vocabulary Tickets

Children save vocabulary tickets in order to go to a center, earn free time, or go to recess. Have each student dictate a word or words that begin with the sound of the day. Write them on small flash cards for him. To earn a reward, the student must remember not only the beginning sound but also the word on the ticket. To extend, have each child use his word in a sentence.

Diane Denison
Columbia, PA

Word Problem Practice

Using illustrations and prices from sale fliers, my students work in pairs to make up word problems. I have students write five problems, one for each basic operation, plus a two-step problem. They also make an answer key. Students exchange papers, solve classmates' problems, and give their work to the writers to check. Children receive one grade for writing and one for problem solving.

Jane Theoharides
Lincoln, ME

Math Drill

I make holders from a piece of construction paper (8½" x 11"). I fold this in half and staple the sides. Then on white construction paper (4" x 7") I write all our numerals from 0 to 10, one numeral per sheet. These are put inside the holder, and each child gets one.

When we play our math games, each child places his cards on his desk. I will give an equation or sentence problem, and students choose the correct numeral to hold up. This gives each child a chance to participate and makes it fun too.

I save the sets from year to year to use with each class until it's necessary to make new ones.

Joan Holesko
North Tonawanda, NY

Fraction Cookies

This recipe requires only a hot plate, and it's a great way to wind up a unit on improper fractions. (Or, adapt this concept to your favorite classroom cooking recipe.)

Mrs. Tyler's Fraction Cookies

$\frac{4}{2}$ c. sugar
$\frac{2}{4}$ c. milk
$\frac{3}{3}$ stick margarine
$\frac{4}{8}$ c. cocoa

Bring ingredients to a boil in a saucepan. Cool slightly. Add ½ c. peanut butter, and 2¾ c. oatmeal. Drop on waxed paper. Makes 1¼ dozen cookies.

Kathi Tyler
Lawton, OK

Spelling Bingo

I give students a blank bingo card for a fun activity to take the place of the traditional spelling pretest. As I read each word, students write it in a space of their choice. After giving all the words, I call words randomly until someone calls, "Bingo!" The winner must say and correctly spell the words that gave him the win. Then everyone checks words as in a regular pretest.

Ginger Hutzell
Hagerstown, MD

Word Rings

To teach the children to recognize a few sight words, I let the child dictate to me the word he wants to learn to read. I write it on a 3″ x 5″ card as the child spells it for me. Then I punch a hole in it and put it on a shower curtain hook. I add a new word any time the child wishes, but he must be able to read the existing words.

We often end up with rather colorful words, such as hulk, motorcycle, superman, cookie, muppet—words that are appealing to the child.

Sometimes we get together in a small group and each child picks one or two words from his ring, makes up a story, and dictates it to me. The child then illustrates the story. These pages are put in a folder to resemble a book. It's surprising how many of the children learn to read their books.

Lynn Klomfar
Gulfport, FL

Graph Study

To help my students understand how to read, make, and interpret graphs, I have them each draw a graph using information on their favorite pets, rock stars, or television shows. Afterwards, each student writes questions about his graph. The class members then exchange papers and try to answer the questions, based on the graph's information. What a challenge!

Patricia Shulman
Aurora, CO

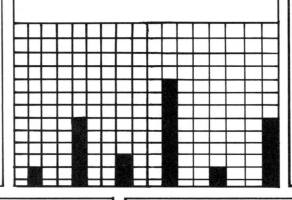

Chain Gang

I get strips of paper 8″ or 9″ long and use them to help my remedial students learn their basic multiplication facts.

We make flash cards on the strips, using crayons or markers. When the student learns his 7 table, for example, he says them. If he gets them all correct, I let him make a chain with the strips.

After all the tables are learned, the chains are really long, and the kids love seeing how they grow. We have a string hung across a corner and use clothespins to hold the chains on.

Mary Northrup
La Grange, TX

Convenient Flash Cards

Make money-saving flash cards out of white paper plates. Program the front of each plate with a skill question, and put the answer on the back. For easy storage and identification, stack all plates in one set together and cut a small wedge. Use a rubber band to keep the set together. After using the plates for a few years, make a new set for yourself, and place the old set on the activity shelf.

Karen Stockstill
Sidney, OH

shapes

number words

numbers

letters

Silhouette Theater

Here's a way to combine your overhead projector with creative writing. Have students write a short story with one or two characters and a setting. They then draw the setting on waxed paper with a black crayon and place it on the overhead projector. Students can cut out shapes of their characters to glue on Popsicle sticks and share their stories in a silhouette production by moving characters above the setting.

Bonnie Pinkerton
Bowling Green, KY

Autograph Book

To encourage my first graders to master the proper letter formation, I construct a classroom autograph book. When they have mastered the manuscript alphabet, they can sign and date the book. We autograph the book again at the end of the year and note our progress.

As an extra incentive, I construct smaller paper booklets for the children to use to collect their classmates' signatures.

Bonnie A. Keating
N. Attleboro, MA

Save Those Boxes!

When you order posters or other large materials from The Education Center, use their large cardboard mailing boxes for various classroom activities:

(1) Cover the box with colorful, self-sticking paper. Attach activities with T-pins to use as a learning center. The box will stand up.
(2) Cut holes in the box, number each hole and use the box as a beanbag toss for math. Students keep a total of how many points they have scored. Students can move closer to the display and toss two beanbags, multiplying the two numbers.
(3) Stand the box on a table or counter, pin some drawing paper to it, and use it as an art easel.

Cora Young
Charleston, WV

Mystery Math

Build some suspense into your daily math worksheets by having each sheet become part of a large mystery character. On the first day, problems might be arranged on a tail shape, the second day on a hat, etc. When students have completed all sheets in a series, they cut out the shapes and glue them together to discover the mystery character.

Laurie King
Wellington, OH

Radio Program

Use a real microphone to add a little zip to oral reading sessions. Label a paper disc with a radio station name, and attach it to the mike. Students play the part of a disc jockey as they hold the mike and read weekly news stories.

Darlene Eddy
Union City, PA

Presidents And Pollsters

To give practice in letter writing, and to promote interest in American history, my students conducted a survey of leading U.S. citizens to find out the most popular president in our country's history.

A cover letter explaining the project, a questionnaire, and a self-addressed stamped envelope were mailed to more than 100 people. More than half of them responded. The survey included three questions, with additional space for comments:

1. Which president do you think contributed the most to the history of our country?
2. What important actions of this man cause him to be your favorite?
3. What characteristics of this man made him a good president?

Current addresses of public figures were located in *Who's Who in America*.

Sandra Steen
Corinth, MS

Lunch Money

Why not put money word problems to a real-life test? After studying and practicing estimating and money, see if your class can go through a mock cafeteria and stay within their limit. My class had a limit of $2.50 each. The children had to choose a nutritious lunch. If you have real confidence in them, take them to a nearby cafeteria, and let them try their wings. In two classes, I have only had one child go over the limit. Not bad in my book!

Brenda McGee
Burlington, NC

Five Senses

To conclude a unit on the five senses, bring your popcorn popper to school. The hot air popper or one which shows the popcorn being popped will be best. As the popcorn is being popped, the children can use their five senses:

    sight: see the popcorn pop
    hearing: hear the popcorn pop
    smell: smell the popcorn
    taste: taste the popcorn
    touch: touch the popcorn as they eat it

This makes a great review lesson for the five senses, and the students love it.

Lucille L. Williamson
El Paso, TX

Model Community

As a culminating activity for work on maps and the community, I have students submit original maps for a model community. We select the best one to construct. We use various sizes, shapes, and styles of wood blocks (made with the help of a shop teacher) and items from home, such as railroad tracks, cars, and signs. I let the child whose model is selected name the town. Save blocks from year to year.

Connie Stark
Jenkintown, PA

Creative Writing Idea

Here's a surefire creative writing idea! Students can make up a daily schedule for their favorite people or characters, like Superman, E.T., or President Reagan.

Linda Rabinowitz
Atlanta, GA

Lima Beans

Write numbers or letters on large, dried lima beans with a fine-line marker, and coat with clear acrylic spray. Use these beans for practice in learning alphabetical order, numerical order, word blends, or for practicing spelling words. Uses are endless and kids will love the "bean box."

Sharon Gullett
Tyler, TX

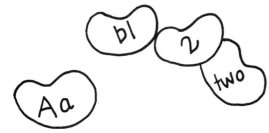

The Price Is Right!

Once upon a time, I had a class who had difficulty with division with remainders. Then it dawned on me that this sort of math is not really different from the crazy game show, "The Price Is Right!"

$$7\overline{)52}$$

"Who has a bid, that when multiplied by 7 is as close to 52 as you can get without going over?" If the contestant is correct, the scorekeepers say, "Ding, Ding, Ding!" If the contestant is incorrect, they say, "Buzz." I also grade in this manner with a "Ding" or a "Buzz" for each problem. Teaching division with a remainder is now something to which we all look forward.

Jill Robbins
Ogden, IL

Silence Is Exciting

Learn the basics of sign language for the deaf. Then introduce a letter sound, and teach its sign. Ask, "Does this word start with a 'w' sound?" Children who hear the sound make a "W sign." Children love the action, and the teachers love the quiet. Then, write a name and have students sign it. Do this with color words also. Find someone in the area to teach a seasonal lesson on signing. See if someone could teach your class a spring song.

Fran Petersen
N. Tonawanda, NY

Correcting Teacher's Mistakes

Drilling multiplication facts can be a boring task. To help students practice in a fun way, pass out copies of a worksheet you've completed that contains several errors. Students circle your mistakes, then determine the final grade.

Debbie Fly
Birmingham, AL

Q-tip Vowels

When teaching vowels, send children to the board and give each a Q-tip in a cup of water. When you pronounce a word, children print the vowel sound on the board. (Mistakes simply disappear!)

Judy Brisbine
Wessington Springs, SD

Multiplication Made Easy!

In order to teach multiplication in a concrete and understandable way, I have found that the plastic rings that hold 6 pop cans together work well. Simply take 2 holders, overlap the 2 end circles and staple them together. Each circle represents a set, with 10 sets in all. Students use small objects, such as beans, in each set.

First, write a multiplication problem on the board and have the students represent the problem, using beans in the sets. Or tell them to put x number of beans in x number of sets, and have them write the problem for that representation. In this way, the students can see, understand, and become proficient at multiplication.

Charlotte Morris
Havre, Montana

Spin And Learn

For a spinner game, I use a plastic margarine or whipped topping dish. The spinner is made right on the lid, and the cards are kept in the dish when not in use. My students love using it.

Patty Zupko
Gulfport, MS

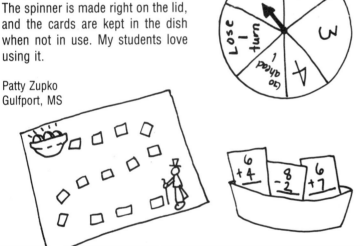

Fun Definitions

A fun project to go with dictionary skills is to have your class complete the following phrases, entitled "Definitions You'll Love But Won't Find in a Dictionary":

Delight is...   Loneliness is...
Relief is...   Discomfort is...
Imagination is...   Appreciation is...

Here are two examples from my students:
  Happiness is knowing your dad is out and you can sit in his recliner.
  Loneliness is staying after school.

Parents love the results!

Brenda McGee
Burlington, NC

Dot-To-Dot With Yarn

For a primary sequencing activity I use very easy dot-to-dot pages with just a few numbers. I laminate each page I plan to use. I push a brad through from the back and tape the head of the brad down on the back.

On the number-one brad, I tie a long piece of colorful yarn and secure it with a dab of glue. Then the child just follows the numbers and twists the yarn once around each brad.

These help teach number sequencing and make cute gifts for children to take home and hang on the wall.

Lynn Klomfar
Gulfport, FL

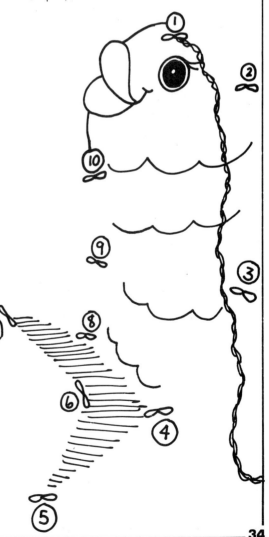

Bulletin Boards

Punctuation Pillows

I created these pillows to make learning punctuation more appealing. Make patterns and cut them out of different kinds of fabric. Fill them with polyester stuffing. Paste eyes and a mouth on each figure, and put the pillows on a bulletin board with appropriate labels and examples. We also play relays with them. Whoever can pick up the correct punctuation pillow gets a point for his team.

Nancy Bell
What Cheer, IA

Mr. T Wants You!

For a motivational bulletin board to display those "A" papers, mount a picture of Mr. T with this caption: Mr. T Wants You To Be a Member of the "A" Team! Hang all those perfect papers around him marked with big "A"s.

Kaye Edwards
Westfield, NC

Bulletin Board Background

For a quick and easy background for a narrow bulletin board, try printed paper towels. Use for larger boards also.

Kimberly Kepp
Lake City, MN

Olympic Skills

Use your students' interest in the Olympics to encourage them to learn basic facts for addition, subtraction, multiplication, and/or division. Enlarge and duplicate symbols for various Olympic sports. Each student chooses and decorates a symbol for a bulletin board. Place silver-foil-covered medals on symbols as students practice a set of facts. When each child demonstrates mastery, present him with a gold-foil medal in a ceremony that includes the national anthem.

Sandy Mercer
Midland Park, NJ

Laminated Material

Laminate 100% cotton material. Then cut into borders for bulletin boards or use a piece to hide an unsightly corner.

Gayle Etter
Vermilion, OH

Laminated Yard Goods

Preprinted, colorful, yard goods material makes a creative display item. Find material printed with Snoopy, Annie, Smurfs, Care Bears, or anything related to a center or unit theme. Laminate it to make a very attractive bulletin board or learning center figure. After it is laminated, the wrong side of the fabric is still pretty enough to mount the figure in a window for a two-sided effect.

Marcille Covey
Lawton, OK

Keep Up the Good Work!

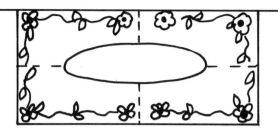

Tissue Box Corners

Get some extra use from an empty tissue box. Many brands use a flower motif on the top. Corners can be cut from the top of the box to be used directly on bulletin boards as decorative corners.

Ann F. Fausnight
Canton, OH

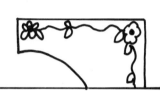

Let's Make A Sundae

To encourage class cooperation and good work habits, I offer an ice cream sundae party as a reward. After a good day, I place a star beside the first letter of the words "Let's make a sundae!" It takes 15 good-work days to earn the party. Sometimes we send invitations home inviting parents to join us. Children can bring their favorite sundae toppings. Since I leave this bulletin board up year-round, we are always working toward another party!

Marsha Goode
Middletown, OH

Portable Bulletin Boards

Cover acoustical ceiling tile with cloth or paper, and add a border. You have an attractive, portable bulletin board for small displays and messages. Tiles can also be used for flannelboards.

Gina Van Leuven
Seminole, FL

Bulletin Board Bummers

Everyone in the school hall will stop to read this bulletin board, which features "bummers" each day. Allow students, faculty, and staff to complete forms and post bummers that begin, "Don't you just hate it when..." Duplicate several forms for each student, and keep blank ones at the bottom of the board for timely additions.

Jo Farrimond
Broken Arrow, OK

Kleenex Box Pockets

Cut empty Kleenex boxes in half and fasten to posters or bulletin boards for durable pockets. For self-correcting flash cards, cut cards slightly taller than the box pocket and write a problem across the top. Put the answer on the bottom of the card so that when it is pulled up, the answer appears in the tissue opening.

Laverne Watson
Warren, AR

Bulletin Board System

A name-tag bulletin board system will help you maintain uninterrupted reading groups. Label a bulletin board with activity areas, and make a name tag for each child. As each student completes his reading work, he chooses to work or view a filmstrip in the library, play a game in a room corner, or work in the hall. After he pins his tag under the correct heading, you can tell in a glance where everyone is at the moment.

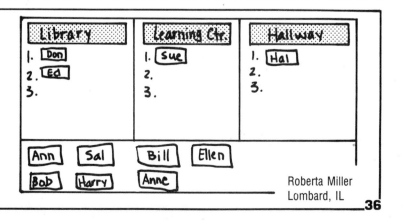

Roberta Miller
Lombard, IL

Bulletin Boards

Finish Your Face

This ongoing bulletin board brightens dull math drills. As each student passes his speed test on each skill, one part is added to his/her face shape. When all levels are completed, children with finished faces receive a math champ certificate from the principal. It's great to see the faces change each week.

Judy W. Jones
Circleville, OH

Egg Carton Letters

Styrofoam egg carton tops are great for bulletin board letters! Trace a stencil on the inside top. Cut out the letters using a sharp, single-edged razor blade. The letters are colorful, durable, and do not fade.

Donna Brides
West Plains, MO

Special Fun Bulletin Boards

I cut apart old children's magazines each month and mount puzzle pages, mixed-up pictures, and riddles (appropriate for the month) on construction paper. After laminating these, I put them on a special fun bulletin board. The children complete the pages with wax crayons and return them to the board when finished. I call my December board "Christmas Capers," followed by "January Jingles" and "February Follies."

Jeane Cowin
Elmore, MN

Extra Bulletin Boards

I use ceiling panels covered with bulletin board paper for extra display boards and centers. You can obtain panels from a building contractor, or look for old ones from remodeling jobs. I display artwork by stapling papers to the boards and leaning them against the wall.

Mary S. Powell
Martinez, GA

Tablecloth Backgrounds

For quick and attractive bulletin board backgrounds, try decorative paper tablecloths. They're durable and easy to place on a bulletin board, and they add bright seasonal and thematic touches to your classroom.

Cynthia L. Myers
Churubusco, IN

Bulletin Board Titles

Use a taut string across the bulletin board to mount cut-out letters straight. Measure at each end of the board, attach string, and pull tight. Place bottoms of letters on the string for easy, straight titles.

Virginia Larsen
Lindenhurst, IL

Good Spelling Makes Cents!

Piggy banks make an attractive bulletin board while providing incentives for spelling and practice in counting money. Each week children can earn a different coin value for passing their spelling tests. Use coin stamps to stamp money earned onto banks. Those who earn the most money at the end of the year (or month) are rewarded.

Carole Betlejewski
Muskegon, MI

Letter Reversals

These cut-out characters serve as reminders to students having trouble with b-d reversals. Attach them to desktops with contact paper, or enlarge and post on a bulletin board or wall.

Lynne West
Rib Lake, WI

Bulletin Board Headlines

Solve the problem of lining up and spacing cut-out letters on your bulletin board! Just cut a strip of the same background paper big enough for all the letters in your headline and glue them on the strip. Then staple the strip to the board, eliminating trial-and-error spacing with pins or thumbtacks.

Claudia Wilcox
Vernon, CT

TV Word Of The Week

This bulletin board promotes vocabulary development through careful listening to TV shows. Each week, students listen for new words while watching favorite programs. They write the words, their meanings, and the shows on which they were heard. A bulletin board TV features a new word each week. Do different activities during the week that use the featured word. Include it on the spelling test. Be sure to feature one word from each child during the year.

Linda Hooks
Riverdale, GA

Calendar Bulletin Board

A math problem a day keeps children working on this puzzle. Make a calendar on which dates come off to reveal math problems. Each day, remove the matching answer piece covering part of a picture or poster mounted on the wall. At the end of the month the entire poster is displayed for your class.

Linda McDonnell
Saginaw, MI

SUNDAY	MONDAY	TUESDAY	WEDNESDAY	THURSDAY	FRIDAY	SATURDAY
9-3 =	8+6 =	12+9=	4	5	6	7
8	9	10	11	12	13	14
15	16	17	18	19	20	21
22	23	24	25	26	27	28
29	30	31				

A School Number Chart

For a colorful classroom number chart, tack large, construction paper fish above the chalkboard. On each fish, write a number and put a corresponding number of paper bubbles coming out the mouth.

Cathie Weaver
Springfield, GA

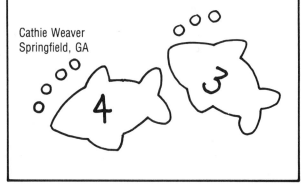

Everyday Reading

To emphasize the importance of reading to my students, I asked them to collect things they read in the course of one day. The students cut out or copied what they read, mounted their selections on cardboard, and posted them on a bulletin board. The children were amazed at the variety of items read: cereal boxes, cash receipts, candy wrappers, traffic signs, etc.

Diane Kramer
Mt. Carmel, PA

Bulletin Boards

Easy Bulletin Board

A plastic window shade makes a super extra bulletin board. Remove it from the wooden roll, and staple or tack it to the cork trim above a chalkboard. These shades are inexpensive and colorful. They can be cut to size and easily wiped clean. Attach a border to finish the bulletin board, and it's ready to use.

Lyn Sullivan
North Adams, MA

Hot Spellers

A motivating bulletin board will heat up spelling skills. Label tagboard thermometers with student names. Mark off a section for each week of the grading period, and post thermometers on a bulletin board. After each weekly spelling test, students color in their scores. A special prize is given to students who score 100 each week.

Sheree McArthur
Liberia, West Africa

Joke Mural

Everyone loves a good joke, especially children. Create a joke mural to liven up your classroom or hall. Have each student fold a small piece of paper. Instruct them to write a favorite joke on the outside flap and the answer inside. Glue completed jokes on a large sheet of paper and have students add illustrations.

Connie Connely
Catoosa, OK

What kind of bean will not grow in a garden?

Jelly Beans

James

TV Guide

Use a laminated poster board TV-set to post educational shows your students watch during the school day. Posted near the television, it is a good reminder for you and your students and will also help a substitute teacher. You can also list afternoon and evening shows that would benefit the class. Wipe off and update as needed.

Barbara Harris
Parkersburg, WV

Television Schedule
Monday
11:00 Electric Co.
Tuesday
9:45 Letter People

Theme Borders

Involve students in bulletin board construction by providing them with strips of construction paper (3″ x 6″ to 8″). Announce the theme of the bulletin board and ask students to decorate their strips appropriately. Use completed strips as an eye-catching border.

Lynn Klomfar
Gulfport, FL

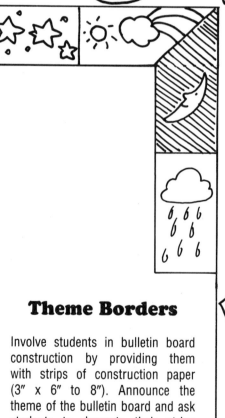

Paperback Board

You can mount a paperback book on your bulletin board by pressing a thumbtack in each corner of the back cover. Place a rubber band around the book lengthwise, leaving the front cover loose. Then just press the book in position on your board.

Lois Cooper
Beckley, WV

Who's Who Bulletin Board

Here's an idea kids of all ages would enjoy. When we talk about human beings and how we change from infancy, the children enjoy bringing in snapshots of themselves as infants. We put the pictures on a small bulletin board. Students try to match the names to the pictures with colored yarn.

Joan Holesko
N. Tonawanda, NY

Trivia Board

This trivia bulletin board will be a popular item in your classroom. Post small bits and pieces of unusual information that take only a few minutes to read. Add new trivia often to encourage students to read for fun and for facts. Students can find fascinating items to contribute in almanacs, record books, newspapers, magazines, and trivia books.

Debbie Wiggins
Myrtle Beach, SC

Who-o-se Paper?

Place an owl on a bulletin board for nameless papers. Helps remind students to include their names!

Rebecca Graves
Burlington, NC

Bulletin Board Holders

Use the plastic containers from ready-to-use frosting for storing bulletin board borders. Roll the strips around your fingers and slide them in. They stay clean and don't get crushed. Cut a piece of the border and tape it to the outside of the container so you can tell at a glance what border is in it. These containers are also great for holding spring-type clothespins and other learning center pieces.

Pat Brown
North Canton, OH

Bulletin Board Responsibilities

Divide a bulletin board into sections and give each student the responsibility of decorating one space. Students mount projects or pictures on separate pieces of paper, then tack them to the bulletin board background.

Julia Ewoniuk
Dickinson, ND

Chalkboard Highlights

Turn a corner of your chalkboard into a handy bulletin board. Frame a section of the chalkboard with a colorful bulletin board border secured with masking tape. Write homework assignments or notices inside the frame. The border increases visibility and prevents assignments from being erased accidentally.

Isobel Livingstone
Rahway, NJ

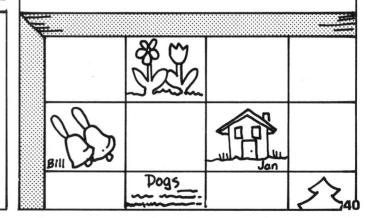

Bulletin Boards

Inexpensive Letters

Make attractive letters for your bulletin boards by using discarded file folders and contact paper. Cover the file folders with the contact paper. Trace letters on the back of the folder, making sure you place letters right side down. Cut out and outline with permanent markers for inexpensive and attractive letters.

Lois Cooper
Beckley, WV

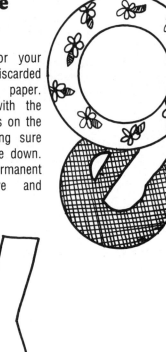

Pellon Characters

Pellon is excellent for making bulletin board characters and letters. Use a permanent marker, and the items can be washed when soiled. They will not fade and tear like construction paper.

Diana Leibrandt
Imperial, NE

Pattern Board Display

Need more bulletin board space? Use a pattern cutting board from a fabric store. Cover with contact paper for a portable display, or even a learning center.

Diane Vogel
Chamblee, GA

Bulletin Board Storage

Trying to keep bulletin board materials organized and in good shape can be easy if you have a central area to store large items. Sort boards and pictures according to months and place them in tall, kitchen-size garbage bags. Attach the bags to hangers with clothespins and hang in appropriate order.

Cathy Chomistek
Indianapolis, IN

Wallpaper Ideas

Wallpaper can solve a lot of bulletin board problems, and its durability ensures that materials can be used year to year.

1. Laminate sheets of wallpaper to use when cutting out letters.
2. Cut seasonal shapes from wallpaper.
3. Back bulletin boards with vinyl wallpaper to eliminate problems with fading and tearing.

Darlene Herrell
Georgetown, OH

Practical Pin Cushions

No more fumbling for the box of pins while putting up bulletin boards! To keep pins handy, tack a flat pin cushion to the wall by each board and you have a ready supply.

Cathie Weaver
Springfield, GA

Hop To It!

Get each child leaping ahead on learning the times tables with this lily pond bulletin board. Number ten lily pads 0-9, and tack them on the board. Each child has a frog with his or her name on it. As a table is mastered, the child moves his frog to that lily pad. Give special awards after each leap and an extraspecial award for getting across the entire pond.

Christine Davidson
Marietta, GA

Aesop's Stories

After reading several of Aesop's fables, help students list the morals on the board. Discuss the morals, then have students write their own stories to fit the morals of their choice. When accompanied by illustrations, the stories will make an interesting bulletin board.

Howard Faulkner
Northport, NY

Staples

Make it easier to remove staples from your bulletin boards. When you put up the board, rock the stapler gently, instead of pushing staples in all the way. Staples stick out just enough to grab.

Mary Dinneen
Bristol, CT

Classroom Cooperation

Encourage good behavior with a classroom character that the students feed each day. Laminate a large cut-out character, and mount it on a bulletin board together with a small container. Have the class name the character. Daily, give each student a predetermined number of dry beans to feed the character. If a child misbehaves, the teacher gets one of his beans. At the end of each day, students feed the character by placing their remaining beans in the container. When the container is full, the whole class gets a reward for their cooperation.

Gayle Cook
Louisville, KY

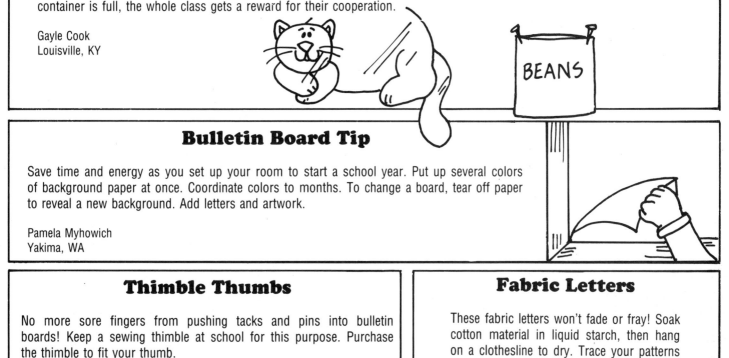

Bulletin Board Tip

Save time and energy as you set up your room to start a school year. Put up several colors of background paper at once. Coordinate colors to months. To change a board, tear off paper to reveal a new background. Add letters and artwork.

Pamela Myhowich
Yakima, WA

Thimble Thumbs

No more sore fingers from pushing tacks and pins into bulletin boards! Keep a sewing thimble at school for this purpose. Purchase the thimble to fit your thumb.

Betty Brooks
Buhl, ID

Fabric Letters

These fabric letters won't fade or fray! Soak cotton material in liquid starch, then hang on a clothesline to dry. Trace your patterns on it, and cut. You'll have nice, stiff bulletin board letters.

Sue Landy
Atlanta, GA

A Drop Of Golden Sun

Let a little sunshine into your classroom on a rainy day. Cut a large sun and individual rays from yellow poster board. On each ray, print a special activity on one side and a number on the other. Laminate sun and rays. Attach rays to the sun, with the numbers showing. On a rainy day, allow students to choose a "drop of golden sun" and look on the back for a surprise activity.

Lisa A. Waters
Philadelphia, PA

Ug The Bug

After children are familiar with beginning consonants, digraphs, and blends, use Ug the Bug to introduce word families. Make a painted egg-carton bug with pipe cleaner antennae. Attach Ug to a bulletin board with his poem and a beginning sound chart. As you give a new word daily, children use the chart to form words that rhyme with it.

Pamela Huntington
Redington Shores, FL

I am Ug the rhyming bug. Here I sit upon my rug. I pick a word and then I sit, and try to find a rhyme for it.

b	bl	br	c
cl	cr	d	dr
f	fl	fr	g

Personal Borders

To make a personal border for our bulletin board, each child writes his name as many times as he can on a strip of 3″ × 8″ paper. Each child can add his own "logo" on the paper strip to add a designer touch. I scallop each strip and laminate to make an appealing personal border for a bulletin board that displays everyone's good work.

Ruth Davis
Clarks Summit, PA

Flying High

Sometimes it's difficult to keep children interested in independent or individually paced programs (reading kits, activity cards, math modules, etc.). Here's a bulletin board idea that doubles as a motivational device. Have each child make a construction paper kite with a crepe paper streamer tail. Each time a child completes an individual assignment, she adds a paper tie to her kite tail. At the end of a month, award a real kite or other small prize to the three students with the most tails on their kites.

Mary Dinneen
Bristol, CT

3-D Bulletin Boards

A nice way to make your bulletin boards come alive is to mount empty toilet paper rolls cut in different lengths to the board. Then mount student projects or pictures onto the rolls, giving the board a 3-D look.

Michelle Rich
Hillside, NJ

Up, Up, And Away With Reading

Hang a huge Superman on a bulletin board covered with comic books for students to read. Change comic books weekly (for a month) to stimulate lots of reading!

Beverly A. Strayer
Red Lion, PA

Newspaper Jumble

To review syllabication rules for end-of-line syllabication, explain to students that most newspapers now use computerized typesetters. The computer is programmed to divide words in the most common place, according to our language rules. Scout the paper for numerous incorrect divisions, some of which are humorous. Or hold a contest to find many of these. Make a bulletin board.
Variation: Have students identify the rule improperly used.

Ann Fausnight
Canton, OH

Color-Word Crayons

Roll and staple poster board into long tubes to make a king-sized display of color words! Attach paper cones to make the crayons' points and black bands to resemble a paper covering. Have all the crayons on the wall, and place a label under each.

Terrell Moore
Bowling Green, KY

Math 500 Rally

Draw a racetrack with a start, finish, and pit stops on a bulletin board. At the start and at pit stops, add envelopes holding sheets of math problems, with more difficult problems at each succeeding stop. Give each student a racing car marked with a name or number. Everyone begins with the start sheet and must answer all problems correctly before moving ahead, one stop per day. I am the official checker. Prizes are awarded both for completing the rally and for finishing with no errors.

Hermine Harken
Greene, IA

The Cat's Meow!

Display the Jiffy Pak bulletin board characters from The Education Center with children's work and your own captions. Choose the cats from the "Absolutely Book Crazy!" Jiffy Pak, for example, to feature with student book reports for "The Cat's Meow!"

Isobel Livingstone
Rahway, NJ

Fabric Letter Pillows

I purchased a pattern for alphabet pillows and put old fabric scraps to work in my room. I sewed special messages to use on bulletin boards. If you don't sew, you could ask parent volunteers for help.

Gina Van Leuven
Seminole, FL

Inflatables

Add a new dimension to displays with small inflatables from shops that sell pool and patio supplies or toy stores. Attach inflatables to the surface with Plasti-Tak or magnetic tape.

Gina Van Leuven
Seminole, FL

Birthdays

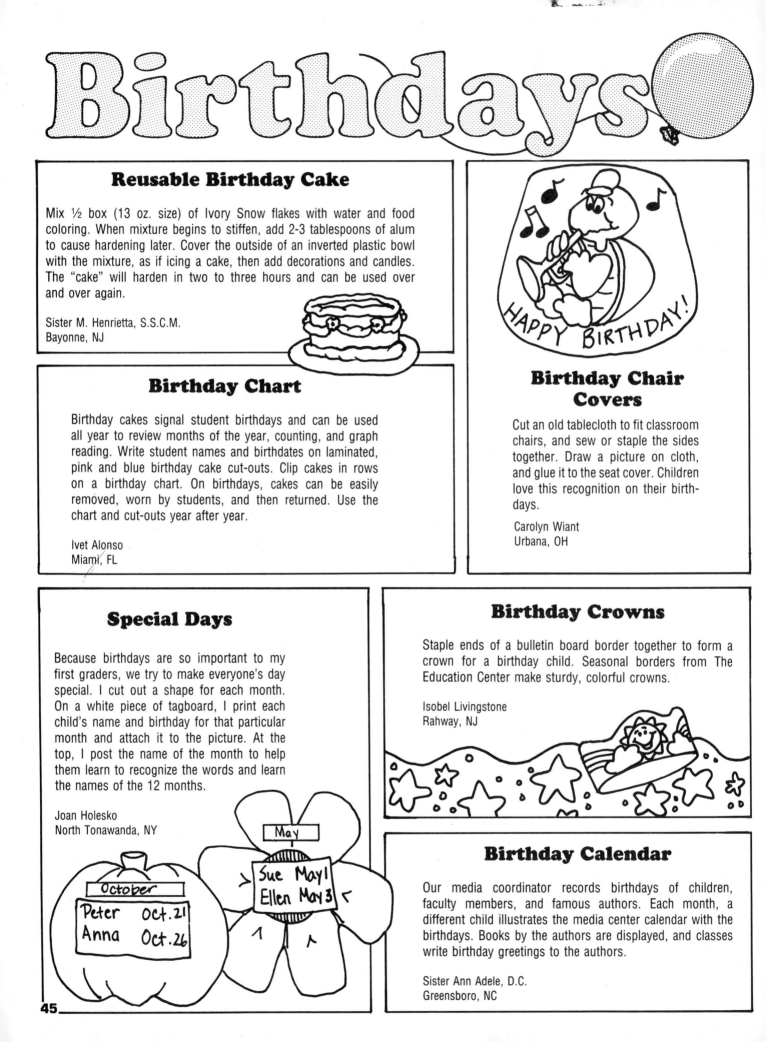

Reusable Birthday Cake

Mix ½ box (13 oz. size) of Ivory Snow flakes with water and food coloring. When mixture begins to stiffen, add 2-3 tablespoons of alum to cause hardening later. Cover the outside of an inverted plastic bowl with the mixture, as if icing a cake, then add decorations and candles. The "cake" will harden in two to three hours and can be used over and over again.

Sister M. Henrietta, S.S.C.M.
Bayonne, NJ

Birthday Chart

Birthday cakes signal student birthdays and can be used all year to review months of the year, counting, and graph reading. Write student names and birthdates on laminated, pink and blue birthday cake cut-outs. Clip cakes in rows on a birthday chart. On birthdays, cakes can be easily removed, worn by students, and then returned. Use the chart and cut-outs year after year.

Ivet Alonso
Miami, FL

Birthday Chair Covers

Cut an old tablecloth to fit classroom chairs, and sew or staple the sides together. Draw a picture on cloth, and glue it to the seat cover. Children love this recognition on their birthdays.

Carolyn Wiant
Urbana, OH

Special Days

Because birthdays are so important to my first graders, we try to make everyone's day special. I cut out a shape for each month. On a white piece of tagboard, I print each child's name and birthday for that particular month and attach it to the picture. At the top, I post the name of the month to help them learn to recognize the words and learn the names of the 12 months.

Joan Holesko
North Tonawanda, NY

Birthday Crowns

Staple ends of a bulletin board border together to form a crown for a birthday child. Seasonal borders from The Education Center make sturdy, colorful crowns.

Isobel Livingstone
Rahway, NJ

Birthday Calendar

Our media coordinator records birthdays of children, faculty members, and famous authors. Each month, a different child illustrates the media center calendar with the birthdays. Books by the authors are displayed, and classes write birthday greetings to the authors.

Sister Ann Adele, D.C.
Greensboro, NC

Chocolate Chip Birthday

Celebrating a child's birthday in your class can be very easy if you make a giant chocolate chip cookie. Spread cookie dough on a pizza pan, and bake. After cooling, break into bite-sized pieces and serve.

Mary Larson
Bristol, CT

Birthday Banner

For each student's birthday, my class makes a birthday banner. On a large piece of bulletin board paper, I write "Happy Birthday" and the child's name in big, fat letters. I also draw a border and other decorations for children to color. I add a birthday message from me and sign it. As children arrive, they sign their names and color in a letter or decoration. When complete, we hang the banner in the hall. Everyone knows whose birthday it is, and at the end of the day, the birthday child takes the banner home!

Lori Wempe
Lindenhurst, IL

Secret Birthday Message

Using a white crayon on white paper, write a personalized message to a birthday child. The message is invisible until the child paints over it with a watery tempera mixture. The secret greeting appears because the paint does not adhere to the crayon message!

Cely Davis
Columbia, SC

Principal's Birthday

On our school principal's birthday, my class planned a special celebration. We made a big paper banner that said, "HAPPY BIRTHDAY!" During art time, the children colored the letters and drew characters or wrote something special to the principal. When the big day came, we put up the banner outside, called to the principal, and yelled, "Happy Birthday!" He loved it, and so did the kids!

Rebecca L. Gibson
Auburn, AL

Birthday Box

To celebrate classroom birthdays in a special way, make a birthday box by wrapping a medium-sized box in gift wrap. Wrap the lid separately so that the box will open without being unwrapped. Put a birthday card and a small gift inside the box. Cards, pencils, and stickers from The Education Center make great gifts! Add a ribbon or bow, and place the box on the student's desk before school. Children can't wait for birthdays, because they all get to share the opening of the birthday box whenever a birthday arrives.

Jeanne Thomas
Cana, VA

Birthday Cakes

To help make a child's birthday special, draw a cake on the board with colored chalk. Add the correct number of candles, then let the birthday child choose the colors for his icing, plate, and candles. Finish by joining the class in a chorus of "Happy Birthday."

Fayla Nanz
Lawrenceburg, IN

Birthday Worksheets

Prepare a birthday worksheet with a cake at the top and room for a birthday story below. Designate areas on the cake for children to add the correct number of candles. Duplicate copies to be used all year. Birthday children may complete their own sheets or choose classmates to complete them as gifts.

Lucy Knight
Washington, DC

MANAGEMENT TIPS

Computer Management

To help manage the use of computers in the library learning center, try this communication tip. Give each child a manila envelope with his name on it. When children go to use the computer, they take their envelopes, with specific instructions or information inside for the library learning center coordinator. As each child finishes with computer time, the coordinator records the program the child has done on the outside of the envelope. Both teacher and coordinator know at a glance where each child left off.

Laura Crosby
Wheaton, IL

Trouble With Directions

If your students often ignore or misinterpret directions on worksheets, try this cure. When the student instructions say circle, have them circle the instruction word. If it says to underline, have them draw a line under that direction.

Paula Hall
Lancaster, KS

Line Up!

Stop segregating boys and girls when it's time to line up! Give each student a class number based on alphabetical order. Calling class numbers in unusual groupings eliminates the race for first place in line. For variety, call numbers 1-12, 13-24, multiples of 3, or odd and even. It's a great idea for class picture lineups.

Paula K. Holdren
Prospect, KY

Take A Number

Have students who are waiting for you to check their work take a tagboard number. Then, call out numbers in order as you are able to check the next paper. Avoids confusion when teachers and students forget who is next.

Barbara Brown
Waverly, VA

Make-Up Work Folders

No more searching your desk for makeup work! Decorate a colored file folder and laminate to make a handy "missed work" holder. Store assignment lists, worksheets, and notes inside for the student to complete and return in the folder.

Sandie Smith
Selma, IN

"Sleep Masks"

Some children just cannot be still during rest time and they usually disrupt the rest of the class. I cut out several "sleep masks" (fake fur, felt, or any soft fabric is suitable) and decorated them with embroidery, fabric scraps, and sequins.

When a child seems particularly restless, he gets to wear a sleep mask. This usually quiets the child down, and once the child establishes a sleeping pattern every day, a sleep mask is no longer needed.

Lynn Klomfar
St. Petersburg, FL

Puzzle Poster

This is <u>the</u> <u>best</u> management tool I've ever used! Mount an animal or bird poster on tagboard and laminate. Laminate a second piece of tagboard of the same size, cut into puzzle pieces, then number each piece. Cover the poster by attaching puzzle pieces with double-faced sticky tape or rubber cement. Call on a student seated at the quietest table to remove a piece and guess what's on the poster. A correct guess earns a treat for the entire group.

Works well for times when you want to settle students—after recess, between classes, or waiting for buses at the end of the day. As the poster becomes clearer, children become very eager to earn a guess!

Diane Lucas
Pittsburgh, PA

RU's To Follow

At the beginning of the year, I told my students there would be no rules this year, only RU's (Are you's?). Are you . . . feeling good about you . . . learning about yourself and other people? Every once in a while we check our RU's. The children enjoy the idea, and it helps them to think positively.

Susan Staats
Chicago, IL

File Folder Labels

To get more life from a file folder, cover the tab with a piece of masking tape. Label a second piece of tape and place it over the first piece. When you're ready to reuse the folder, remove the top piece, and either label the bottom piece or apply more tape and label it.

Lois Cooper
Beckley, WV

Cracker Jack And Cracker Jill

To encourage good behavior in my class, each child's name is put in a bowl, boys in one and girls in another. As long as a child follows our rules, his name is kept in the bowl. On Friday, the two children whose names are drawn get a box of Cracker Jacks to become "Cracker Jack" and "Cracker Jill." It's a small price per week that really pays off!

Diane West
Big Horn, WY

Pocket Pal Variations

When I make a Pocket Pal game for my class, I prepare extra sets of game cards and program them for different skill levels. I store the extra sets in labeled envelopes. Pieces for each set are coded on the back to avoid mix-ups. The same games may be played by groups of students at different levels of mastery by changing the skill cards.

Debbie Hawkins
Atwood, IL

Mr. Tuttle

Put up this clever poster to discourage young children from tattling on each other. If a child approaches to tattle, tell him to go tell Mr. Tuttle. At first, students will actually talk to Mr. Tuttle. Soon they begin to see the humor in talking to a poster and understand what tattling is.

Beverly Heath
Fayetteville, NC

MANAGEMENT TIPS

Homework Assignment Sheet

To make assigning homework easier, design a weekly homework assignment sheet. Fill in the week's tasks, duplicate the sheet and give it to the students each Monday. Encourage students to post their homework assignment sheets on the refrigerator or other visible place at home so that family members are aware of the daily assignments. A great planning hit with students and parents!

Regina L. Toliver
Richmond, VA

Suggestions

A combination wipe-off memo board and corkboard hangs in our classroom. Students all write suggestions for improving our surroundings on the board. Fascinating!

Ann Hudson
Forest, VA

Study Carrels

Make 2 carrels by cutting a large cardboard carton in half lengthwise. Remove the top and bottom and cover the cardboard with colorful contact paper. I use several carrels with children who are easily distracted. The carrels can also be used to set up centers by clipping materials on with clothespins.

Linda Shell
Athens, OH

Conference Schedules

When parent conference days are in progress, hang that day's schedule outside your door.
>   7:00-7:15   Ms. Graves
>   7:15-7:30   Mr. Ackers
>   7:30-7:45   Ms. Lee
This procedure saves on interruptions and confusion.

Mary Dinneen
Bristol, CT

Daily Date

To eliminate the constant question, "What's today's date?" I laminate cards labeled with the month, day, and date. Each morning we clip the current date on the wall with E-Z clips as a reminder all throughout the day.

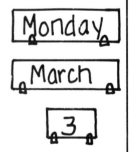

Margaret Leyen
Iowa Falls, IA

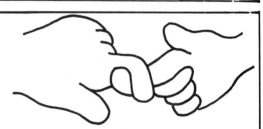

Silent Signs

My students use some nonverbal signs to give me messages without the interruptions of asking:
>   Two thumbs up - "My work is finished. May I go to a center?"
>   Pointer fingers hooked - "Can I ask a buddy for help?"
>   Hooked finger - "May I leave the room to get a drink?"

Sr. Ann Claire Rhoads
Emmitsburg, MD

Student Checkers

As an alternative to self-checking materials, I allow a designated student to keep track of students who have completed a given task. When a new set of learning materials is put out, the children enthusiastically set to work. The first child to complete each series of tasks correctly becomes the "checker." His name is written on a laminated "checker" card, which is attached to the activity.

Jane Cuba
Redford, MI

Ornament Hangers

This is a real money saver for teachers who like to hang children's work from the ceiling or from wires stretched across the room. Rather than bending paper clips to make hooks, use Christmas ornament hooks. They're inexpensive and don't break when you bend them. I can let the kids take their art home to hang—hook and all!

Patricia Luttmann
Lansing, MI

Freebies

It's hard to find time to write letters requesting free classroom materials. Let it be a writing assignment for students! It will provide them with a good opportunity to address envelopes and write business letters, and they'll love getting items in the mail.

Connie Connely
Catoosa, OK

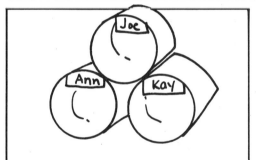

Mailboxes

Instead of simply passing out graded papers, I ask my students to bring in empty coffee cans, which we decorate, label with names, and stack into a mailbox unit. At the end of the day, my paper monitors simply place papers in the correct mailboxes. The students love the idea of receiving "mail!"

Jeri Facklam
Lebo, KS

Easter Basket

Bring in a large, wicker Easter basket to use when distributing and collecting children's papers. My students love to pass our papers because they get to carry the basket. I use the basket all year long. It holds papers I've finished checking until they are passed back.

Annette Mathias
Partridge, KS

Lesson Plan Labels

If you write your lesson plans in ink, mistakes can be a problem. Try this trick for last-minute changes. Instead of liquid paper, apply a small, self-sticking white label over the mistake. Eliminates the mess of liquid paper and the time of rewriting plans.

Mary Dinneen
Bristol, CT

Teacher's Helpers

Label a file folder for each day of the week. In each one, store daily seat work and other needed papers. Save space by stacking folders atop one another. Any substitute teacher will thank you for being so organized.

Kathy Graham
Filer, ID

MANAGEMENT TIPS

Working Together

Students will encourage each other to work together in this seating arrangement. Place 4 to 5 desks together in small groups. Have each group choose a name and leader. Groups work to earn points each week by bringing in all homework and signed notes, or by working quietly. Points may be exchanged for rewards.

Harriet Kramer
Ormond Beach, FL

For The Substitute

Most of the time, teachers do not know they are going to need a substitute the next day. I find that a "substitute pack" is a great help to the person who comes in to take my place. Inside a manila envelope are headbands for each child, with his or her name on them in large letters, easily visible and requiring no pins or tape to wear. I also include copies of a couple of coloring sheets for the children to use while the substitute is counting lunch money, etc. The final thing I include is an information sheet listing names of dependable children, classroom rules, and some suggestions for games the children especially like. Every substitute has said this packet was especially helpful.

Helen Burkard
Beckley, WV

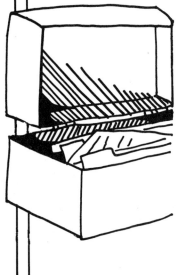

Idea Box

When I did my student teaching, I started an idea file. Using an old recipe container, I divided it into sections for all the months of the year, reading, math, language, poetry, science, social studies, art, safety, etc. Whenever I see something that would be a good idea for use in my classroom, I make a note about it, draw a picture, or clip the magazine article. These items are filed in my idea box for later use. It's great to help stir up some new ideas throughout the year!

Joan Holesko
N. Tonawanda, NY

Workbook Corners

My first and second graders have difficulty finding pages quickly. When they complete a workbook page and I finish checking it, I trim the corner. The children can then turn right to the next assignment.

Margaret Leyen
Iowa Falls, IA

Stoplights

In order to help my children remember what they are to be doing at any certain time, I made a stoplight. When the light is on green, the children are allowed to be out of their seats to gather materials, work at centers, etc. When the light is on yellow, it is discussion time, and the children are to be in their seats and listening. Our red light means that it is work time and the children are to be in their seats working quietly.

Michelle Lee Hesse
Ontario, CA

Textbooks On Tape

For students in your classroom who are below grade level, tapes of science and social studies texts can help them keep up. Older students or PTA members may volunteer to make such tapes. Prerecorded books can be obtained from the Society to Prevent Blindness or similar groups.

Kathy Beard
Keystone Heights, FL

Sub Survival Kit

Provide a survival kit for substitute teachers in your classroom. Include copies of school and class rules with procedures to follow if they are broken. List names of dependable students, students with special requirements, favorite class games, listening activities, or art projects with materials. Throw in good behavior awards, a good book to read to the class, and a candy bar for the sub. The kit will help the substitute teacher enjoy a productive day with your class, and children will look forward to surprises you have planned for them.

Laura Crosby
Wheaton, IL

Tape Recorder At Workshop

At make-and-take workshops, I use a tape recorder to facilitate making items shared there. It is easy and less expensive than using a camera to record centers. When I have a center partially finished, I explain remaining details on tape so I can complete it later. Then I am free to make another center.

Maxine Bishop
Fairfield, IL

Book Checkouts

Keeping track of classroom book checkouts was a headache until I came up with this easy system. Label a book card pocket for each student. Paste pockets on a large piece of poster board. When a child checks out a book, he puts the book card in his pocket. When he returns the book, he removes the card and puts it back in the book. You can tell at a glance who has a book out.

Jo Farrimond
Broken Arrow, OK

Music Box Change

When children are working in various centers, it's often hard to begin a class without confusion. To make a smooth class change, I simply wind a music box and let it play. Students know that they should be ready for the next class to begin when the music ends.

Elaine Plemons
Calhoun, GA

Organization Tip

Eliminate a lot of wasted time collecting and distributing papers. Collect work from the previous day early the next morning. Have one child call the order of the papers. Children line up alphabetically and place their work on a table. Papers are then already in order for recording grades. At the end of the day, place graded papers (still in order) on a table, and have children come up alphabetically to pick up their work.

Karen Mullen
Lafayette, IN

Winter Weather Help

During the start of the winter season, have each child write his name on a clothespin. On days when boots are worn, each child clips his boots together with his clothespin. This makes boots readily identifiable, especially when more than one student has the same color boots!

Linda Terranora
Westerly, RI

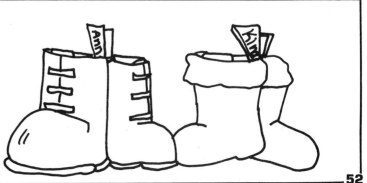

MANAGEMENT TIPS

Acetate Overlays

Laminated file folders with acetate overlays protect and extend the use of individual worksheets. Use bookbinding tape to attach liftup overlays to the folders and insert sheets under the plastic. Laminating the folder makes it more rigid and prevents corners from curling or tearing. This is not only a paper-saving device, but also avoids the need for making copies of the same material year after year.

Betty Huffman
Zanesville, OH

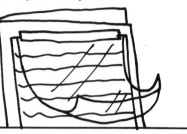

Quota Of Questions

Encourage "lazy listeners" to become self-reliant and stop asking questions that have already been answered. Draw a large question mark on index cards and give several to each student who frequently asks unnecessary questions. They may use each card to ask one question. When they run out of cards, they can no longer ask questions. Helps them make wise choices and save questions for important matters.

Paula Holdren
Louisville, KY

Directions In A Flash

Write directions you usually repeat orally on large flash cards. Signal time for instructions by flashing the lights to get student attention. Hold up appropriate cards, such as stop work, clear your desk, line up, sit down, come up, and recess.

Annette Mathias
Partridge, KS

Student Dictionaries

Solve the problem of frequent spelling questions by making each child his own dictionary. Students make covers the first day of class and attach them to index cards with shower curtain hooks. When a child needs a word spelled, he flips to the right page and whispers to the teacher, who writes it down. Dictionaries are sent home the last day of school, with yarn in place of the curtain hook.

Robin Turner
Arlington, TX

Worksheet Cover

I use worksheets in units of ten with my students. I create a cover sheet for the booklet with an illustration suitable for recording completed work. When the student finishes a sheet, he colors a section on the cover—my signal to check the page. I add a smiley face to show successful completion of the worksheet.

Margaret Leyen
Iowa Falls, IA

"X" Marks The Spot

Keep your classroom neatly arranged by putting an "X" with marker or tape under each front-row desk. Students can line up other desks easily if the first one is in the correct place.

Debbie Wiggins
Myrtle Beach, SC

Smile Stickers

During a test or difficult assignment, I place smile stickers on students' desks. Reminds each one that I'm smiling because I know he can do well!

Julie Tillotson
Vicksburg, MS

Communication Game

Here's one game you will enjoy as much as the students. Periodically, I tell them that for the next 30-40 minutes they may communicate any way except by talking. They may use sign language or hand motions, write notes, mouth the words, etc. I stress that no form of talking or whispering is allowed! The kids really enjoy the note writing since it's the only time I allow them to do so. It's interesting to see what new ways they can think of to communicate.

Gale Martin
Sugarland, TX

Remembrance

To help me remember to give students homework sheets or letters to parents, I place a string along the bulletin board edge. Then I attach a clothespin to it. On their way out, the children can get their papers. This visual reminder keeps all of us from forgetting.

Arnetra Townes
Norlina, NC

Homework Jar

Solve the problem of no-name papers. Have students write their names on both upper corners of their homework papers. Cut off one corner of each when the papers are turned in and place in a homework jar. At the end of the week, draw 2 names and reward winners with a no-homework weekend!

Julie Gaynor
Baltimore, MD

Handwriting Hint

To help children with spacing between words, have them turn their papers sideways and write between the lines.

Ann Fausnight
Canton, OH

Homework Excuse Note

If you have students who do not turn in work, have them write an excuse note. Let students know it will be on file to look at when a question about low grades comes up.

Lynn Franklin
Savannah, GA

Reading Management

This management idea involves parents in your reading program and boosts communication between school and home. Duplicate a guidesheet for each story you will teach. The guidesheet should include a list of all assigned work and skills covered. Those skills not mastered are circled. Completed work is stored in an individual paper envelope labeled as shown. At the end of a specified period, send the reading packet and guidesheets home with a note from you to the parents. The note should state the intent of the packet and ask that the parents review the guidesheets and completed work with their child. Parents then sign the packet and return it to school.

Susan Black
Mercer, PA

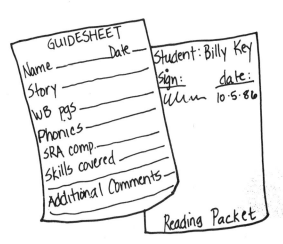

MANAGEMENT TIPS

Student I.D. Numbers

In order to quickly see whose work is missing and to record grades rapidly, give each student an identification number. Assign numbers to a name list alphabetized by last names. Students write their names and numbers on all work. When collecting papers, place them in numerical order. Instead of looking for a name in your roll book, go down the I.D. number list.

Helene Croft
Chatsworth, CA

Class Ringleader

If your students ask when it will be their turn to be class leader, use a circus wall as their visual cue. Have children cut out circus characters and line them up in a circus parade with a student name card below each character. Put a ringleader with top hat in the center ring. The leader's name is placed on the ringleader and name cards are moved up at the end of each day. Each child can count how many days until his turn to be ringleader.

B. Blackburn
Boiling Springs, NC

Name	Report Cards	New Crayons	Show & Tell	Field Trip Permission
Mark		✓	✓	
Anne	✓			✓
Kay		✓	✓	

Record Keeping

Need an efficient way to keep track of who brought back report cards, permission slips, or items for an art project? Duplicate a class list with columns for your returns. Label the top of each column. As a child brings back an item, check off his name.

Marsha Konken
Sterling, CO

Roster Checkoff

Finding it difficult to keep up with student papers? Label a file folder for each class assignment. Clip a duplicated copy of your class roster to the outside of each folder. Students check off their names when they place completed assignments in a folder. A quick glance at the roster lets you know who has turned in his work.

Mary Needham
Clarkston, WA

Keeping Kids Quiet In The Library

Issuing "library licenses" prompts good library behavior. During the class visit to the library, I record the quietest workers on paper. On our return to the classroom, each quiet worker gets a library license minicertificate duplicated on a ditto master. Students who receive a given number of licenses earn a prize or a privilege.

Carolyn Bolz
Riverside, CA

This is to certify that _____ knows how to work quietly in the library

Friday Folders

Each Friday, send folders home with a sample of the week's work. Include tests, notices, and worksheets. Inside, staple a reading record of books read in spare time and a comment sheet for parents to sign. On the front of the folder, children attach stickers, which are given each week for tests on which they received a perfect score.

Friday Folder ☺ Billy

Patricia Fahey
Wayside, NJ

Do Not Disturb

I placed a Do Not Disturb sign next to me so students knew when they could not interrupt. It was so effective that I decided to make a sign for each child. No one may disturb a student whose sign is up. If someone does disturb him, the disrupter pays a penalty. It was very effective for children who found it hard to finish work.

Gail Edelman
Macungie, PA

Reserved

To avoid arguments and students' fears of losing their turns at an uncompleted game, place a Do Not Disturb sign with each learning center. If a student is called away from the center, he can secure his place by putting a sign on the unfinished game or activity and be assured that it will be waiting undisturbed when he returns.

Nancy Hall
Chicago, Il

Lucy Lost

To solve problems with lost-and-found clothing, create this eye-catching display. Draw Lucy Lost on cardboard, and dress her with these lost items. Change frequently so students or parents can recognize lost-and-found clothing.

Janet Myers
Baltimore, MD

Tape-A-Test

Save time when making up tests for absent students. Whenever an oral test such as spelling is given, and a student is absent, tape the exercise as you give it. On his return, the absentee uses headphones to take the test at his convenience.

Helen Mak
Gothenburg, NE

Roll-A-Job

Here's an interesting job chart. List jobs down one side of a piece of poster board, and cut top and bottom slits on the other side. On a piece of adding machine tape twice as long as the distance between the slits, write a list of students' names twice. Thread the tape through the slits, and fasten the ends together to form a circular, repeating list. Each week, allow one child to select his job for the week. Pull the circular list until his name appears opposite that job. All the other names will fall in place beside a job for the week.

Jenan Merrill
Columbia, TN

Reading Lesson Master Plans

Instead of spending hours writing detailed reading plans for each group, try making a master copy of your lesson plans and duplicate it. List the skills for each story and the materials to be used. On each reading group's copy, record the date each skill is taught, which materials are used, and who needs extra help.

Diane Fox
Seffner, FL

Story Name The Beaver's Trip		Page Numbers: Pupil edition 15-17	
New Vocabulary	Silent Reading		Discussion
Skills	Workbook Pages/Worksheets	Games/ Filmstrips	Key Words for Seatwork
1. Literal Comprehension 2.	p. 25	word puzzle	whistled, jumped

MANAGEMENT TIPS

Ditto Album

If you have a lot of dittos but never have time to use them, here's a solution that will save duplicating time and expense. Get a 100-page magnetic photo album. Fill its pages with your dittos. Children do work right on the plastic, using a wipe-off crayon. These can be checked and used by other students. If your class is large, buy two albums for more rotation.

Terri Noboa
Miami, FL

Colored Clothespins

To help locate papers quickly, I use brightly colored clothespins instead of paper clips to secure student work (blue for math, yellow for reading, etc.) The clothespins are easier for my first-grade helpers to handle, and I can identify papers at a glance.

Connie Luginsland
Waverly, KS

Job Applications

My students apply for the classroom jobs of their choice on a monthly basis. I hand out "Job Squad Applications" which have spaces to list previous experience and reasons for wanting the job. When more than one child wants the same job, I use these applications to make a decision. Students demonstrate a real desire to do their best on the job.

Patricia D. Shulman
Englewood, CO

Folders For Reading Papers

Provide a colored pocket folder for each student. Label pockets "Take-Home Papers" and "To-Be-Done Papers." At the end of the day, students put completed work in the to-be-done pocket and turn folders in. I check work and place papers in the appropriate pockets. I am the only one who may put papers in the take-home side. When the folders are passed out, students know immediately which papers need corrections. Extra bonus: only one thing to return to each child.

Maxine Bishop
Fairfield, IL

Sharing

To ensure that every child gets to share something with the class once a week, I make a sharing chart with places for 6 names for each weekday. Each child chooses a day of the week, and this remains his sharing day all year. To encourage good listening, I allow class members to ask only 3 questions of each person. Everyone gets the experience of facing the class on a weekly basis, and sharing time takes a maximum of 15 minutes.

Patricia Luttmann
Lansing, MI

Help Stop The Wiggles

Help students keep movement to a minimum as they sit in a small group. Tape a circle to the rug where everyone will sit. Children try not to wiggle off the circle.

Sister Margaret Ann
Emmitsburg, MD

Color-Coded Clocks

If you have students leaving for music, physical education, or art classes at different days and times, try this color-coded clock system to help them remember. Each morning, put a colored sign with the day of the week up on the board. Each student has his clocks pasted in the front of his folder. If he has a clock the same color as the sign on the board, he knows he goes to a class that day and matches the time on his clock to the classroom clock.

Karen Young
Bunker Hill, WV

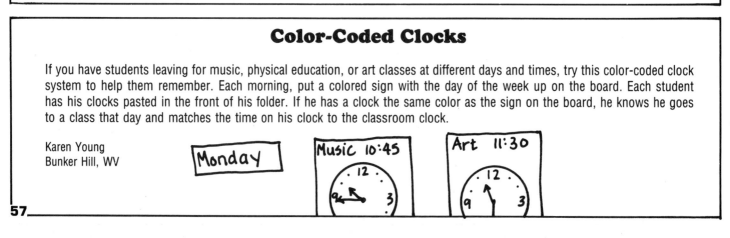

Record Sheets

Record sheets will prove invaluable in keeping track of parent-teacher meetings. Duplicate enough sheets to have 1 to 2 per student. Each time there is communication between parent and teacher (letter, phone call, conference, home visit, etc.), record it on the student's chart. The issues discussed, steps taken toward problem solving, and progress should be included.

Kathy Gales
Tampa, FL

Date	Type of Contact	Contact Initiated By	Summary	Conclusions
Oct. 4	Progress Conference	Teacher	Strengths: ___ Weaknesses: ___	

Center Wheel

To manage a small group of students working independently at centers, construct this rotating device. While you work with one small group, and a second group works with an aide or does seat work, a third group can see at a glance the center assignment for each member. To construct the wheel, slide the circle marked with center names and/or pictures into the vertical slit on the square, so that only half of the center names are showing. Secure with a brad. List all students, coded to their small groups, outside the circle so that one from each group is at the center at a time. Rotate the wheel one space when it's time to change center assignments.

Adrienne Hamlin
Dawson, GA

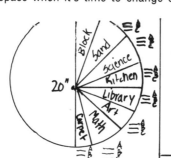

Teacher Aides

Upper-grade students can serve as teacher aides and help in many valuable ways. Allow all students, rather than just the exceptional, to participate by selecting helpers through an interest inventory and by teacher recommendations. Aides can correct papers and put up bulletin boards, as you might expect, but can be given greater responsibilities, such as conducting story hour, supervising games and outdoor play, tutoring, and helping children select library books. You'll find that student aides with these abilities can really be a boon to a busy teacher!

Paula Holdren
Louisville, KY

Show And Tell Wheel

Here's an easy way to manage show-and-tell. Cut 2 poster board circles. On one, draw a face and cut out the mouth. Line the other as shown, and attach it under the face with a brad. Turning the wheel, write names on the teeth. Rotate weekly to reveal new "show-and-tellers."

Patti Wright
Omaha, NE

Learning Center Management

Take snapshots of your current centers and mount them on poster board. Under each picture make a slit and put paper clips for the number of children who may use the center at one time. Place laminated cards with each child's name in a container by the chart. Students insert their names in the clips under their chosen centers.

Cathie Weaver
Springfield, GA

MANAGEMENT TIPS

Name Charts

Keep student name charts looking new all year! Laminate a blank sheet of poster board, then write names on tagboard strips. As students switch reading groups or move away, strips are easily attached and removed from the poster board with double-faced sticky tape.

Jane Cuba
Redford, MI

Flag Wavers

Instead of gazing out at a classroom of raised hands waiting to be identified, use this flag-waving management technique. Each child places a piece of plastic clay in the bottom of a Styrofoam cup and makes three flags—red, green, and yellow—from Popsicle sticks and construction paper. The children use the color-coded flags to signify that they need help (red), that they are finished with their work (green), or that they are at a center (yellow).

Judith Gale
Flagstaff, AZ

Mr. Behavior Bear

To encourage good behavior, I set a bear on the chalkboard ledge. Mr. Behavior Bear doesn't like to see children get their names on the board for misbehavior. For a first offense, write the child's name on the board as a warning. Further disobedience warrants a check mark. Students with no check marks are rewarded at the end of the week. Children start each week with a "clean slate."

Deb Stock
Chariton, IA

The Sharing Bag

To solve the problem of show-and-tell on a daily basis, try using a drawstring sharing bag made of denim or other suitable material. At the beginning of the school year, send a letter home to parents telling about the sharing bag and how it will be used during the year. Every class member, including the teacher, gets a turn to take the bag home and choose something special to bring the following day. All are encouraged, in this manner, to wait their turns and to share souvenirs of travels, favorite books, articles of interest from newspapers or magazines, unusual items, or collections. Toys are discouraged except on toy day, the day after Christmas vacation, when every child may bring in one favorite toy or game received as a gift. Children can give clues to motivate others to guess what's inside before letting it out of the bag.

Duane Graber
Hesston, KS

Our Helping Team

"Our Helping Team" is the simplest method to distribute classroom jobs ever! After discussing the importance of teamwork, give each child a bat cut-out to label and place under the job of his choice. Changing job assignments will take only a few minutes at the beginning of each week!

Linda Johnson
Louisville, KY

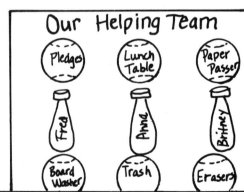

Quiet Lines

If students are noisy while waiting in line, tell them that someone is going to earn a trip to the front. Slowly, give clues describing a well-behaved student. See how quiet they all become while listening for the winner!

Mandy Daniels
Phoenix, AZ

Good Behavior Chart

Encourage students to be on their best behavior. Discuss and agree upon class rules. Then provide this laminated chart. At the end of the day, if a student has followed all rules, he colors a box by his name. Boxes are colored Monday through Thursday, and special treats are given Friday for those with four colored boxes. My class plays educational games for a treat.

Michelle Hawkins
Berea, KY

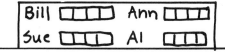

Reading Group Schedules

To eliminate the endless morning cries of "What are we going to do today?", post daily reading charts. Divide a bulletin board into sections, one for each reading group, and label with group names or animals. Each day, post assignments for the groups, in the order they will be assigned. Tasks could include teacher–directed instruction, seat work, centers, and informal reading, and they can be varied from day to day to prevent boredom.

Tommie Sue Schlinder
Harrisonburg, VA

Great Grader

When grading a group of papers that call for objective answers, I place an acetate sheet over the first one and circle the correct answers. Then I lay the sheet over the remaining papers and check at a glance. Using different, colored wipe-off markers for each group of papers makes the job a snap!

Barbara Grubb
Crockett, VA

Textbook Selection Committee

Involve your students in future textbook selection as an interesting, independent assignment. Place texts under consideration at a center, along with specific questions for the students to answer, such as:

Read pages 25, 50, 75, 132, and 200. How many unfamiliar words did you find?

Does the book progress in difficulty from front to back?

Are there any stories/topics of special interest to you?

After the class has had a chance to review the different texts, discuss them and take a vote on the favorite. Go back to your textbook committee with some real feedback!

Ann Fausnight
Canton, OH

Noise Meter

I made a noise meter for my kindergarten room to keep the noise level down. Cut a cardboard semicircle and divide into 3 equal pie shapes. Color red, yellow, and green. Attach a movable hand. When the class is quiet, the hand is on green. If they start to get noisy, I place the hand on yellow. I very seldom have to move the hand to red, but when I do, all heads go down on desks for 1 minute. Then we reset the meter.

Sharol Foxhoven
Iliff, CO

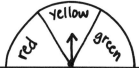

CN = Careful And Neat

If a student completes a paper carefully and neatly, I write "CN" in the top, left-hand corner. Students save CN's until they have enough to cash in for specified rewards. I collect CN's once a week, count them for each student, and mark through the CN so it can't be used again. This procedure takes only 5-10 minutes and encourages better handwriting.

Jean A. Kaschak
Kirkersville, OH

MANAGEMENT TIPS

Neater Worksheets

To save time when using ditto master units, tear off the top sheet. Replace it with a sheet of regular, loose-leaf, ruled notebook paper. Secure it with paper clips at the top. This helps keep your lines of writing straight and can be used on the ditto machine just like a regular master.

Tilda Sumerel
Spruce Pine, AL

Ticket Reward System

Prepare a name card for each child, and place all the cards in a deck. Cards remain in the deck unless the child misbehaves. Students who still have cards in the pile at the end of the day earn good behavior tickets that may be exchanged for prizes. You might provide a treasure chest of toys worth 5, 10 and 20 tickets. Vary the system by announcing a double-ticket day, when each ticket is worth twice as much.

Deborah DeLuccia
North Haledon, NJ

Clapping For Quiet

When your students are too noisy, or you just want their attention, clap a rhythm with your hands. The class then imitates the rhythm and waits quietly for another. Repeat rhythms until the whole class is listening. Then give the necessary instructions, and they're back to work!

Kristi Pedersen
Barron, WI

Pencil Savers

To help my students keep track of their pencils, I give each child a sticky dot from The Education Center and have him write his initials on it. I wrap the dot around the top half of his pencil. When I find stray pencils around the room, I place them in a can for lost pencils, ready to be picked up the next day.

Rhonda Thurman-Rice
Tulsa, OK

Paper Cup Motivators

This tip will motivate children to work harder than ever! Label 5-ounce paper cups with student names, and place them on the windowsill. Mark each cup with a line about ¾ of the way up. Each time the class follows a rule, does good work, or follows directions, drop a bean in the cups. When the cups are filled to the line, reward children for their efforts with a goodie of your choice.

Beverly Bippes
Madison, NE

Super W.A.T.T.

In order to motivate students to be prepared, cooperative, hardworking, and considerate of others, I have developed an award called the SUPER W.A.T.T. This is an acronym for Willing Anytime to Try. The award is not based on grades; instead it motivates students to always give their best efforts and show good manners.

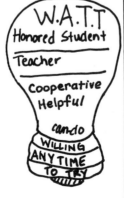

Sharon Sandy
Lorain, Oh

Everlasting Permission Slips

Instead of writing one permission slip after another, make several laminated ones. Leave blanks for a name, destination, and date. Students fill in the information with a grease pencil and wipe slips clean when they return. Slips can be used again and again.

Rebecca L. Gibson
Auburn, AL

Check-In Board

Several teachers in my school use this method for taking the lunch count and recording absentees.

Stain or paint a piece of plywood (30" × 20"). Every six inches or so, screw in a cuphook. Either hang it from the ceiling, put it on a signpost for a floor stand, or prop it on the chalk tray.

Write the name of each child on a key tag, or use labeling tape to stick each child's name under each cuphook.

As the children enter, they can "tag in" by putting their tag into a box labeled "hot lunch" or a box labeled "cold lunch." The day's leader then counts the tags and makes the appropriate notations on the daily absence list.

I find the students love doing this and really keep a close eye out for mistakes! It certainly takes a load off the teacher also!

Buckley Johnson
Wethersfield, CT

Quiet Cleanup Time

To shorten and quiet down desk cleanup time, set a timer for about 3 to 5 minutes. Challenge the children to see if they can all finish before the timer rings, working so quietly they can hear it ticking as they work.

Fran Petersen
N. Tonawanda, NY

Self-Correcting Activity Cards

Save time by making your activity cards self-correcting. Back pairs of activity cards with matching wallpaper or gift wrap. Makes cards more durable too!

Margaret Maxwell
Oregon City, OR

Smile Magic

Here's a way to encourage desk neatness. Cut out large, bright circles from oaktag, add smiley face features, and laminate. During a periodic after-school desk check, place a face on each neat one to reward the owner. The next morning, the children turn in the large faces and draw in small ones by their names on a wall chart. After earning smiles on three consecutive desk checks, the students may take home the large faces. This really works!

Betty Dale
Wellsboro, PA

Ready Pencils

This sharp idea saves time and interruptions. So that children won't have to stop to sharpen pencils, keep a can of sharpened pencils in your room. If a child breaks his point, he goes to the can, takes a fresh pencil, and puts the broken one in the can. After a few days, assign a monitor to sharpen the pencils in the can.

Vita Campanella-Feldstein
Brooklyn, NY

Behavior Reports

This self-report behavior chart is a good way to communicate with both parent and child about classroom behavior. Periodically, confer with each child about his behavior, then help him fill out a behavior report to be sent home. Parents are given an opportunity to respond, and returned reports are filed for future reference—an invaluable tool for documenting student behavior problems and progress.

Connie Connely
Tulsa, OK

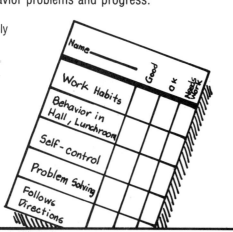

Answer Key

Save time correcting papers and give your students immediate feedback by providing an answer key for reading, spelling, or math worksheets. Students mark their errors and write the number wrong on the tops of their papers. Next, they must redo the ones missed to make the paper 100% correct. This method lets them practice self-directed learning techniques and turns each paper into a success!

Nancy Lach
Mandan, ND

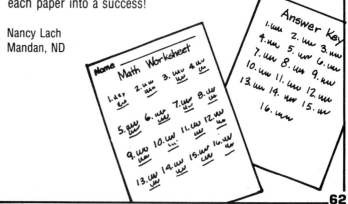

MANAGEMENT TIPS

Watch The Clock

To help children learn the daily schedule and cut down on the incessant "What's next?", draw clock faces on the board with tempera paint. Label each clock with the activity beginning at the time indicated. (Add the hands daily so you can be flexible.) Children watch the clock and match up times to figure out what is coming up next. Class changes run as smoothly as clockwork!

Sister Margaret Mary
Greensboro, NC

No More Hand Mix-Ups

To help children remember their right and left hands, remind them that their left hand will make an *L*.

Connie Miller
Tulsa, OK

Bonus Night

Once a week, I have a bonus night—no homework. The catch is that I make the announcement *after* I've collected the work for the day! Those who completed their work are excused from homework that night. This surprise gives students a good reason to finish homework. It's a real booster! Any student who needs extra credit can always do the work that night.

Diana West
Big Horn, WY

Quicker With Stickers

For years we've all saved ourselves a few seconds by using gummed return address labels on our letters. Here, however, are some additional ways you can use these labels to save time in the classroom.

1. Give a label to each student at the end of the year so that they can drop you a line during the summer.
2. Place a label on any manuscripts submitted to magazines like *The Mailbox*, or on ideas you share with other teachers.
3. Use labels on books or other materials you need to identify.
4. Identify objects in the classroom which may be borrowed throughout the year.
5. Take labels to workshops and meetings and exchange with people who are to send you information.

Tilda Sumerel
Spruce Pine, AL

A Good Right Hand

Dreaming of a private secretary? Get one—one of your students. Instead of spending valuable time passing back papers or "mailing" them yourself, fix a box with a folder for each child, and appoint a secretary to file the papers you have corrected. Although the children are responsible for visiting their own mailboxes, they may not do so when the secretary is filing.

Sister Myra, SND
Ft. Wayne, IN

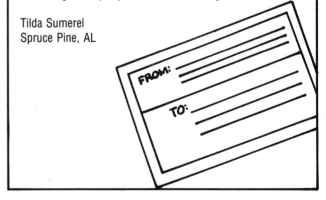

Housecleaning Time

Whenever our classroom looks particularly untidy at the end of the day, I declare a 60-second housecleaning time. One child, the clock-watcher, gives the signal to start. Children spring into action, picking up scraps and straightening desks, games, bookshelves, and centers. In one minute, the children are back in their seats, and our room looks great!

Helen Newton
Schwenksville, PA

Reading Motivator

To motivate children to read, cut a commercially prepared certificate or award (one per student) into 6 to 10 strips. Number the backs of the strips for easy reassembling and place in individual envelopes labeled with student names. For each student, glue one-half piece of ditto paper to an unusual construction paper shape, label with the student's name, and mount on a bulletin board. Each time a student reads a book, glue a strip from his envelope to his shape. Students will enjoy watching their certificate near completion each time they read a book. When the certificate is completed, add an attractive sticker, and send the certificate home. Also a great way to motivate good behavior.

Mary Whaley
Kentland, IN

Answer Key File

To save valuable teaching time, keep an answer key file. Write answers to coded worksheets and centers on index cards and store in a file box by subject area. Students use the code on their activity to locate the proper key, then check their own work.

Ruby Pesek
Lake Jackson, TX

Good Work Habits

In first grade, I use a construction paper folder each month. It has a calendar on the front. Each day we add the date. The children put all their seat work papers in it. Things they must do are:

1. Write name on all papers.
2. Put date on folder.
3. Work must be completed correctly and neatly.

If all is right, they not only get a treat from our treasure chest, but they also get a star on that day on their calendar. Students work hard to see how many stars they can get in a month. Treats can be candy, balloons, or stickers.

Fran Petersen
North Tonawanda, NY

Numbered Cards

If you have problems determining which child had his hand up first for help, try using a numbered card system. Hang a set of brightly colored poster board cards numbered consecutively (1 to 35) on a nail or hook in your room. If a child needs individual help, he gets a number and takes it to his seat. This allows you to roam from child to child as their numbers come up or to call children to your desk in order.

Tommie Sue Schlinder
Harrisonburg, VA

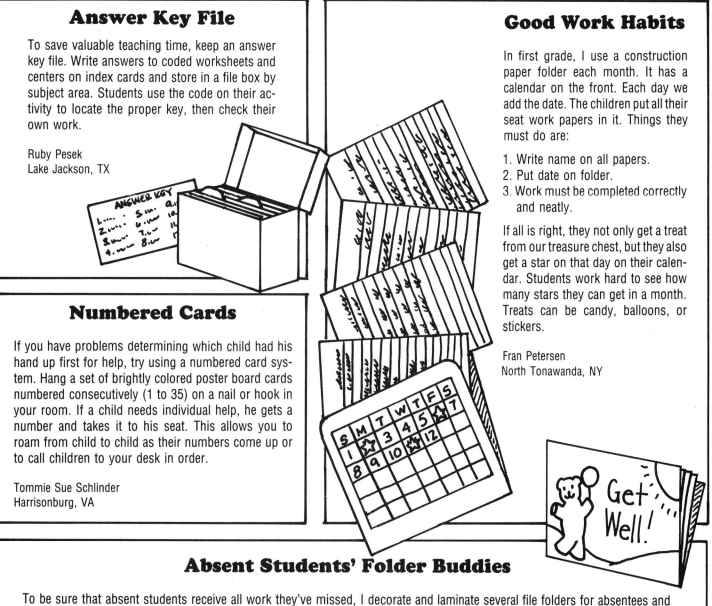

Absent Students' Folder Buddies

To be sure that absent students receive all work they've missed, I decorate and laminate several file folders for absentees and keep them on my desk. Decorations include pictures, puzzles, and best wishes. After attendance is taken, I assign a buddy to put a folder on each absent student's desk and to be sure all assignments are placed in it. All I do is double-check at the end of the day.

Kathryn Irwin
Lewisburg, PA

MANAGEMENT TIPS

Clean Room Tickets

It's easy to have a clean room at the end of the day if you ask students to bring a certain number of tickets as they line up to leave. Tickets are scraps of paper found around the room. Ask one child to be the ticket taker and stand by the door with the wastebasket. The number of tickets can be adjusted according to the amount of paper that needs to be picked up.

Carol McWilliams
Minneapolis, MN

Doodle Stack

Need to jot down a reminder in a hurry? Keep a stack of scrap paper handy. Each week, assign one child to write notes as you think of them and place them in your "doodle stack." By designating note-takers, you won't need to interrupt your lessons.

Mary Dinneen
Bristol, CT

Reading Contest

To make any reading contest a challenge for everyone, I have three first-place winners, one from each reading group. Each student competes with others on his level. Winners are determined by the number of pages read.

Bernice Miller
Chattanooga, TN

Catch-All Bucket

I use a small, plastic bucket as a catchall in my kindergarten. When little things (paper clips, erasers, etc.) are found, they're placed in the bucket without a word being said. Then at the end of the day, I select a child to put everything in its proper place.

Lynn Klomfar
Gulfport, FL

Speeding Tickets

Keeping my students from running in the hallway or classroom was a constant chore. I solved this problem by issuing speeding tickets to students caught running. For each ticket given, the student has a privilege revoked. For example, I took minutes off recess as payment for a ticket. My students slowed down considerably.

Jill Fitch
Bloomdale, OH

Focus On Feelings

During the winter semester, boredom often sets in and tempers become short. A thoughtful way to ease tensions is to focus on feelings, getting pupils talking to each other and thinking about feelings. Divide students into pairs, and suggest topics for small group discussion:

How do you feel when....

your team loses?	you are in a strange place?
you can't fall asleep at night?	you get new clothes?
you are line leader?	it's the night before the first day of school?
you are student of the week?	your friends argue?

Select other appropriate topics, and have students go beyond happy-sad-tired-scared to develop their thoughts. Encourage students to contribute situations to share. Poetry, short stories, or pictures about feelings are possible culminating activities.

Paula K. Holdren
Louisville, KY

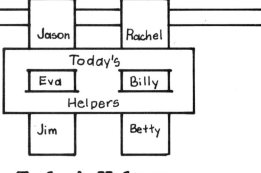

Today's Helpers

Here's an easy way to designate new class helpers each day. Make a 4" x 7" poster board rectangle with two windows. Cut slits. Insert two, 2" strips labeled with student names. Every morning, move the strips to the next names. If a student is absent or tardy, move on to the next name.

Laura Pledger
Baytown, TX

Happy-Face Reminder

I made a happy-face sign that tells students when I am free to talk to them or answer questions. On the reverse side, I drew a face with a red diagonal line through it to remind them not to disturb me when I am busy with another student or group.

Kathryn Folino
Cincinnati, OH

Note To Parents

One way to make sure that your notes go home and straight to the parents is to write the message on a ditto master and let each student add a decoration before you duplicate the sheet. They're enchanted with the "magic" of the ditto process, and the note goes right to the parents to show off the best decorations!

Patricia Luttmann
Lansing, MI

Helper Box

For a real timesaver, ask several older students to come to your room every morning before school to help with simple clerical tasks. Place a helper box near the door, and fill it with tasks you'd like your helpers to do. Older volunteers can pass out papers, check timed tests, run errands, staple dittos, or take down bulletin boards.

Karen Johnson
Columbus, OH

Seat Work Record

Help young students keep track of daily assignments with individual seat work records. At the beginning of the week, tape a record sheet to each student's desk. Each morning as directions are given, students mark the boxes of the assigned work. As a student completes a task, he checks it off on his sheet. Award a foil star for each day of completed work. Send sheets home on Friday.

Mary Needham
Clarkston, WA

	Math	Reading	Spelling
Monday	X✓	X	X✓

Handy Names

Label each student desk by writing a child's name in permanent marker on a strip of clear contact paper. Place on the fronts of desks. Names appear to be written directly on the desks, but the strips peel off easily. They are visible from the front of the room and are a real aid to substitute teachers when passing back papers.

Alice Phillips
LaFarge, WI

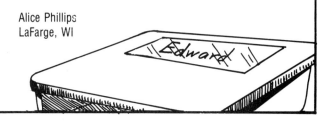

Projection Excitement

Use the opaque projector to enhance lots of classroom lessons. Project a reading selection on the wall for each reading group. Project worksheets onto the blackboard, and have children work the problems. This saves you the time and paper required to reproduce worksheets.

Rebecca L. Gibson
Auburn, AL

Daily Work Chart

At the beginning of the week, give each student a folder with this chart stapled inside to record and keep daily work organized. As they complete assignments, students check the appropriate boxes, place work in their folders and continue. At the end of the day, they draw how they felt and turn in folders.

As I evaluate the work, I either put a sticker over the student's check mark, write "not finished" in the box, or write "see me" if changes are needed. Each Friday, students take folders home so parents see weekly progress.

Dea Butcher
Aurora, CO

Week of :	Seat work	Work book	Center	Today's Work
Monday	✓	✓	✓	☺

MANAGEMENT TIPS

Confidential Box

A "confidential" box kept on a table provides students with a chance to sound off about their concerns. All comments are encouraged, and only the teacher reads them. Children may or may not sign their names. Comments can be extremely helpful in revealing students' personal needs.

Rebecca Graves
Burlington, NC

Movie-Rated Grades

Want to try a new grading scale for fun? See if you can apply the movie rating scale to your students' grades.

X-Excellent
G-Good
PG-Pretty Good
R-Review

Merleen Ivey
Jackson, MS

"Check-Out" Area

Ungraded work piling up on your desk? Set up a classroom "check-out" area for students to use to check their work. Use clothespins to hang answer keys for worksheets, centers, etc. from locker handles. Provide colored pens and allow each student to mark his own paper. (We have a rule that students must leave their pencils at their work area.) Provides immediate feedback and saves time too!

Jill Stine
Dayton, OH

Interruption Hat

While I am working with a group of children, I have the problem of constantly being interrupted by other children. In order to stop this, I wear a hat when I am working with a group. The children are not allowed to interrupt me when I am wearing my hat. If they need help, they ask others in the class until I remove my hat.

Michelle Lee Hesse
Ontario, CA

Personalize Your Property

To personalize materials you often loan to other teachers, carve the reverse of your initials on a gum eraser. Dip in ink or tempera paint and initial all your belongings— centers, posters, duplicating master books, magazines.

Lynne West
Rib Lake, WI

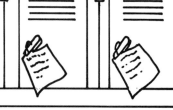

Bill Of Rights

Draw up a student bill of rights and post it in your classroom to encourage student cooperation and respect for each other. Emphasize that the rights students have are designed to guarantee the welfare and learning of all. If a student does not observe another's right to hear, have him write a paragraph entitled, "I will not interfere with my classmates' right to hear."

Darlene Shelton
Collierville, TN

How To End The Day

End the school day on a positive note. Gather children together in a circle. Discuss the activities of the day. Compliment each child on something he or she did well. On 3" x 5" cards, record each child's favorite activity. Every day, children take these cards home to show to parents.

Peggy Mills
Bethlehem, PA

The Listening Tree

To encourage good listening habits, I make a listening tree. I attach cut-out construction paper shapes to a small tree branch. On the back of each shape, I write a special surprise or award. Before students go home, I identify the best listener of the day, who is sent to the listening tree to choose a surprise.

Sharon Johnson
Blacksburg, VA

The Penmanship Club

Because my pet peeve is a sloppy paper, I've created the Penmanship Club! All students begin the year writing in pencil. When they demonstrate that they can produce neat work (no torn corners, errors completely erased, uniform writing, margins), then they may join the Penmanship Club. At the sign-up ceremony, I play a tape of parade music, and the child signs the Penmanship Club members list and receives a certificate and a pen. He may now use a pen for all subjects except math. At any time, I can place a member on probation. Of course, by the end of the year, all students are members, but this really gets even the sloppiest of kids to try.

Jill Robbins
Ogden, IL

Thirsty?

Here are two ways I minimize the problem of getting drinks during class time:

1. Each child receives a cup to keep on his desk if he is thirsty. This saves water, and there are surprisingly few spills.

2. Rather than send my whole class to get water after gym, I walk around the room, reading a story. I tap a few children at a time to get water. There's no waiting in line, and when the story is done, so are the drinks!

Marian Bronero
Waldwick, NJ

Crayon Matching

When children have to draw lines for a matching activity, have them use different colored crayons. It's easier to check and more attractive.

Paula Luce
Seminole, FL

Line Up

Students line up quickly for lunch when they know someone will have a chance to move to the front of the line. After they've lined up, call out a number. The person in that position gets to move to the front!

Ann Hudson
Forest, VA

Book Slips

To keep track of books read by individual students, give each child a supply of duplicated reading slips. When a child reads a book, he fills out a slip, gets a parent's signature, and places it in a file box. Every few weeks, go through the box and record books on reading records.

Lois Cooper
Beckley, WV

Happiness Is ... Reading A Book!

name _____ has read _____ title

date finished _____ parent's signature _____

MANAGEMENT TIPS

Freeze

To keep kids quiet while I'm handing out papers, I call out directions for them to follow. Examples:
—Put your right hand on your heart.
—Look at the ceiling.
—Put your left leg over your right leg.
—Freeze.

Rhonda Knodle
Oakes, ND

Center Management Chart

Here's a management chart with movable pieces that you use all year long. Draw columns for student name strips and center times. Use paper clips to fasten names on the chart and to form hooks for center circles made from cardboard mailing tags. To show children the center assignments for the next day, hang a second circle by each name and flip it over at the end of the day.

Joanne Sperry
Decatur, IL

Job Chart

List all your students' names around the edge of a cardboard circle or pizza round. Use a brad to attach an arrow in the center, and add a soda pull tab for hanging. As a job or errand arises, turn the arrow to the next name. This passes work around more than weekly helper assignments, and it provides a handy class list students can copy when needed.

Geraldine Fulton
Sedgewickville, MO

Credit Cards

To promote and reward reading in my classroom, I use a credit card system. When a child reads a book and can tell me about it, I initial a square on the credit card. When all ten squares are signed, the child may cash in his card for a homework assignment of his choice.

Debbie Fly
Birmingham, AL

Music In The Classroom

I've discovered that music can work wonders in the classroom. Many times when we are doing written work, I put a record on in the background. I've found that this quiets any undercurrent of talking and calms down the restless kids. It's also great for teaching music appreciation. We start the year with popular music and gradually build up to modern music played by symphonies and the classics. My kids are hooked on Baroque music!

Linda Geller
Venice, FL

"I Don't Have A Pencil!"

Here's a way to end the pencil aggravation. Make each child a token labeled with his/her name. When someone needs to borrow a pencil from you, he places his token in the pencil can. When he returns the pencil, he takes his token back. This way I know exactly who has and hasn't returned the borrowed pencils.

Karen Davis
Jacksonville, FL

At The End Of Your Rope?

Instead of scolding when students fail to follow classroom rules, try playing Hangman. Make large tagboard cut-outs that can be clipped together with bent brads. (See illustration.) Children will know you're getting "closer to the end of your rope" as you add a piece for misbehavior. Celebrate when you've all made it through the day without completing the Hangman!

Diane Denison
Columbia, PA

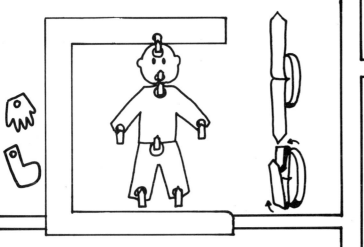

Workbook Record Keeping

Attach a ditto to the back cover of your students' reading workbooks. Number it to correlate with the pages in the workbook. Each time a page is completed and graded, record the score next to the page number. This gives your students a personal record and allows you to send graded work home immediately.

Marjorie S. Martin
Elyria, OH

Exercise For Alertness

Morning exercise makes students more alert and ready to work. It's especially important in winter when children spend a great deal of time indoors. Start the day by exercising together to the students' favorite songs. The teacher begins as leader with warm-up exercises, then chooses a child who, in turn, chooses another. The students enjoy creating new exercise steps and improvising with old ones.

Pamela Barni
Bloomsburg, PA

Multiplication Tables Tip

After you have introduced the basic concept of multiplication and are ready for the students to tackle the facts, have them memorize the 9's first, then work backwards to the 1's and 0's. The children will learn the difficult facts while they are still motivated and eager. Later, when their interest wanes, only the easier ones will be left to master.

Pat Hill
Grand Saline, TX

Tie-Dyed Tee Shirts

Looking for an easy way to keep up with your students on field trips? Tie-dye tee shirts in the same color for your students to wear. Use different colors if your class will be divided in groups. These are also good to wear during school-wide "field days."

Ruth Fields
Ayden, NC

Worksheet Check System

Every time I run multiple copies of a worksheet, I place them in a file folder labeled as to the type of activity, the source, page number, etc. On the front of each folder, I attach an index card. When a worksheet is removed for assignment to a particular child, I write the child's name on the card. This prevents giving the child the same worksheet several times.

Nancy Scroggins
Bunker Hill, IL

MANAGEMENT TIPS

Desk Top Duty

To solve the problem of keeping desk tops clean, keep several pump squirt bottles filled with water and a little liquid cleaner. Each day before the children leave their seats for free time, have them clean their desk tops. Gets your whole class involved in keeping a room you're all proud of!

Mary Dinneen
Bristol, CT

Library Award

Each Friday, the librarian chooses the best-behaved class of the week and presents it with a plaque naming that class "Library Class of the Week." This award may be displayed on the classroom door before being passed on the next week.

Martha Jones
Lynchburg, VA

The June Box

To discourage children from bringing toys and trinkets to school when inappropriate, I display a box where confiscated toys reside until June. The subtle reminder of the "June Box" is enough for kids to keep toys at home. I have never had to use the June box in eleven years of teaching!

Paula K. Holdren
Prospect, KY

Wink!

Keep student attention with a blink of an eye. Tell children to watch closely during a lesson for your wink. The child who catches you winking gets a point for his team.

Linda Moya-Mendez
Hixson, TN

This coupon is good for 3 problems off the arithmetic assignment.

With this coupon you may subtract 2 sentences from the English assignment.

Work—Off Coupons

In this age of coupons and trading stamps, this idea can be used to motivate and interest youngsters. Run off copies of several work–off coupons.

Give these coupons as a reward for excellent work, great effort, good control, or whatever you wish to reinforce. They may then be used when a child needs to shorten an assignment. He simply attaches the coupon to his paper.

Helen Found
Leroy, NY

Recording Game

When you introduce a new game or learning center to your class, turn on your tape recorder. Place the instruction cassette and tape recorder with the new materials. Any student who forgets what to do may listen to your directions again.

Debbie Hawkins
Atwood, IL

Go-Fer Button

As each child in your class takes a turn as the teacher's helper, have him place a "Teacher's Go-fer" button on his desk or wear a Go-fer badge. When the chore is completed, he passes it on to his neighbor. Everyone will get a turn, eliminating arguments about helping out!

Diane Fox
Seffner, FL

Who's Here

Wise, old owls know who's absent. As each child enters the room in the morning, he removes his owl from a tree display and puts it in a box. At a glance, I can see who's absent, and I save time by not calling roll.

Martha Jones
Norcross, GA

Request For Names

Send homework home to sick students via the neighbors! At the beginning of the year, send home a note asking for the names and school room numbers of children who live nearby. Then when a child is absent, send work home with the student listed. Most students return to school in step with the class!

Karen Mullen
Lafayette, IN

Bubble Gum Box

To cut down on absences and tardiness, keep a bubble gum box in your room. Students who haven't been absent or tardy all week get a piece of bubble gum from the box on Friday.

Nancy Davis
Tulsa, OK

Happy Note Box

Disturbed by the negative comments students make about each other? Approach the problem from a positive standpoint. Make a hole in the top of a decorated shoe box and place paper and pencil beside the box. Whenever any member of the classroom (including the teacher) sees another member doing a kind or thoughtful deed, he writes it on paper and drops it in the box. Only positive remarks about good deeds are allowed. On Friday, the box is opened, and the happy notes are read aloud. The praise is enjoyed by all, and the children search for nice things to write about each other. As a result, there are more smiles and less frowns in the classroom.

Mrs. Rebecca Graves
Burlington, NC

Have A Ball!

To solve the problem of whose turn it is to use the classroom ball at recess, I made a poster featuring a large ball. A strip labeled with a student's name is placed in slits cut in the ball. When recess is over, the child who used the ball removes his name, pulls the next name out of a storage pocket, and puts it in place to indicate who will use the ball the following day.

Mary Dinneen
Bristol, CT

Have a Ball at Recess Today!

Easy Seating Chart

Use a magnetic photo album with sticky pages and clear overlays for showing your seating arrangement. Type students' names on cards, then position the seating chart as you wish.

Carol McWilliams
Minneapolis, MN

In The Black Or In The Red?

When I am recording student grades in my record book, I use two pens. One pen is black and the other red. Grades above 75% are recorded in black. Grades below 75% are written in red. This alerts me quickly to students with many low grades who need interim reports sent home.

Amelia K. Burns
Willoughby, OH

MANAGEMENT TIPS

Breathe In ... And Hold It

To quiet an unruly group, or to ease the transition between activities, I ask children to take a deep breath and hold it. Have them release the breath, and say, "Let it out slowly, and take another one. Keep breathing quietly as you listen to my directions."

Sr. Madeleine Gregg
Portsmouth, RI

Award-Winning Idea

Over the years, I have collected a large file of awards that I use to recognize student progress. Since every student receives many awards during the year, here is a system to avoid duplication. File awards in a shoe box with cardboard dividers. Clip a blank sheet to each pack of certificates. When I use an award, I jot the student's name on the paper, preventing later duplications!

Jane Cuba
Redford, MI

First Name File Folders

We are required to save samples of students' work during the year. Since my aide doesn't know the students' last names and children rarely write their full names on papers, I label and alphabetize folders using first names. The aide, a volunteer, or even a student can file the papers easily.

Cyndie Morris
Winter Haven, FL

Seat Work Folders

Make an organized seat work folder with four pockets for each student. Label pockets as follows: "New Assignments," "Fix," "See Me," and ☺ for work to be taken home. Eliminates the need for lengthy instructions.

Kathy Beard
Melrose, FL

A Personal Record

This handy record-keeping chart shows both completed work and what needs to be repeated. List any classroom activities, then duplicate sheets for each student. When work is completed, I fill in the date and the number correct. I can also mark out activities a child is not to do.

Debbie Hawkins
Atwood, IL

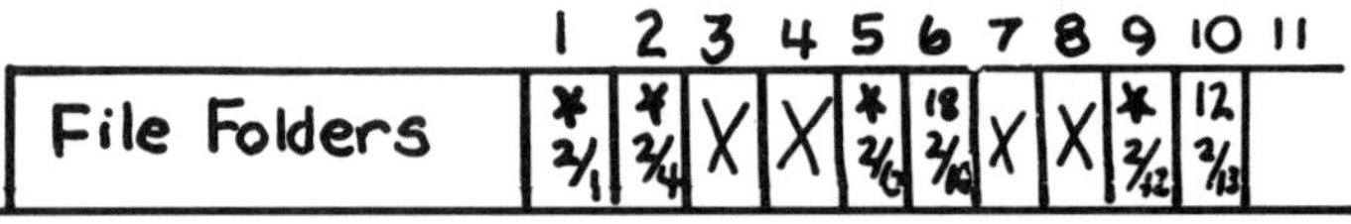

Reading Order

No more quarrels over reading order! Decide which child will read which page during reading time by drawing page numbers from a hat, or by taping page numbers under chairs before students take their seats.

Mary Lee Hitch
Lenoir City, TN

Halve Your Grading Time

Save time by grading two students' papers at once, comparing them one to another instead of an answer key. This works only with answers to questions other than true/false or other two-choice formats. Odds are against two students missing the same items. If answers disagree, check closer to see if one or both made an error.

Debbie Hawkins
Atwood, IL

Following Directions

Following directions seems to be a problem with many second graders. I've found one helpful trick. I have a "Directional Center" that I leave up on my bulletin board all year. (See illustration.) I change the chart paper in the middle of it each week when new directions are given. It has been successful!

Carolyn Kanoy
Winston-Salem, NC

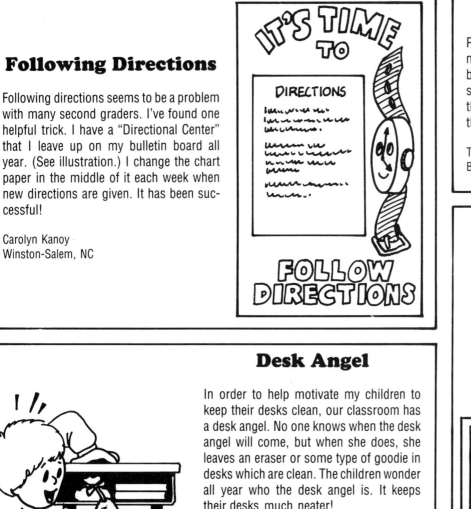

Magic Trash

Play Magic Trash when your classroom needs a pick-me-up. Choose a secret scrap before children clean up. As they collect scraps, carry the trash can around to find the winner with the magic trash. (You get the prize—a clean room!)

Terrell Moore
Bowling Green, KY

Surprise!

Each Monday I print the word "Surprise" on the board. If the class becomes disruptive, I give a warning. The next time, I erase one letter. If any letter is left at the end of the week, we have a surprise on Friday.

Diana West
Big Horn, WY

Desk Angel

In order to help motivate my children to keep their desks clean, our classroom has a desk angel. No one knows when the desk angel will come, but when she does, she leaves an eraser or some type of goodie in desks which are clean. The children wonder all year who the desk angel is. It keeps their desks much neater!

Michelle Lee Hesse
Ontario, CA

Time-saving Tip

To save time passing out seat work, have students pick up papers before class starts. After you lay out the day's work on a table, children take a paper from each pile and go to their seats. Then they label each sheet with name and date, arrange according to a list on the board, and put the papers in their work folders.

Linnette Pugh
Harrisonville, MO

OPEN HOUSE

Indian Tales

The American Indians told tales explaining the reasons for the existence of things around them. When my class is on the Indian unit, we also make up tales. Each child selects a characteristic of one animal to explain in a story and illustrate. The finished tales go into a large book to display on parents' night.

Betty Bowlin
Chesterfield, MO

Alison
How the Bunny Got His Ears
Once there was a bunny. He didn't have any ears. They were little. It rained and his ears got so big that he couldn't walk. The sun came out and his ears became just right.

Brian
How the Bird Got His Beak
Once there was this bird who kissed too much. His mouth got stuck and that's how the bird got its beak.

Recycled Bulletin Board

Don't throw away those shapes you cut out and labeled with students' names on your September "Welcome back!" bulletin board. Recycle them as decorations on the children's work folders or as a desk name tag for parents' night.

Claudia Wilcox
Vernon, CT

John
Math Worksheets

Picture Display

Keep students in the picture! Arrange a large, multipicture display of student photographs, showing children at work and play during the school day. Keep current by adding photos throughout the year. Parents and visitors can view, at a glance, their children and friends.

Laura Braden
Pasadena, TX

OUR CLASS

The Quiet People

As a fun surprise for parents on open house night, greet them with this class of "quiet people." Several days prior, ask parents to send a set of their children's old clothes, but don't tell them why. The students stuff the clothes with newspaper, add cardboard portraits of themselves, and set the "quiet people" in their chairs. What an eye-opener for open house!

Betty Bowlin
Chesterfield, MO

Potluck, Anyone?

Get the whole family involved in the classroom. Plan a family potluck supper! Questionnaires, reminders sent home, and phone calls gather information and spread excitement. The first graders at Northern Hills Elementary School tried the idea and had a huge turnout.

Lisa Rae Anderson
Norfolk, NE

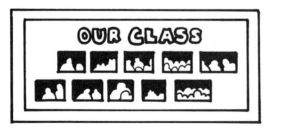

Open House Display

Have a brainstorming session on a topic such as "How I Learn Best," or "What Makes a Good Parent." Then assign students to illustrate each accepted idea on a sheet of paper, and bind the pages together to form a book. Put it out for display at your PTA open house.

Susan Chisari
Orlando, FL

Classroom Guest Book

What do parents and other visitors to the classroom do when they visit? The classroom host/hostess or the child whose parent is visiting takes the three-ringed, loose-leaf guest book to that visitor. There is a place for them to enter date, name, and address. Other inserts include "Let's Get Acquainted" sheets which were completed by students the first week of school. This gives the guest an idea of the background the students bring with them. Other pages include poetry written by students, letters sent home to parents, creative writing, current newspaper clippings of students and school activities, and any other examples the teacher deems would be of interest to visitors, parents, or students. Great for actively involving your visitors!

J. Royce Brunk
Hesston, KS

Open House Bulletin Board

For an unusual open house bulletin board, have each student fold a piece of notebook paper in half horizontally. Students write a self-description on the front and an acrostic on the inside. Staple papers to the board, and ask parents to find their child's description. (You may want to type descriptions so that handwriting won't give them away.)

Melissa Noonkester
Christianburg, VA

Chalkboard Welcome

If you're looking for an interesting and easy display for a parents' meeting or open house, use your chalkboard. Write "Welcome, Parents" in big letters, and allow each child to draw a picture with colored chalk. Have students autograph their artwork.

Connie Connely
Catoosa, OK

Free Frames

Inquire at local frame shops for discarded or irregular mat boards. These colorful, free frames make students' drawings or paintings special. They also make an attractive display for a special occasion at your school.

Clarese Rehn
Lake Villa, IL

Toothpaste For Brighter Desks!

Use toothpaste to remove water spots on wooden desks and chairs. It also makes the room smell nice.

Meg Hedrick
Abilene, TX

Stories About Kids

For a daily penmanship and language practice, have the children write complimentary stories about each other. Then compile the paragraphs into a special book for parents' night.

Connie Connely
Catoosa, OK

Fingerprinting

If your community does not have a program for fingerprinting children, you can begin your own. You will need fairly heavy, nonporous, white paper and black printer's ink. At the top of the paper, list the child's name and date of birth. Print the fingers individually for each hand, and then do the fingers of each hand together. Do the thumbs separately. Send these home with the parents. Encourage them to keep fingerprints in a safe place in the event that the police would need them to help identify a lost or hurt child.

Ellen Javernick
Loveland, CO

Arts & Crafts

Chinese Jacks

To cut corners and save money when making class booklets, I provide my students with colored plastic rings called "Chinese Jacks." Found in most toy or discount stores, they are cheaper and more eye-catching than regular notebook rings.

LaDonna Hauser
Wilmington, NC

Yarn Needles

Many craft ideas require expensive (and easily lost) yarn needles. I make my own quickly and inexpensively using a spool of wire that is flexible but stiff. Bend 5-inch pieces of wire in half, then insert a pencil in the looped end and twist. This needle works well for prepunched sewing projects, and you can easily make needles for the entire class!

Jane Cuba
Redford, MI

Clock Shop

After completing a unit on time, have children make their own clocks at home. Provide materials such as paper plates, paper fasteners, and oak tag. Stress that they are to use their imaginations and any materials they find at home. The finished products will make a great display, and you might even vote for favorites!

Diane Jones
Newtown, PA

Game Making

Even younger students can help with game making. Give pupils a blank game trail with directions to make up a game on any topic—animals, people, household objects. Let them glue pictures cut from old books or catalogs on the trail. Especially good as readiness activities, these games can be used in the classroom or can be sent home for additional practice with parents.

Mary Hood
Shevlin, MN

Spelling Magic

Try a little magic to teach spelling words! Have students write words on white construction paper with white crayon. Then have them paint over the paper with thin tempera paint. Words will appear like magic!

Debi Kruse
Fort Wayne, IN

String A Number Line

Take a piece of tagboard and cover with contact paper. Punch ten sets of holes along the top and bottom. Make a set of 10 circles and label them with the numbers 1 to 10. Make a set of 10 circles with pictures depicting 1 to 10 items. Using a shoestring, the child strings the numbers in order along the top, and he strings the pictures at the bottom.

Carolyn Wiant
Urbana, OH

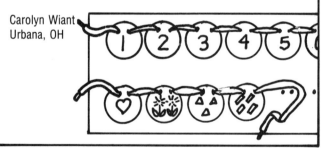

Tempera Paint Containers

To make paint containers large enough for several students to use, cut plastic milk containers (the half-gallon or gallon size) about two inches from the bottom. To reuse, simply rinse them out.

Deane Beverly
Pawcatuck, CT

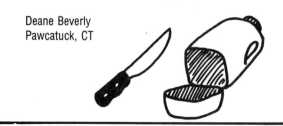

Using A Kwik-Twist Paper Drill

The paper drill, which can punch through papers up to ½" thick, is useful to make a booklet. Stack pieces of paper, fold in half, and punch 2 holes along the fold. Tie with yarn. The drill can also reinforce folded workbooks with a staple in the center in the same fashion.

Eldonna Ashley
Richwood, OH

Rubber Stamps

Make your own rubber stamps by cutting shapes from tire inner tubes and rubber cementing them onto small wooden blocks. Children enjoy leaf shapes, dinosaurs, and animals for decorating their papers.

Mary J. VanderPoppen
Seattle, WA

Pretty Bulletin Boards

To encourage children who continually fail to finish their work and to reward the children that always finish, I use a monthly art project.

At the beginning of each month, on a large piece of poster board, I draw the outlined shape of something seasonal, such as an Easter egg.

As each child finishes his work paper and brings it to me, I give him a piece of colored tissue paper (about a one-inch square). He takes the tissue paper to the art project, folds it around the bottom of a large primary crayon (see illustration) and pastes the tissue on the Easter egg.

No one wants to miss pasting on a piece, and as the outline becomes nearly filled in, students become eager to get it finished. This really helps motivate everyone to finish work, and I get a pretty, new bulletin board every month!

Lynn Klomfar
St. Petersburg, FL

Nose-y Bookmarks

After reviewing library rules, make tagboard bookmarks that really hold the place. Children cut out a tagboard figure and cut around the nose so it will fit on a page. Decorate with yarn and wallpaper scraps.

Deb Dye
Marion, IN

Disappearing Act

Help your students perform a real disappearing act. Children write their names with chalk on black construction paper. Then they spray with hair spray and watch their names disappear and return.

Clara Presutti
Wheeling, WV

Giant Crayons

Melt broken crayons in a muffin tin in a hot oven. Let cool, and pop out of muffin tin. You have large crayons which are very useful.

Barbara Blackburn
Boiling Springs, NC

Furry Fellows

Instead of drawing pictures and attention getters on tagboard, cut them out of furry material. It lasts forever! This also works well for making tactile letters and numbers.

Cathy Whittle
Nashville, TN

Be A Good Egg

Decorate your room and instruct your students at the same time with large eggs cut from colored paper. Provide an assortment of lace, ribbon, sequins, flowers, etc.

Let your students decorate the eggs and think up appropriate messages to promote good behavior or other desirable character traits.

Fran Petersen
N. Tonawanda, NY

Timely Time Lines

To help children remember important dates in history and visualize sequential relationships, I have them draw time lines on cursive writing sentence strips. Children divide the strips into 3 inch units and illustrate each with an important event from our discussions. At the end of the unit, children have a meaningful study tool and a satisfying souvenir.

Paula Holdren
Louisville, KY

Stamp Out A Warning

Children will enjoy alerting others to safety hazards with posters they've made using alphabet rubber stamps and various colors of ink. Students use the stamps to write a message and then make an eye-catching picture to finish off the poster. Emphasize the need for a short, catchy slogan for each safety poster.

Shirley Liby
New Castle, IN

Slide Show

After your class has finished reading a story, make your own slide show. With the class, plan a series of pictures to illustrate the plot, and write a sentence caption for each picture to tell the story. Tape the captions and photograph the drawings on slide film. Don't forget to serve popcorn!

Mary Ann Kaufman
Sayville, NY

Clean-Up Fun

After an art project, when the floor is littered with scraps of paper, we play Scrap Race. I'll say a color, and all the children must pick up only scraps of that color and put them on their tables. Then I'll call another color, and only those colored scraps may be picked up and placed on the table. This goes on until all scraps are gone, and the table with the largest pile of scraps wins. The winners are allowed to go to lunch first or get an extra five minutes of play. This really helps to get all the mess cleaned up quickly, while reinforcing color recognition.

Lynn Klomfar
Gulfport, FL

Yarn Dispenser

Containers for baby wipes are compact, efficient dispensers. The hole in the top is perfect to pull yarn through, and refilling yarn is easy. Have parents with babies save these for you.

Sharon John
Loring, MT

Tracers

Avoid making tracing patterns every year. Make patterns to trace on 12" x 18" oaktag, laminate, and then cut out. Patterns stay in good shape for several years.

Mary Dinneen
Bristol, CT

Crayon Bags

Crayon boxes never seem to last past the first month of school. To keep crayons from being lost or broken, give children a small plastic bag to use as a container for their crayons.

Mary Dinneen
Bristol, CT

Classroom Banners

Save cardboard gift wrap tubes to make hanging banners. Use poster board, bulletin board paper, or felt material, then glue on cut-out letters and art. To make smaller banners, use paper towel tubes.

Debbie Wiggins
Myrtle Beach, SC

Coloring With Chalk

To color large bulletin board characters, games, and posters, save your markers by using chalk. After coloring, wipe artwork with a tissue. Laminate the pieces, or spray them with hairspray to stop smudging. This also makes coloring these large characters much faster.

Debbie Kuzman
Slickville, PA

Tube Collection

Gather up a sizeable collection of cardboard tubes from Christmas gift wrap, kitchen wrap, or tape. Have pre-school and kindergarten children paint them with various colors of tempera paint. Coat tubes with a nontoxic clear finish if desired. Children may arrange tubes in artistic designs, count them, or sort them by color or size.

Lucy J. Knight
Washington, DC

Book Catalog Uses

Librarians and school secretaries receive many colorful book catalogs, which are often discarded. Ask them to save these for your class. The catalogs are sources for pictures of familiar book "friends." Have students cut out book characters for bookmarks or glue several pictures on construction paper and laminate for place mats.

Cathy C. Bonnell
Phoenix, AZ

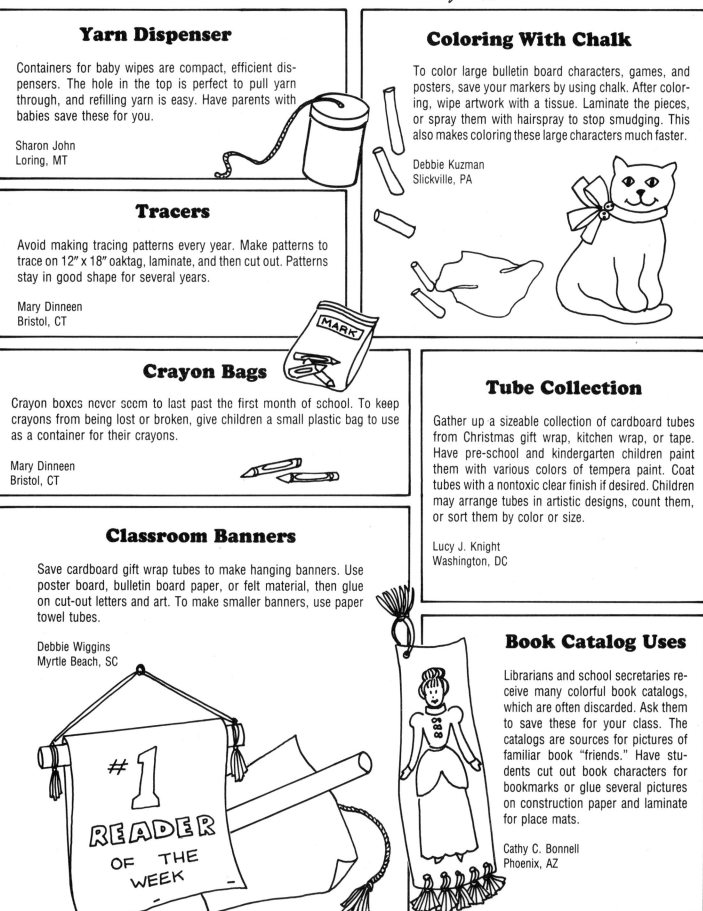

Yazoo The Yardstick

Children can make their own colorful yardsticks by pasting 36 one-inch circles on a tagboard strip. To show the divisions by foot, make the 1st, 12th, and 36th circles out of a contrasting color. When completed, children can use their yardsticks to measure objects around the room. Younger children might enjoy a story about Yazoo meeting his friends (circles) and special friends (contrasting colors).

Joan Blanco
Pompano Beach, FL

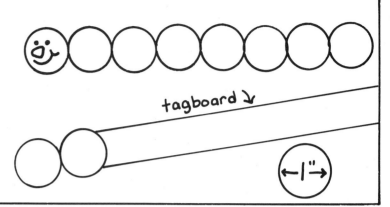

Bumper Sticker Campaign

Begin your own classroom publicity blitz on basic skills by having your students design their own bumper stickers. Provide strips of solid-colored contact paper and permanent markers, along with sample slogans to get the students started: "Reading Is My Thing," "Make Magic With Math," "Science Is Out Of This World," etc.

Vurna Turner
Greensboro, NC

Art Gallery

To display children's art, stack three boxes that are covered with material. Staple flat art to the sides, and use the top for 3-D art.

Sr. Margaret Ann
Emmitsburg, MD

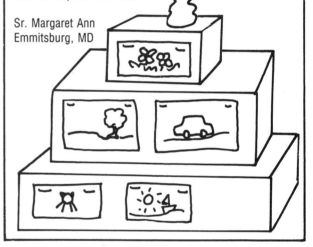

Squirt-Top Paint Bottles

Is a squirt of tempera paint all you need? Save plastic, squirt-top, liquid detergent bottles. Mix tempera paints at the beginning of the year, and store them in these clean bottles. You'll save time when paint is needed for art projects or small touch-ups.

Kathy Dykes
Stanford, KY

Flannelboard Help

To make flannelboard cut-outs more permanent, use the cool-seal laminating film to cover the front side of your picture or figure. Glue the felt to the back side. No more worries about letting the children touch!

Carol Kondras
Boca Raton, FL

Nail Brushes

Don't throw away old brushes from fingernail polish bottles. Clean them in nail polish remover and use as paintbrushes for those hard-to-reach places.

Meg Hedrick
Abilene, TX

Easy Washup

Keep a can of laundry soap by the sink for easy washup after art activities. Teach children to place 1 finger in the flakes before washing. It takes less time, less soap, and results in less mess!

Marcia Backstrom
Bethel Park, PA

Monster Bag Puppet

With a little bit of imagination (and construction paper), your students can turn a plain bag into their favorite monster. Each child cuts, then glues, a construction paper face onto the bottom of a small lunch bag. They then add another piece of paper for Cookie Monster's body and attach cut-out eyes. Children can feed their puppets cut-out cookies that are labeled with sight words, numbers, colors, etc.

Karen Adams Stone
Goodland, KS

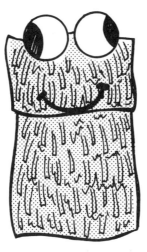

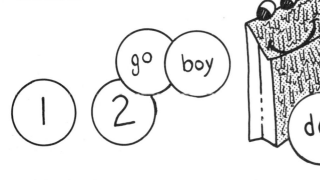

Special Paint

Mix a little egg yolk, dry detergent, and food coloring to make paint that will stick to a shiny surface such as glass, foil, or freezer paper.

Bonnie Pinkerton
Bowling Green, KY

Easy Gluing

Use empty fingernail polish bottles to store glue. The small brush prevents children from getting too much glue on their projects, and that saves on your glue!

Bonnie Pinkerton
Bowling Green, KY

Glue Dispenser

If you have difficulty pouring glue from those gallon containers into small glue bottles, try this idea. Put glue in an empty syrup or dish detergent container. The squirt top makes it easy for children to refill their own glue bottles.

Barbara Ihnen
North Manchester, IN

Classroom Art Paper Dispenser

Install a cafe curtain rod as a dispenser for a big roll of shelf paper or freezer paper in your art center. Hang a pair of blunt-nosed scissors nearby so that children can help themselves.

Bonnie Pinkerton
Bowling Green, KY

Monofilament Fishing Line

I use monofilament fishing line under the chalkboard for displaying artwork and papers. Run the line through the center spring of short, colored clothespins to have a ready way to hold up work.

Dorothy Simmons
Memphis, TN

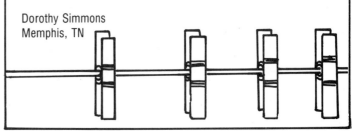

Refrigerated Contact Paper

Put contact paper in a refrigerator for a few hours before using it to cover games. Then the paper is less sticky and much easier to use.

Debbie Hawkins
Urbana, IL

Draw What It Says

Give each student two sheets of paper. On one he writes descriptive directions for a drawing. On the other, he draws what he described by following his own directions. Students exchange directions and follow them. The author and artist compare pictures. If drawings aren't similar, they review the instructions and how well each person followed them.

Rebecca Webster Graves
Burlington, NC

1. Draw a circle the size of a quarter.
2. Draw 2 eyes, a nose, and a mouth in the circle.
3. Draw a top hat on top of the circle, and darken it.
4. Draw a circle the size of a 50¢ piece under the first circle letting it touch but

Wanted Sign

Have you ever wanted to do a classroom art activity, but didn't have enough of one item? Post a Wanted sign outside your door, and watch the supplies come in. Put a sample of the needed item and the number you want with the Wanted sign. Keep a daily count posted of how many you have collected to avoid an overflow. The whole school enjoys the involvement and it makes your job a breeze!

Rebecca L. Gibson
Auburn, IL

WANTED
130 1-gallon
milk jugs (plastic)
— EMPTY, CLEAN, AND DRY —

Noodle Coloring

Whenever we do a project with macaroni noodles, I color the noodles first, using Easter egg coloring packages. The noodles come out with bright coloring, ready to string, sort, count, etc.

Eleanor Messner
Dalton, PA

Magic Marker Tubs

Are your children always losing magic marker caps? Pour plaster of paris into a margarine tub. Place markers upside down ½" in the mixture, before it hardens. Keeps markers together and prevents loss of caps.

Connie Connely
Catoosa, OK

Glue Caps

When children need only a small amount of glue for a craft or art project, pour the glue into a soft-drink bottle cap. Students won't get as messy and caps can be thrown away at the end of a project.

Rebecca Graves
Burlington, NC

Vinyl Smocks

Make inexpensive, long-lasting painting smocks from vinyl upholstery material. Use a piece about 36″ x 15″, and cut a hole for the head 10″ from one end. The short end hangs in back, while the long end protects the entire front of a student. These smocks take less than a minute to cut out, they clean and store easily, and they never ravel along the edges. Many upholstery shops will gladly donate short pieces of vinyl material.

Pauline Lawson
Morristown, TN

Shopping Bag Costumes

Shopping bags are an inexpensive, simple alternative to costumes. Use the large ones with the heavy handles, cut out the bottoms, and decorate. The child steps in and pulls a handle over each shoulder.

Lynn Klomfar
Gulfport, FL

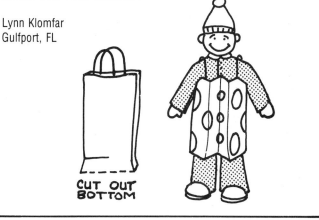

Language Unit Windows

For each language unit, choose 7-8 vocabulary words, and tape a simple picture for each word to the outside of your classroom windows. Have children trace the drawings on the inside of the windows and paint them with water-base paint. Your room will be brightly decorated, and your students will benefit from both fine motor practice and language expansion.

Kim Zimmerman
Tulsa, OK

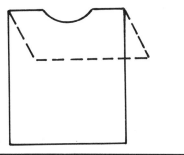

Color Town

At our Color Town center, kindergarten or preschool children can practice their coloring skills. Set up at least one desk or table in a colorful area of the room, and furnish it with suitable coloring books, worksheets, crayons, watercolors and markers. Allow children to try different color media together.

Lucy J. Knight
Washington, DC

Math Drill Sheets

Motivate your students and liven up math drill sheets at the same time. After writing several rows of math problems on a ditto, have a student decorate the bottom of the ditto with his own artwork. Be sure students add their signatures to their pictures.

Connie Connely
Catoosa, OK

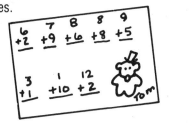

Read And Grow

Encourage reading to bloom with flowers that grow taller with each book read. Cut a large, colored, construction paper flower with a yellow circle glued to its center for each child. Use an X-Acto knife to make two parallel slits in the center. Cut green tagboard strips the width of the flower slits, and insert the strip through the flower from the back. Write a child's name on each flower.

As the child completes a book, slide his flower up the stem, and write the number of books read on the center of the green strip. These work best if hung on the wall. Children enjoy taking flowers home when they are fully grown.

Myrna Kokales
Aberdeen, SD

The Cardboard Kids

Invite the "Cardboard Kids" to your class for role-playing, holiday programs, and unit or book reviews. Make these stand-up characters from a large cardboard refrigerator box. Select a boy and a girl of average size from your class. Have these children lie down on the cardboard, leaving 6″ above each head. Outline the figures in pencil, and then trace with a marker. Use an X-Acto knife to cut holes in the cardboard for heads. Students add cut-out clothing, including hats and props. The children take turns putting their faces behind the Cardboard Kids and answering questions from the audience. We have made Indian kids, pilgrim kids, and Abraham Lincoln, among others!

Jane Skaryd
W. Sayville, NY

Art Ideas

Art period can be trouble-free. Here are two ideas to help spruce up any art class:

1. Wipe out sticky hands during activities requiring glue. Keep a damp sponge at each worktable to clean messy hands. Eliminates disruptive traffic to and from the sink.

2. To make a clean stamp pad that produces quality prints, lay two pieces of felt in an aluminum pan. Pour or brush thick tempera paint onto the felt, allowing the paint to be absorbed. Let children press different kinds of Styrofoam packing pieces onto the pad, then onto paper. Repeated stampings will produce an interesting design.

Nancy Seate
Goldsboro, NC

Quilted Book Reports

In addition to a half-page written summary of a book, each of my students recreated a scene from his book on white drapery lining fabric that is coated to prevent water stains. The coating kept felt-tip or fabric markers from bleeding when the scene was colored. After coloring, students stitched the scene, batting, and backing together using long basting stitches. For remaining squares, students submitted possible sketches. Those chosen by a selection committee were completed as outlined above. I used school colors for connecting strips. The hanging was assembled by a quilt-as-you-go variation on my sewing machine and is now a conversation piece hanging in the school hallway. Hint: try to find parents willing to do the time-consuming stitching on the sewing machine.

Betti Birkenmeier
Jackson, MO

Coaster Awards

Make easy and inexpensive awards by stapling paper coasters to construction paper ribbons. Decorate with colorful markers.

Barbara Hosek
Canoga Park, CA

Band-Aid Boxes

After the cardboard boxes fall apart, store crayons in empty, metal, Band-Aid boxes.

Margie Kirk
Antigo, WI

Math Monsters

Here's a quick activity that requires only paper, crayons, and imagination. Students create their own artistic monsters by listening and following oral directions such as:

"Give your monster a green, square body."
"Put 5 orange eyes on the head."
You may be surprised at the different pictures!

Denise Cox
Greenville, NC

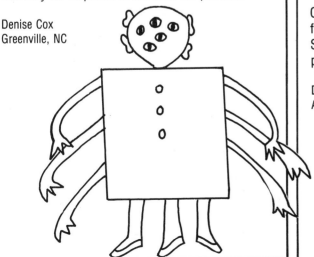

Room Mother's Apron

As a personal remembrance for room mothers, make each one a cobbler-style apron. Have students autograph the apron and let them embroider the outlines with colored thread. The room mothers will enjoy such a special gift, and the children will be quite pleased to see the mothers wearing the aprons at the next party.

Mary Hurley
Holly, CO

Paper By The Truckload

Check at your local printing shop for leftover and scrap paper available for teachers. You'll probably find pieces in all colors, sizes, and weights. Stock up on large and small scraps to make flash cards, games, and art projects.

Debbie Hawkins
Atwood, IL

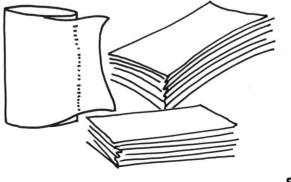

State It In A Poster

When studying letter writing, have each student write and mail a business letter to a state tourism office, allowing six to eight weeks for responses. Then, have each student construct a poster about the state, using library books, maps, and encyclopedias for more research. Poster illustrations should include a basic outline map showing the capital city, major bodies of water, and three of the state symbols (flag, bird, flower, tree). Challenge students to add more information.

Sandra Steen
Corinth, MS

Glue Containers

Encourage students to conserve on the amount of glue used by putting only as much as they will need on small cardboard squares used for pats of butter. Give each child a toothpick to apply glue. Working with a toothpick helps improve coordination and development of small hand muscles.

Connie Luginsland
Waverly, KS

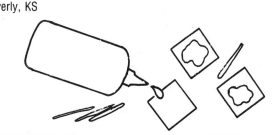

Paint On Windows

For a different and exciting art lesson, let your students paint on the windows. Just add dish soap to tempera paint, and paint as usual. I've used this idea to decorate windows with Halloween fence posts, Christmas scenes, and Valentine's Day hearts. Cleanup is easy— just use water.

Chris Berens
Bolivar, OH

Kindergarten Slide Show

As a culminating activity to our circus unit, my students made their own slide show. I bleached the color out of old slides (straight bleach), rinsed them in clear water, and dried them overnight. Each child was given two blank slides and an assortment of fine-tipped magic markers to draw his favorite aspect of the circus. I encouraged them to press hard to make the colors more brilliant. The next day each child identified his/her own slides as they appeared on the screen. The show was enjoyed by all.

Marsha Konken
Sterling, CO

Nonsmear Chalk

To make chalk art pieces easier to work with, dip chalk into sugar water before drawing. Finished art will not smear.

Bonnie Pinkerton
Bowling Green, KY

Nonaerosol Spray Bottles

Use nonaerosol spray bottles for spatter painting, instead of old toothbrushes. Students lay objects that they have found, such as leaves, rocks, or paper clips on their papers. Then they spray the papers lightly. They can remove or rearrange the objects and spray with a second color of paint. For a different touch, they may use seasonal shapes and colors of paint. Put the spatter design on plain brown wrapping paper if you want to use it as gift wrap paper.

LaDonna H. Hauser
Wilmington, NC

Puppet Power

Puppets and children pair up for reading and speech development. Have children make puppet characters to "speak" for vowel and consonant sounds. Obtain small bags from a grocery or specialty store so puppets fit little hands. Use puppets while reading stories or word cards in a group. When a student comes to an unfamiliar word which has the same vowel or consonant sound as his puppet, he manipulates his puppet and says the word.

Rhonda Thurman-Rice
Catoosa, OK

Musical Art

Have children draw pictures while listening to music. When the music stops, each child passes his paper to a neighbor. Continue the music. Children add to their neighbor's picture and pass their artwork on each time the music stops. Choose holiday music, works by famous composers, or sound tracks from current movies as themes if you wish. Display the group efforts around the classroom so students can admire the creativity of their classmates.

Linda Rabinowitz
Atlanta, GA

Grease Pencil Remover

To remove grease pencil or crayon marks from a laminated surface, use silver cream polish. It works just like an eraser!

Margaret McCandless
Mentor, OH

Reading Center Pillows

To make our library center more comfortable and more personal, my children helped make toss pillows for the center. Each child drew herself/himself on an 8″ x 8″ square of un-bleached muslin. The picture was colored heavily with wax crayon and ironed between waxed paper. I sewed the squares together with scraps of bright gingham and backed them with plain muslin. The pillows were stuffed with discarded panty hose.

Carol Lambert
Slippery Rock, PA

People Cracker Pins

Cute pins can be made from People Crackers found in the pet food section at the grocery store. Just glue on a pin backing and use Modge Podge to coat the dog biscuit.

Ann Hudson
Forest, VA

Alliteration Photos

The copy machine makes good black-and-white copies of class photos. Have students cut out photograph copies, mount them on construction paper, then write an alliterative phrase for each one.

Kathleen Hutchinson
Beaverton, OR

Art always ate apples in April.

Sally saves stamps sometimes.

Mighty Man Or Monster?

Students draw a hero or a monster. Then they answer questions that you've provided, using complete sentences. They're amazed to discover they've written a story.

1. What is his name?
2. Where is he from?
3. What powers does he have?

4. Is he a "good guy" or a "bad guy"?
5. Would you like to be this monster/hero?

Bonnie Dennis
Blacksburg, VA

Write A Drawing

After your students have written short stories or poems, have them copy their work in the shape of whatever object they wrote about, using their words to form the outline of the shape. Good practice in both creative writing and art!

Shirley Liby
New Castle, IN

I really like our old car. It is rusty, but I love it because the car is tan and red. We have had a lot of great times in it before.

Chunky Crayons

Use stubs of old crayons to make large, chunky crayons. Spray the inside of a push-up deodorant container with Pam. Melt stubs and pour wax into the opening. When hardened, push up to break the seal.

Diane Billman
West Carrollton, OH

Rubber Cement Dispenser

To make using rubber cement easier, put the cement in a small oil can (the kind used to oil bicycle chains). This way you can squirt out just enough. If the cement becomes too thick, add a little thinner. This way you can buy the large can that doesn't come with a brush and save money.

Heidi Harper
Blacksburg, VA

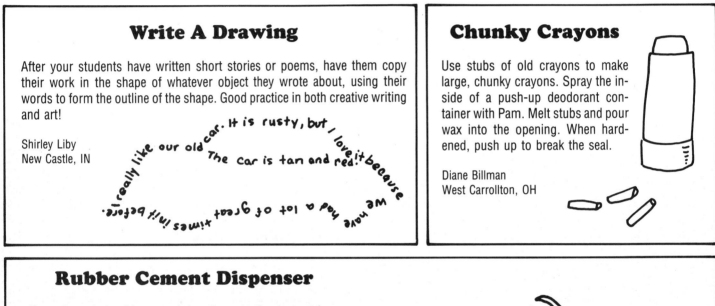

Place-Value Pockets

Have each student glue four pockets on a piece of poster board. Instruct them to write the numerals 0 to 9 twice on 20 slips of white paper. When the teacher calls a number, students form it by placing the number slips in the pockets. Add more pockets and slips for larger numbers.

Sylvia McFeaters
Slippery Rock, PA

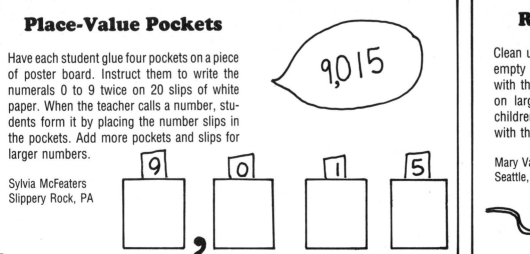

9,015

Roll-On Paint

Clean up sloppy painting times with empty roll-on deodorant bottles. Fill with thinned tempera paint and use on large pieces of paper. Remind children to shake the bottles often—with the caps on!

Mary Vander Poppen
Seattle, WA

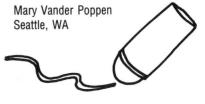

Detergent Bottles

Plastic detergent bottles can be cut into sturdy clock hands, pointers, game pieces, and badges. Students can decorate plastic circles with waterproof markers, stickers, or cut-out pictures. Add double-faced carpet tape on the back for badges, or punch holes in circles to string for a necklace.

Virginia Larsen
Lindenhurst, IL

Accordion Greeting Card

Children create this greeting card for someone who is ill or moving away, or someone who deserves congratulations. Cut 12″ x 18″ art paper in half lengthwise, then fold it accordion-style at three-inch intervals. Pass folded papers for each child to write or draw his greeting on a 3″ x 6″ section. Cut off unused sections, tape in one long strip, refold, and add a to/from label on top. Tie with colored ribbon. The recipient will be impressed with the lengthy card.

Rowena L. Brooks
Stanfield, NC

Calligraphy Markers

Instead of buying the expensive double and triple markers that are out on the market now, make your own. Using a razor blade or art knife, cut notches across the point of a wide-tipped marker. Use your new calligraphy pen to do quick, fancy lettering on centers, to create pretty stripes and plaids, or to do an interesting border around a poster.

Vurna Turner
Greensboro, NC

Cleaning Work Tables

An easy way to get those dirty work tables clean is to let children finger-paint on the tabletops with shaving cream. They'll have loads of fun, the tables will be clean, and the room will have a good, fresh smell.

Jo Farrimond
Broken Arrow, OK

Plastic Pack Holders

Plastic, six-pack drink holders make great mobiles. Tie a string to each ring and attach your pictures. Much softer and lighter than coat hangers.

Christine Davidson
Marietta, GA

Seascape

When studying the ocean world, we turned our entire classroom into a beautiful seascape. We made fish and creatures stuffed with newspaper to hang from the ceiling, crepe-paper seaweed to dangle in the corners, and shells to tape to the floor. Creating this environment really involved my students in ocean study.

Betty Bowlin
Chesterfield, MO

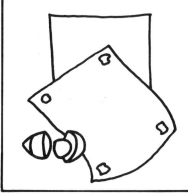

Stick 'Em Up

Make any surface a display board to accompany a lesson by using sticky putty. Use it on chalkboards, bookcases, filing cabinets, or a projection screen. It makes flannelboard figures stick on any surface too. When the lesson is over, remove the pictures and putty to use again.

Linda L. Skadeland
Melbourne, FL

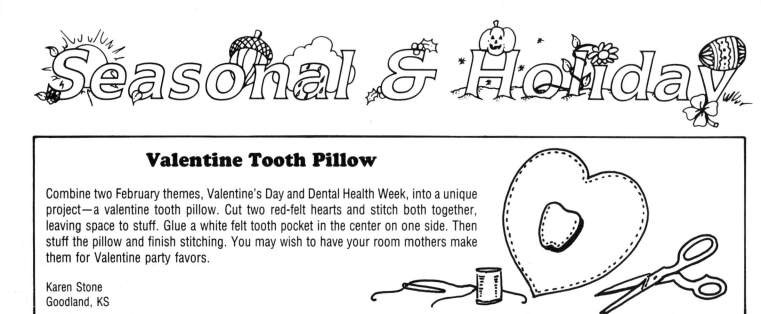

Valentine Tooth Pillow

Combine two February themes, Valentine's Day and Dental Health Week, into a unique project—a valentine tooth pillow. Cut two red-felt hearts and stitch both together, leaving space to stuff. Glue a white felt tooth pocket in the center on one side. Then stuff the pillow and finish stitching. You may wish to have your room mothers make them for Valentine party favors.

Karen Stone
Goodland, KS

Valentine List

Children can make a valentine list to take home by alphabetizing their classmates' names. About 2 weeks before Valentine's Day, have students write their names with dark crayons on 4" x 18" strips of paper. As a class, arrange these strips in two columns, one for boys and one for girls, and alphabetize by last name. Children then copy the names on a valentine worksheet, complete with the teacher's name and a special note to parents.

Mary Dinneen
Bristol, CT

Sweet Tooth Estimates

For Valentine fun and estimation practice, fill a jar with candy hearts. Let children estimate the number of pieces in the jar. The student whose estimate is closest to the actual number receives the jar and candy.

Darlene Shelton
Memphis, TN

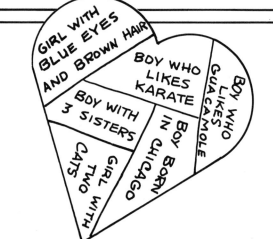

Biographical Valentine

This Valentine's Day activity will help students get to know their classmates better. Divide a heart shape into several sections, label them with descriptive phrases as shown, and duplicate for each student. Children interview each other to find someone to fill each category.

Debbie Wiggins
Myrtle Beach, SC

Famous Pairs From Books

For great Valentine's Day mobiles, try the following activity. During a class discussion, have students list as many famous pairs as they can. The only requirement is that these famous people or animals must be found in books. List as many pairs as there are students in your classroom, more if possible. To get you started, a few are Paul Bunyan and Babe, Romeo and Juliet, Ramona and Beezus, Henry and Ribsy, Hansel and Gretel, Little Ann and Old Dan, and Cinderella and Prince Charming. Number each pair. Each student draws a number to select his famous pair. The student must find a book in the school library in which the couple can be found. Using the card catalog, the student lists the book title and call number. After finding needed information, students make mobiles using heart pieces about their famous pairs, listing book titles, call numbers, and the couples' names. A sketch of the famous pair completes each literary valentine.

Sandra Looper
Ada, OK

Nursing Home Projects

My class makes monthly projects for a local nursing home. Not only do the children love it, but the adults are just thrilled! October spiders are Styrofoam balls painted black. We add pipe cleaner legs. We make February Valentine flowers by pasting paper hearts on Popsicle sticks. The sticks stand in clay lumps inside a shoe box lid.

Mrs. L. Szyarto
Howell, NJ

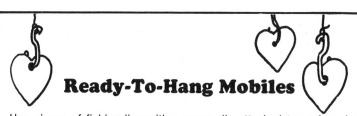

Ready-To-Hang Mobiles

Use pieces of fishing line with a paper clip attached to each end to hang seasonal objects in your classroom. Suspend the lines from the ceiling, using tape, nails, or tacks. Punch holes in items such as leaves, eggs, valentines, shamrocks, or snowflakes. Hang them on the bottom clips, and enjoy.

Rebecca Webster Graves
Burlington, NC

Valentine Mailbox

Each year, every student in my class designs and manufactures his or her own Valentine mailbox. I also have my own box for cards—a standard rural mailbox covered with red and white dotted swiss and white-felt hearts. The children enjoy the teacher's box as much as I do!

Marla Budd
Dresden, OH

Valentine Pencil Treats

As a special treat for my students, I cut out large hearts for Valentine's Day and write an individual message on each. Instead of drawing an arrow through the heart, I punch two holes and insert a Valentine's Day pencil from The Education Center.

Laura Crosby
Glen Ellyn, IL

Valentine Message Math

Get more mileage out of boxed valentines by printing math problems on the reverse side. Laminate the cards, and have students complete problems with a grease pencil.

Pamela Biery
Belmont, WV

Valentine Tree

Provide a valentine tree so students can choose activities themselves. Place a branch in a clay pot full of plaster of paris. Hang paper hearts labeled with activities on each branch with clothespins. A student selects a heart, pins it to himself, and does the chosen task. Change the tree to suit the season by writing choices on cut-out apples, Easter eggs, or Christmas ornaments.

Nancy Smith
Lockbourne, OH

The Valentine Voice

Children produce colorful valentines with this listening activity. Duplicate a sheet with 20 numbered outlines of valentine hearts. Tape-record instructions from the "Valentine Voice" for decorating valentines. Students listen to the tape and follow the directions to decorate each heart.

Patricia Shulman
Englewood, CO

"DRAW LACE AROUND HEART #1 ..."

"DRAW STRIPES IN HEART #2 ..."

Words From St. Patrick

Use large sheets of construction paper for quick and easy wall decorations. Give each sheet a theme, such as "Words From St. Patrick," and let students add their thoughts with crayons. Makes an instant project for any holiday.

Susie Frost
Omaha, NE

Paper Plate Clocks

To make learning to tell time more fun, each child is given a plain white paper plate and a green ditto with 12 numbered shamrocks and the hands for the clock. Students cut and paste the clocks together. This helps them learn the correct position of the numerals. When we are finished, we make a display off our clocks and set them at different times to show the special things we do throughout the day.

Joan Holesko
N. Tonawanda, NY

9:00 a.m. We come to school.

Pots Of Gold

Leprechaun coins motivate students to complete their work and fill their pots with gold. At the beginning of March, read the class a story about the leprechauns and their hidden gold. Give children a pattern to cut out, fold, and staple to make their own pots. Punch holes on each side, attach yarn for a handle, and hang each pot from the chalkboard ledge. Make gold coins from yellow construction paper.

As each child finishes an assignment, he gets a coin to put in his pot. At the end of the week, everyone counts and turns in his coins for a reward! Your leprechauns will keep working right up to Easter vacation.

Linda Gwardiak
Mobile, AL

A Leprechaun Visit

Plan a surprise visit from the leprechauns! On the night before St. Patrick's Day, turn over a few desks and chairs in your classroom. Paint green footprints on the floor and hide a little, green-felt hat. Place a piece of green candy taped to a shamrock cut-out on each child's desk. Leave notes from leprechauns to students. The next morning there will be plenty of excitement as children discover the evidence. Follow up by writing stories entitled "The Day I Met A Leprechaun."

Annette Mathias
Partridge, KS

Dear Class,
When I was dancing in your room, I lost my green hat. Would you look for it? If you find it, please leave it by the door.
Thank you,
Pat Leprechaun

WHO WILL BE THE BEST SHENACHIE?

Shenachies

I introduce Irish storytelling the first week of March with a shamrock-covered bulletin board, "Who Will Be The Best Shenachie?" Students try to discover the meaning of "shenachie" as I tell stories during the following weeks. If they do not guess, I let them know that it's an Irish word for story-teller. They make up their own stories, and I reward my shenachies with pipe cleaner shamrocks.

Jody Cowen
Chandlerville, IL

Shape-Pictures With A Value

Draw a holiday picture, or any picture of a topic you're studying, using only basic shapes. Assign each shape a value, and have students add up the value of the squares, triangles, or circles in the whole picture!

Patricia Liguori
Paterson, NJ

□=10 ○=3 △=5

Natural Egg Dyes

Natural Easter egg dyes can be found right in your own kitchen: beets, coffee, tea leaves, green vegetables, strawberries, blueberries, and onion skins. Boil the natural substance in just enough water to cover. Strain and add a few teaspoons of vinegar to the water. Place boiled eggs into the water for coloring.

Tomia Fingerle
Ocala, FL

Plus And Minus Cut-Outs

Do your students have trouble distinguishing between addition and subtraction word problems? For a quick activity, give each student a seasonal cut-out with a plus sign on one side and a minus sign on the other. Read word problems to the students, then ask them to hold up their cut-outs to display the side with the appropriate sign. This reinforces both word problems and listening skills.

Cyndy Sanford
Oak Grove, VA

Extraspecial Paper

Children love using open worksheets instead of regular paper for spelling tests and math assignments. For instance, team Easter egg and bunny sheets, and have children copy examples from their math books onto the eggs.

Isobel Livingstone
Rahway, NJ

Words In A Basket

Motivate children to learn new words. Have them make construction paper Easter baskets. As each child learns a new word, he writes it on a paper egg and adds it to his basket.

Lori Stein
Shattuc, IL

Green Hair

Grow some green hair for spring! I have children draw a colorful face on a Styrofoam cup and add potting soil, grass seed, and water. By the end of the week, our bald-headed men have grown hair. By the next week, our men need haircuts, so children take them home.

Joy E. Herbert
Mays Landings, NJ

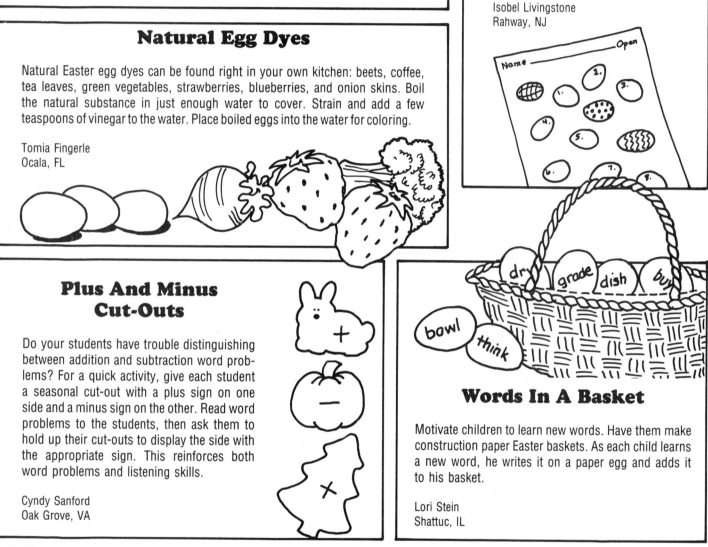

Coleus To Share

Each fall, I bring a huge, healthy coleus to decorate my classroom. The students care for it through the school year. In early spring, each child roots a cutting. The new plants are ready for Mother's Day gifts by May. They're special gifts for mom, plus cuttings from a plant we've enjoyed all year.

Paula Holdren
Louisville, KY

Grandparent's Day

As a special activity every year, my class celebrates Grandparent's Day. Students invite their grandparents to visit our class, where they are entertained with skits, songs, decorations, and refreshments. Contact your local Council on the Aging or senior citizens' group for students without grandparents. The children record taped interviews with their grandparents. Later, we replay the tapes and discuss their comments, which are then compiled in a class newspaper. The finished newspaper is sent home to students and grandparents to remind them of a happy get-together.

Paula Holdren
Louisville, KY

Mother's Day Coupon Booklets

Using a paper cutter, cut colored construction paper into 4" x 12" strips, then cut white paper into 3" x 11" strips. Students use 2 color strips as covers and 10-15 white strips. Staple at one end, or if using 5-6 sheets, fold in half and staple. Discuss and list on the chalkboard chores students could perform for their mothers. Students decorate the covers, then fill out each coupon.

Martha Hein
Madison, IN

Mother's Day Project

Use language arts class to create Mother's Day booklets. Allow about 2 weeks to give the students ample time to do activity pages, proof, and rewrite. Use a ditto for each page. When booklets are completed, each child has a special gift for mom.

Sentence Starters

1 — My mom loves me when . . .
2 — My mother looks pretty when . . .
3 — My favorite thing about my mother is . . .

Sylvia McFeaters
Slippery Rock, PA

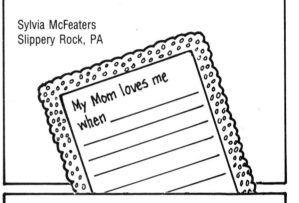

Mother's Helper

For Mother's Day, I have each child draw a flower on construction paper. In the center of the flower, the children glue pictures of themselves. On each flower petal, they write chores they will do to help mom.

S. McGahey
Belleville, MI

January Perk-Ups

Do you get as restless as your students do in January? This idea might perk up your month. Make a January calendar on a ditto. Each school day should be assigned a special theme. Examples of special days are hat day, T-shirt day, blue jeans day, hot chocolate day, gum day, and favorite record day. Send the calendar home with the children before Christmas vacation. This way children look forward to coming back to school after the holidays. I've found that attendance is high during January since students don't want to miss a day of perk-ups.

Rhonda Zinter
Aberdeen, SD

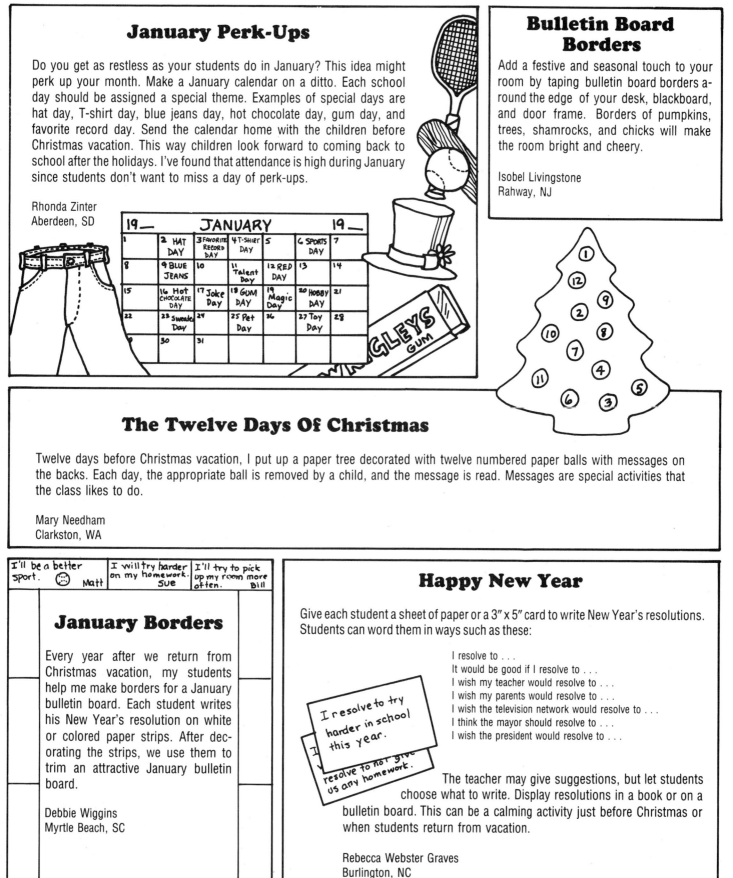

Bulletin Board Borders

Add a festive and seasonal touch to your room by taping bulletin board borders around the edge of your desk, blackboard, and door frame. Borders of pumpkins, trees, shamrocks, and chicks will make the room bright and cheery.

Isobel Livingstone
Rahway, NJ

The Twelve Days Of Christmas

Twelve days before Christmas vacation, I put up a paper tree decorated with twelve numbered paper balls with messages on the backs. Each day, the appropriate ball is removed by a child, and the message is read. Messages are special activities that the class likes to do.

Mary Needham
Clarkston, WA

January Borders

Every year after we return from Christmas vacation, my students help me make borders for a January bulletin board. Each student writes his New Year's resolution on white or colored paper strips. After decorating the strips, we use them to trim an attractive January bulletin board.

Debbie Wiggins
Myrtle Beach, SC

Happy New Year

Give each student a sheet of paper or a 3" x 5" card to write New Year's resolutions. Students can word them in ways such as these:

I resolve to . . .
It would be good if I resolve to . . .
I wish my teacher would resolve to . . .
I wish my parents would resolve to . . .
I wish the television network would resolve to . . .
I think the mayor should resolve to . . .
I wish the president would resolve to . . .

The teacher may give suggestions, but let students choose what to write. Display resolutions in a book or on a bulletin board. This can be a calming activity just before Christmas or when students return from vacation.

Rebecca Webster Graves
Burlington, NC

Footprints

Children are fascinated with this fun, tactile experience. Place a large piece of black paper on the floor next to a pan of white tempera paint and a pan of rinse water. Each student removes his shoes and socks. He places his feet in the white paint, then on the black paper. The next step is into the rinse water! The footprints make a great Halloween bulletin board.

Bess Anne McKnight
Jonesboro, AR

Pumpkin Patch Winners

On October 1, I make a bulletin board with Charlie Brown and Snoopy waiting for the Great Pumpkin in an empty pumpkin patch. At a center stocked with orange and green paper, crayons, and magic markers, each child makes a pumpkin to put in the patch.

Two or three days before Halloween, I place a number behind three different pumpkins. Children guess which pumpkins have numbers behind them and write their names on their choices. On Halloween, we take the pumpkins down. The winners receive a small prize.

Sr. Margaret Ann Wooden
Emmitsburg, MD

Spooksville

To make your room look really spooky for Halloween, tie black yarn together to make a spider web. Add a felt spider and hang on a door or window.

Karen Stone
Goodland, KS

Guess What

A guessing contest adds excitement to a class Halloween party. Count as you fill a small jar with candy corn. Glue a Halloween favor on the jar lid. Have each child write his name and his guess of the number of candies on a slip of paper. The winner gets the jar of treats!

Eleanore Zurbruegg
Memphis, TN

Holiday Puzzles

To make quick and inexpensive giant puzzles, I buy holiday posters from The Education Center for less than $1.00. I glue a poster to poster board, then cut it into big puzzle pieces for my kindergarten children. I color code the pieces and store them in a Zip-Loc bag.

Katrina Lockridge
Radford, VA

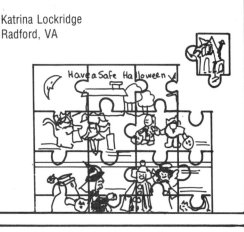

Halloween Treat

Here's a fun treat for your Halloween party. Prepare frozen orange juice or orange Kool-Aid. Cut the tops off black licorice sticks for children to use as straws.

Annette Mathias
Partridge, KS

Cat Tales And Scary Stories

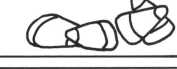

Have children write Halloween tales and decorate them with imaginative art. Mount stories on light-colored construction paper. Add tails, ears, hats, or anything that illustrates the topic.

Sr. Ann Claire Rhoads
Emmitsburg, MD

Trick-Or-Treat Bag Awards

Designate a task or behavior for each day during October. Each child who achieves the daily goal gets a paper lollipop in his trick-or-treat bag posted on the board. Make lollipops from colored circles that are glued to Popsicle sticks. On Friday, students with four or five lollipops choose an item from a grab bag.

LaDell Doss
McGehee, AR

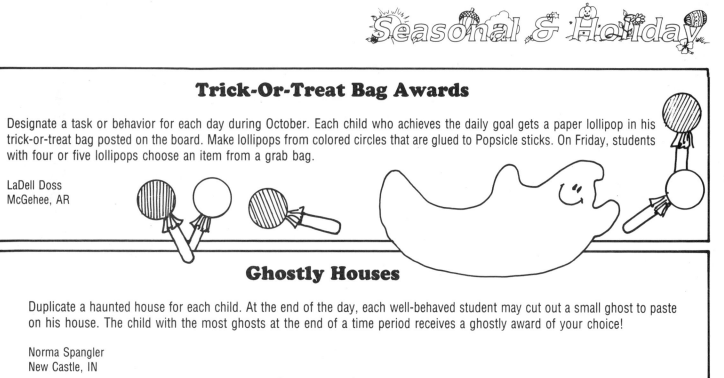

Ghostly Houses

Duplicate a haunted house for each child. At the end of the day, each well-behaved student may cut out a small ghost to paste on his house. The child with the most ghosts at the end of a time period receives a ghostly award of your choice!

Norma Spangler
New Castle, IN

Sticker Treaters

For Halloween treats that please parents and children, purchase small treat bags and fill each with several Halloween stickers. Hand out to students and trick-or-treaters.

Pamela Myhowich
Selah, WA

Read At Home

Motivate your class to read at home! Outline a 3' x 3' piece of rat wire with a seasonal shape and hang. For each 15 minutes students read at home, they get to fill a hole in the wire with tissue paper. Children must bring prepared slips signed by parents to show minutes of reading time. They'll try to complete the shape quickly, and you'll have an attractive room decoration!

Sue Richardson
Altavista, VA

Draw A Jack-O'-Lantern

Motivate math or spelling practice with a jack-o'-lantern drawing contest! Begin with 2 pumpkin outlines on the blackboard. Using 11 strokes, 2 teams compete as members take turns to draw 1 stroke for each question answered correctly. First team to complete its figure wins!

Rebecca Graves
Burlington, NC

Apple Month Treat

For Apple Month in October, we top homemade bread with crockpot apple butter. To make apple butter, each child brings apples from home. We core, peel, and cook them in the crockpot all day, savoring the aroma! The next afternoon, we mix the following into the crockpot: 8 cups applesauce (made the day before), 3¾ cups sugar, 2 tsp. cinnamon, 1 tsp. cloves. The crockpot is turned on high heat at 2:00 p.m. and stirred hourly. I take it home with me. At bedtime, I turn it on low. The apple butter is ready in the morning. We taste it, then serve apple butter in the cafeteria one day.

Beverly Strayer
Red Lion, PA

Halloween Fun

Halloween is a special time for students. Try these holiday activities:

1. Provide each child with a cut-out pumpkin. Each time a child completes an assignment or goal, he adds a facial feature to his pumpkin. Children enjoy watching their pumpkins turn to jack-'o-lanterns.

2. Write riddles on seasonal cut-outs and place in a reading center. Put answers on the back.

3. Write seasonal words on a poster board web. Prepare task cards to go with the web.

Debbie Fly
Birmingham, AL

Super Story Starter

To motivate my creative writers, I draw a sectional picture on a transparency and write a descriptive word or phrase in each section. We discuss the words, and then the students receive a duplicated copy of the picture. They write an original story, using as many of the words as they can, and color in each section of the picture as they use the word.

Betty Bowlin
Chesterfield, MO

Haunted House

Create your own spooky haunted house. Divide the class into groups of two or three students. The class chooses rooms to make, including an attic. Each group designs their room in a box, decorating it with such things as L'eggs containers. When rooms are finished, fasten boxes together on a table, with a background of dark blue paper for a sky.

Nancy Neubauer
Staunton, IL

Flying Witches

For a cute Halloween party decoration, draw a simple outline of a witch and cut it out of black construction paper. With a hole puncher, make two holes at the bottom edge of the witch and slide in a lollipop, with the candy part at the back. With the sucker in place, the witch looks like she is riding her broomstick across the sky!

Joan Holesko
N. Tonawanda, NY

Light The Jack-O'Lantern

Reinforce good health habits with this clever Jack-O'Lantern. Enlarge the pattern shown, and make the folding pumpkin from orange construction paper. Cut out the facial features. Fold in half and glue along the edges, leaving the top half open. Now make two circles (one yellow and one black) to slip inside. When a student is not observing good habits, display the black circle. Light up the pumpkin when everything looks good. Works well for almost any skill.

Wilma Heiser
Falls City, NE

front ➚   ← back

Holiday Motivators

Use the invitations to your classroom holiday parties as incentives. To gain entrance to the party, each student must earn 10 feathers for his turkey, spell out "Happy Halloween" on his pumpkin's teeth, etc. Helps the children get their work done during high-excitement seasons!

Diane Vogel
Chamblee, GA

Turkey Times Review

For a colorful November display, students color turkey pictures as they master multiplication tables. Give each child a copy of a turkey. When two multiplication tables are mastered, he colors the designated feather. After all feathers are colored, he fills in the body. No student wants the last incomplete turkey on the board.

Louise Peters
Hillsborough, NC

Drill Fun

Write facts on seasonal cut-outs. Display a large, corresponding shape on the bulletin board. When a student has mastered all the facts, he may add his name to the large shape.

Lois Vogel
Versailles, IN

Thanksgiving Center

During the month of November, I put up a small tepee purchased at a crafts fair. Inside I put Thanksgiving games, books, and other materials. The children enjoy crawling in and out of their Thanksgiving tepee to get the activities.

Rhonda Zinter
Aberdeen, SD

Cornucopia Award

On November 1st, let each child trace and cut out a cornucopia. Hand out ditto sheets of fruits and vegetables. At the end of each day during the month, good workers get to select one food to color, cut out, and staple in their cornucopias. It's fun to watch the horns of plenty fill up with the "fruits of hard labor" as the month progresses.

Joan Holesko
N. Tonawanda, NY

Thanksgiving Menu

My class made up a menu of foods they would like to eat on Thanksgiving Day. Each child then wrote his/her own version of the recipe for one of the foods. I compiled the kids' recipes and sent home copies to parents, who enjoyed the child's-eye view of Thanksgiving. (Don't forget to caution that none of the recipes are guaranteed to work!)

Brenda McGee
Burlington, NC

Deviled Eggs

Things you need: eggs
salt
lettuce
red stuff
What to do:
Hard boil your eggs at 100 for 25 minutes. After eggs are ready, get shell off and cut in half. Sprinkle salt and powdered red stuff on egg halves. Then arrange eggs on a platter. Put lettuce around sides of platter.

Susan Sheffield

Turkey Feathers

Students earn the right to color and cut out duplicated turkeys through good behavior or completed assignments. Further efforts earn wallpaper feathers for the birds. (Some paint stores will give you old wallpaper samples.) Mount the turkeys on construction paper and display until Thanksgiving. Then send home with an explanation on the back of how the turkeys were earned.

Molly Buchanan
Gloucester, VA

Winter Reminder

After the holidays, keep the tree you used for holiday decorations up as a daily reminder to students to keep wearing their winter protective clothing! Have students donate items or use lost-and-found items to outfit Ed Evergreen in winter clothes. Add eyes, a mouth, a belt, mittens, a hat, a scarf, and maybe even a vest to bring it to life. An attractive decoration and a good reminder to the students!

Carolyn Wilhelm
Maple Grove, MN

Santa's Sack

Guess what's in Santa's sack! Place articles in a large red sack as students observe. Then ask them to recall as many items as possible. Vary the game by passing around the sack so each child can guess what's inside by feeling.

Kathy Beard
Keystone Heights, FL

Poinsettia Patch

Use a paper tablecloth decorated with poinsettias for a bulletin board background. If students can read the words on this board, they add paper poinsettias labeled with their names. Change the activity so students get more than one chance to put a poinsettia in the patch.

Ruth Davis
Jermyn, PA

Perfect Christmas Tree

On December 1, I gave each child a large, green, Christmas tree shape to hang in the room. To decorate their trees, children earned ornaments for perfect papers. Each day, during the last few minutes of class, I passed back graded papers and let children count up their total of perfect papers. For each perfect paper, they collected paper ornaments from me to glue on their trees. I had boots, balls, stars, and candy canes ready. The last day, we added glitter to create a tinsel chain. This was a painless way to raise everyone's scores and create a fantastic art project at the same time!

Sharon Wright
Overland Park, KS

Christmas Knox Blocks

For an easy but elegant Christmas snack, make cherry and lime Knox Blocks squares and serve them together on a toothpick.

Knox Blocks
4 envelopes unflavored gelatin
3 boxes (3 oz.) flavored Jello
4 cups boiling water

Put gelatin and Jello in a bowl. Add boiling water. Stir. Pour into oblong cake pan. Refrigerate. Cut into 1" squares.

Nancy Lach
Mandan, ND

Holiday Book Exchange

Include reading in your holiday festivities. Have each child bring one gift-wrapped book from home. Students choose one of these book packages from a sack. Each child is delighted to take a new book home to enjoy. For students without books, you can supply bonus books from book club orders.

Pamela Myhowich
Selah, WA

Popcorn Party

The days before a holiday are exciting, but it's difficult for children to settle down. To encourage good behavior, announce a popcorn party for the last day of school. Each day that a child behaves, he adds a section to a cut-out holiday shape. On the day of the party, each child gets one scoop of popcorn for each section he has earned.

Nancy Neubauer
Staunton, IL

Santa Claus Soup

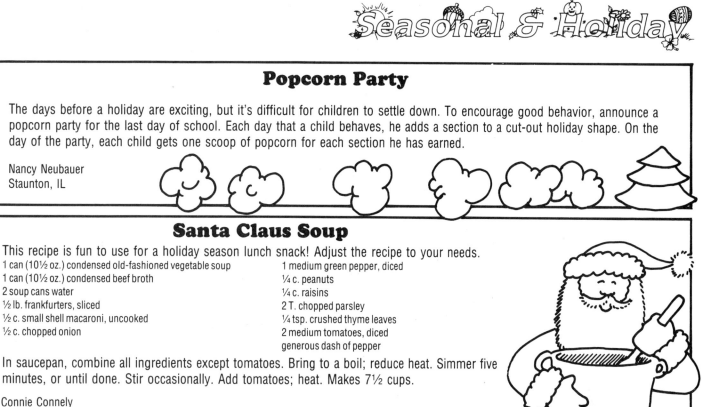

This recipe is fun to use for a holiday season lunch snack! Adjust the recipe to your needs.

1 can (10½ oz.) condensed old-fashioned vegetable soup
1 can (10½ oz.) condensed beef broth
2 soup cans water
½ lb. frankfurters, sliced
½ c. small shell macaroni, uncooked
½ c. chopped onion
1 medium green pepper, diced
¼ c. peanuts
¼ c. raisins
2 T. chopped parsley
¼ tsp. crushed thyme leaves
2 medium tomatoes, diced
generous dash of pepper

In saucepan, combine all ingredients except tomatoes. Bring to a boil; reduce heat. Simmer five minutes, or until done. Stir occasionally. Add tomatoes; heat. Makes 7½ cups.

Connie Connely
Tulsa, OK

Wrap It Up!

Need rolls of Christmas wrapping paper? Let children draw and color different scenes on a long roll of white bulletin board paper! Send some home. Parents love it too.

Rebecca L. Gibson
Auburn, AL

Christmas Hints

Shortly after Thanksgiving, I make up a list of educational materials and games that can be purchased in the local department stores. I list the materials according to skills and send it home to parents. The list gives them ideas about materials that can help their child and is very helpful before the holiday season.

Sandra McGahey
Belleville, MI

Summer Snowman

Plan ahead for a summertime snow surprise. Make a 12″ snowman and freeze him in foil. Bring him out at the end of the year, and read *The Summer Snowman*, by Gene Zion.

Sr. Margaret Ann
Emmitsburg, MD

Christmas Coloring Sheets

Take home extra Christmas worksheets for children of friends and relatives to enjoy when they visit you.

Debbie Wiggins
Myrtle Beach, SC

Print Your Own Ornaments

Have children draw simple pictures on the bottom of Styrofoam meat trays and cut them out. After painting the shapes quickly with a thick tempera mixture, they print them onto construction paper of a contrasting color for beautiful greeting cards.

Nancy Johnson
Greensboro, NC

Holiday Puzzle Letters

These puzzles provide practice in letter writing. Have each child write to a friend and paste the letter on lightweight cardboard, or let them write on the inside cover of an old Christmas card. Cut puzzles apart, place them in envelopes, and mail them with an explanatory note for a holiday surprise.

Carol Gillespie
Chambersburg, PA

Advent Santa

Count down the days until Christmas with an Advent Santa. Draw circles on a cut-out Santa's beard, and label them with dates. Each day, cover a circle with a cotton ball until Santa's beard is full and Christmas is here!

Lois Elfvin
Ringoes, NJ

Postmark Geography

Around the first of December, I ask my students to cut out postmarks from Christmas cards received by their families and bring them to school. After the holidays, we draw a big U.S. map, sort through the postmarks, then use an atlas to correctly attach each postmark. When we're through we have an attractive display as well as a valuable lesson in geography.

Paula Holdren
Louisville, KY

Dear Santa

Primary and intermediate teachers work together in this Christmas writing project. Put a large Santa on a Christmas bulletin board with a decorated mailbox and the phrase: "Dear Santa: I want . . ." All the primary grade children are encouraged to write Santa telling what they want for Christmas and then to deposit the letters in the mailbox. At the end of the day, intermediate teachers take the letters and have their students answer them, pretending they are Santa! What great writing experience for both the primary and intermediate grades! And the little ones get so excited about getting an answer to their letters.

Marie Brown
Bristol, CT

December Guests

Every day in December, invite two students to be your guests of honor at lunch! Buy a package of Christmas napkins and a set of paper place mats from a card store. Laminate two place mats for your guests and set places next to you. By the Christmas holidays, each child should have a turn to share a special lunch and special conversation.

J.K. Jacob
Baton Rouge, LA

Dazzling Display

No room for a Christmas tree in your classroom? Make a gigantic, breath-taking decoration by hanging hundreds of Christmas balls on a fishnet suspended from the ceiling!

Verena Harp
Pineville, LA

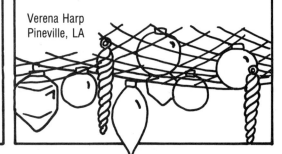

Caring And Sharing

Have students make Christmas cards for area senior citizens. We use old holiday cards to design ours. Make as many as possible, and present them to an area senior center, a retirement home, or to individuals. Older citizens are very happy to know that students care about them.

Carolyn Allison
New Cumberland, WV

Musical Gift Exchange

Play Pass the Present this year for your Christmas gift exchange. Arrange children in two circles, one for girls and one for boys, and put on a Christmas record. When the music begins, children pass their grab bag gifts to the left. When the music stops, children keep the gift they are holding. Make sure each person has a gift other than his own before allowing everyone to open their presents.

Mary Graham
Atlanta, GA

Santa's Surprise

Use old Saint Nick to keep kids on their toes! Each day, when a student completes all class assignments, he may put his name on Santa's list. At the end of the day, record the students' names that are on the list on a separate chart. A blank list goes up each day. The students whose names appear on Santa's list the most times get a surprise.

Debbie Retzlaff
Fort Knox, KY

Holiday Word Cubes

Write the letters in "Christmas" on small, wooden cubes and have children rearrange the cubes to make words. Children see how many words they can spell using the letters. Moving the letters around on cubes is easier for primary children than visualizing the possible combinations.

Mary Lee Dorsey
Littleton, CO

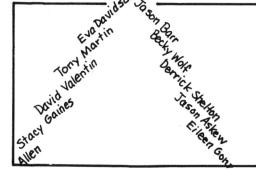

Outline Signatures

Place thin paper over a tree or snowman outline so children can see the shape. Then have them sign their names in pencil and go over them in ink. Students must judge the space that names will need. Some may want to practice writing their names in the air first.

Rebecca Webster Graves
Burlington, NC

A Letter From Santa

My children were elated to receive personal replies from Santa! I asked students to write letters to Santa with parents' help. As children brought their letters in, we read them and placed them in a large envelope to mail to Santa. Our eighth-grade "Santas" addressed their personal replies to children in care of the school and saved used stamps to paste on the envelopes. Each child took home a cherished letter.

Sr. Margaret Ann
Emmitsburg, MD

Super Workers

This bulletin board can be changed monthly to fit holiday themes. After a student completes his daily work, he gets a cut-out, writes his name on it, and puts it on the board. The child gets immediate reinforcement, and the teacher can see who needs to finish work. At the end of the day, students remove cut-outs to be ready for the next day.

Sharon Franke
St. Joseph, MO

Silent-Reading Picture

To spice up silent reading, I make a sectioned holiday picture. Each day that we read, I call on a different student to color in a section of the design. My students love to see the picture completed. At the end of each month, I post a new picture and select a student to take the completed one home.

Laura Henricks
North Judson, IN

Christmas Tags

Save Christmas gift tags and program the backs with vocabulary words or math facts. Store them in a pretty Christmas gift box for a holiday activity center.

Connie Connely
Catoosa, OK

Punctuation Contest

Build a Christmas bulletin board while you practice punctuation. Hold a contest several weeks prior to the Christmas holidays. Each time a student makes a perfect score on a punctuation paper, he adds a cut-out to the board—a stocking, tree ornament, snowflake, etc. For an added incentive, allow students who make six perfect scores to skip all punctuation assignments until the contest is over.

Beth Holder
Kinston, NC

Letter From Santa

This creative writing idea is good for self-concept and vocational thinking. Read a letter from Santa telling children that Santa's elves are sick. He needs people about their size to help get ready for Christmas! Discuss jobs elves do. Then have children write to Santa applying for a particular job and stating why they would be good at that task.

Sarah Gustafson
Okeechobee, FL

Sugar Plums

After reading *The Night Before Christmas,* your children can have their own "visions of sugar plums." To make sugar plum treats, stick marshmallows with toothpicks and dip in warm milk. Roll in red or green Jello mix and eat!

Connie Connely
Catoosa, OK

Merry Christmas Wish

Wondering what to do with those extra prints of school pictures? Use them to decorate the school hallway with Christmas fun. Have students glue their pictures on a piece of paper and draw a Santa, elf, or reindeer body around it. If you still have extra prints, cut out a large Christmas tree and glue faces on as ornaments. Students can sign their pictures as a Merry Christmas wish from your class.

Diana Roberts
College Park, GA

Paper Chains

Each day in December that a child exhibits good behavior, he adds a loop to his chain. Children take chains home to decorate their Christmas trees.

Mary Lafser Via
Roanoke, VA

Styrofoam Ornaments

Cut out pictures from old Christmas cards and glue them to the bottom of Styrofoam meat trays. Then cut around each picture, punch a hole, and thread with bright yarn. Nice for a bulletin board, a mobile, and take-home gifts.

Nancy Johnson
Greensboro, NC

Bulletin Board Time-Saver

For January's bulletin board, I cut a huge snowflake from white paper and surround it with students' poems. When February arrives, I shape the snowflake into a lacy heart for an instant valentine poem display.

Mildred Holsema
Lafayette, IN

Christmas Cookie Bake

For holiday cookies with a different twist, have children shape refrigerator cookie dough into numbers or letters of the alphabet. Children can display and identify cookies before eating them.

Rhonda Thurman-Rice
Tulsa, OK

Monthly Straw Wreath

Decorate your classroom door for every month of the year with a commercially produced straw wreath. Add brightly colored bows and small seasonal decorations each month. Enlist student and parent help in gathering decorations: felt cutouts, plastic figures, buttons, small toys, cake decorations.

Carole Pippert and Sandy Docca
Silver Spring, MD

The Gift Box

To encourage good behavior before the holiday vacation, I bring in a large gift box decorated with Christmas paper. I cut a slit in the top. When children do especially well in their work or show good manners, neatness, or study habits, I put their names in the box. Later, a drawing is held for 2 or 3 wrapped surprise gifts!

Arnetra Terry
Palmer Springs, VA

Snowmen For The Birds

When the snow is right for building snowmen, bundle up for an outdoor nature activity. In teams of five or six, make several snowmen on the playground. Give each dapper snowman stick arms from which to hang pinecone bird feeders. Make feeders the previous day by stuffing cones with peanut butter and rolling them in birdseed. Attach colorful yarn to hang feeders from the snowmen.

Kathleen Baily
Bristol, CT

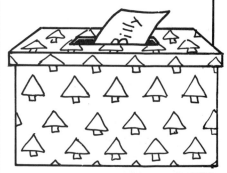

The Twelve Days Of Christmas

Use this enrichment activity the last 12 days of school before Christmas vacation. After an activity is completed, students color an ornament, cut it out, and paste it on the tree.

Sandra McGahey
Belleville, MI

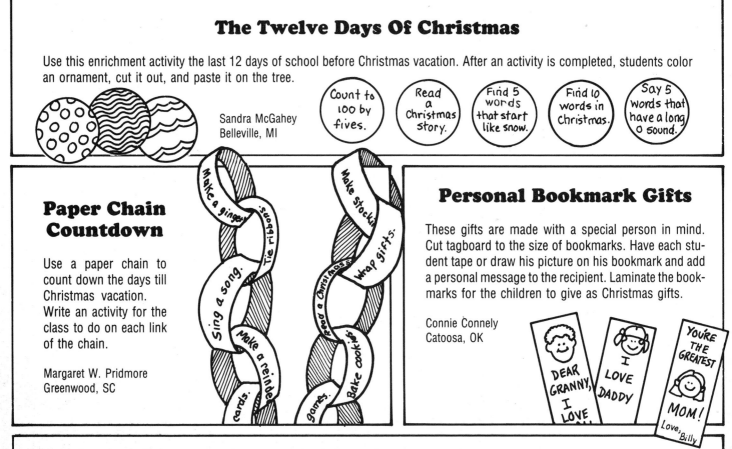

Count to 100 by fives.

Read a Christmas story.

Find 5 words that start like snow.

Find 10 words in Christmas.

Say 5 words that have a long O sound.

Paper Chain Countdown

Use a paper chain to count down the days till Christmas vacation. Write an activity for the class to do on each link of the chain.

Margaret W. Pridmore
Greenwood, SC

Make a gingerbread.
Tie ribbons.
Sing a song.
Make stockings.
Read a Christmas story.
Wrap gifts.
Make a reindeer.
Bake cookies.
Play games.
Make cards.

Personal Bookmark Gifts

These gifts are made with a special person in mind. Cut tagboard to the size of bookmarks. Have each student tape or draw his picture on his bookmark and add a personal message to the recipient. Laminate the bookmarks for the children to give as Christmas gifts.

Connie Connely
Catoosa, OK

DEAR GRANNY, I LOVE

I LOVE DADDY

YOU'RE THE GREATEST MOM! Love, Billy

Holiday Helpers

Encourage your students to pass on the holiday spirit by starting a Santa's Helpers club. Let students sign up to help any teacher in your school who needs an extra hand in setting up projects, tutoring, etc. Before a helper is allowed to assist a teacher, he must have exhibited good behavior during the day, and he should have completed all required work.

Helene Sparaco
Middleburgh, NY

Snowy Day Activity

To get children out for a bit of fresh air after a snowfall, fill plastic squeeze bottles or spray bottles with water to which you have added food coloring, and let kids draw on the snow or "paint" a snowman.

Bonnie Pinkerton
Bowling Green, KY

Dazzling Winter Border

For eye-catching bulletin boards, cut a border in a desired style. Then spray on artificial snow, and add silver or colored glitter while still wet. Really brightens dreary, winter days.

Sr. Ann Claire Rhoads
Emmitsburg, MD

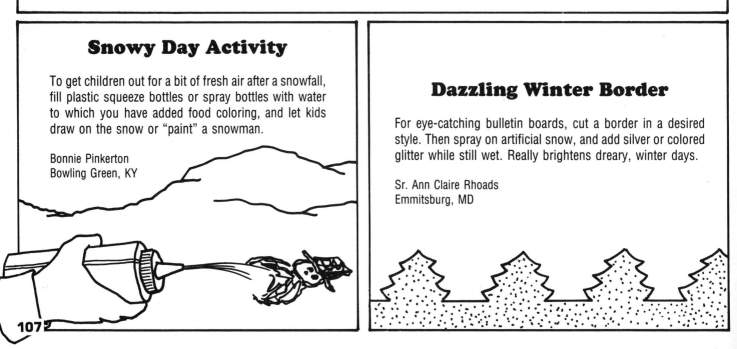

Poems On Tape

Have students practice their favorite holiday poems, then record them for your listening center. They might also include original poems. To extend the activity, have each student prepare a question sheet based on his poem, then post the sheet in the center.

Pat Smith
Atlanta, GA

Holiday Listening Game

This auditory association game is a good holiday time-filler for primary children. Ask "Which does not belong?" Then name two holiday vocabulary words and one unrelated word. Example: bell, reindeer, egg.

Jo Farrimond
Broken Arrow, OK

Scrambled Shapes

Two of our readers came up with variations on the same idea. Kathy Kuehn runs duplicates of seasonal shapes and scrambles one of the week's spelling words on each. At Halloween, the shapes are ghosts, witches, and cats. At Christmas, she uses trees, Santas, deer, etc.

Marilyn Janssen also cuts out holiday shapes, but programs them with scrambled seasonal words. For example, she labels a Christmas tree shape with the letters "osty" for her students to rearrange into the word "toys."

Kathy Kuehn
Amery, WI

Marilyn Janssen
Lorraine, KS

May Basket Treats

The custom of hanging little flower-filled baskets on doorknobs on the eve of May Day came from Great Britain. The object was to leave the basket before being discovered, a foolproof way to keep away evil spirits. Our class decided to vary the custom a bit and make baskets filled with candy for a nearby nursing home. This gives children a chance to do something good for someone else.

Mrs. Rebecca Graves
Burlington, NC

Contract For Holiday Fun

Write up a contract for holiday fun involving a variety of skills and activities. Place copies of the contract, all materials, and directions in a center for students to work on independently.

Adeline Greco
Palm Springs, CA

Seasonal Three-Ring Binder

Store worksheets for a particular month in plastic cover sheets in a three-ring binder. Provide a nonpermanent marker when you display the binder of the month for students who need an extra challenge. Some students will work the same sheets several times!

Verena Harp
Pineville, LA

Spring Clouds

For textured, spring clouds with silver linings, use artificial snow spray. Add glitter to give raindrops a special sparkle. These same materials make dazzling unicorn horns and wings.

Sr. Ann Claire Rhoads
Emmitsburg, MD

Hands Up!

Use a holiday rubber stamp collection as an incentive for students to finish their work. Assign a stamp and ink color for work to be done each day. As students turn in completed work, they stamp their right or left hands, using the assigned color and stamp. Children love to be stamped, and by a glance you can tell who has completed what!

Karen Bellis
Stover, MO

LEARNING CENTERS

Center Assignment Chart

Are your students confused about their center assignment? Divide a poster board square into sections according to the number of centers you have. Put a center number in each square. Then clip a clothespin with the student's name on it beside the center he or she should complete.

Barbara Ihnen
Silver Lake, IN

Oilcloth Gameboard

Use permanent markers and oilcloth to make durable, basic gameboards. Use an overhead projector to transfer the desired design onto the cloth. The gameboards can be rolled or folded for easy storage and wiped clean with a damp cloth.

Lois Cooper
Beckley, WV

Magnetic Tape Calendar

Use the side of a metal file cabinet for a classroom activity calendar. With colored tape, rule off 31 blocks. Have students design poster board numbers and month titles to cut out and back with small pieces of magnetic tape. For special events and holidays, create special magnetic markers. The children enjoy updating the calendar each month and learn their months and holidays quickly!

Vurnalynn Turner
Greensboro, NC

Showers Of Good Work

For an April display, trace the outline of a giant raindrop onto a ditto master. Create a worksheet on the raindrop. Duplicate it on light blue paper, and have students cut it out after completed. Hang on a bulletin board for a "shower of good work."

Audrey Cook
Susquehanna, PA

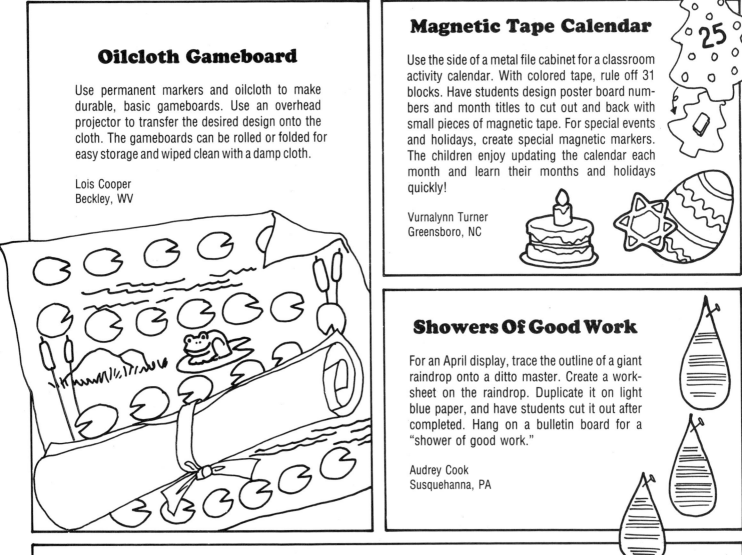

Recycling Gift Wrap

I decorate manila envelope centers with backgrounds of eye-catching gift wrap paper. Anytime I'm at a party or someplace where they're throwing away wrapping paper, I save it! It also can be laminated to use for game pieces.

Rhonda Thurman-Rice
Catoosa, OK

Versatile Cookie Sheet

Take an old cookie sheet to school to use as a center for magnetic letters and numbers. Cookie sheets also keep glitter, glue, or paste off desktops and tables. They are great surfaces for tracing letters in fingerpaint, Jell-O, or cornmeal.

Janis Tysko
Athens, OH

What Is A Friend?

For a focus on friendship, share "What Is A Friend?" — compiled by Lee Parr McGrath and Joan Scobey — with your class. Then ask the children to write their definitions of friendship. These can be written on large pieces of paper and posted on a bulletin board or compiled into a booklet that the kids will love.

Rebecca Graves
Burlington, NC

Tickets To The Learning Station

When assignments are completed, my students get out their tickets to learning stations and free-time activities. Each activity is numbered. When a student completes one, I punch his ticket on the corresponding number. When all are punched, a child may go back to his favorite activities for a second punch. Stations and activities are changed monthly to spur new interest and enthusiasm.

Carole Betlejewski
Muskegon, MI

Friday's Letters

Each Friday, the children in my class write letters to me. They use correct letter form and may write whatever they wish—what they liked or didn't like during the week, problems with friends, questions about school-work, etc. Letters go in a "Friday's Letters" mailbox. Over the weekend, I answer each letter so children receive a reply on Monday. This gives children who have a hard time opening up an opportunity to express themselves.

D. Shelton
Memphis, TN

Open-Ended Gameboard

A colorful gameboard can be created quickly from gift wrap paper. Cut a piece of gift wrap and a piece of poster board the same size. Attach the gift wrap to the poster board using rubber cement. Make a game trail around the gameboard with either gummed paper or construction-paper pieces. Add a clever title and special directions on a few trail spaces. Be sure to laminate for durability. For playing, supply directions, cards with a skill to practice, and pawns such as space creatures or cars found in the party supplies section of a store.

Deborah Smith
Mechanicsville, MD

Alphabetizing Board

To help students in alphabetizing, cut 10 slots across the width of a one-foot piece of 2" x 4" board. Each slot should be 1" deep to hold up index word cards. Sand the rough spots, paint, and the board is ready for any sequencing activity.

Debra Roe
El Dorado Springs, MO

Razor-Cut Stories

Use stories from old books, magazines, or workbooks to get students writing. Decide on a skill you wish to focus on, such as an ending to the story, a beginning, or a change in the plot. Cut out that part from each story. Paste the remaining story in a file folder. Add directions, and have students complete stories on their own papers. Cut-out people in pictures are fun for art!

Sr. Ann Claire Rhoads
Emmitsburg, MD

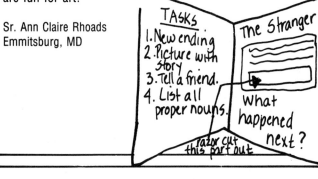

Quick, Fun File Folder

I collect kids' meal boxes from fast-food chains for a source of a quick file folder. Games, puzzles, and mazes are on all sides of these boxes. Cut out the activities, glue to a file folder, and laminate. Provide answer keys if desired. These would be great to complete during the summer.

Susan Reinagel
Benton, MO

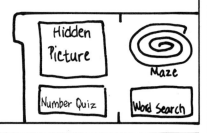

Album Jackets

Don't throw away those old record album jackets. Cover them with white paper, decorate, and use as a learning station sign. Or cover the inside and add artwork for a great, easy-to-store gameboard.

Elizabeth Cole
Annapolis, MD

The Formula For Super Storage

Have mothers and friends with babies save formula cans for you. They're neat for storing game pieces, making banks, or holding learning centers. Unlike Pringles cans, they stack easily and don't roll, and they are sturdy.

Rhonda Thurman-Rice
Catoosa, OK

Writing Rodeo

Create a center with a rodeo flair for handwriting practice. Display cowboys holding penmanship worksheets that get children to write names of famous cowboys, ranches, Indian tribes, or western films. I changed the worksheets weekly and had a special treat for those who tried them all. It was difficult to find people and places that my students would recognize, so we made name identification part of the activity too.

Michael R. Bond
Olamon, ME

Medicine Bottle Pawns

Commercially produced games often provide small, cut-out figures to use as game pieces. Preserve these paper pawns for years of use by placing each one inside a small, clear medicine bottle. They don't tip over, and they last forever!

Mary Dinneen
Bristol, CT

Lost-And-Found Pieces

Keep a lost-and-found box for misplaced center and game pieces. When a student finds a center part that doesn't belong, or if he's missing a piece, he automatically goes to the lost-and-found box.

Rhonda Thurman-Rice
Catoosa, OK

Open Gameboards

Keep a collection of open gameboards handy, along with sets of playing cards on various skills. Students select the board they're interested in, and you select cards for the skill you want to reinforce.

Joanie Warner
New Bedford, CT

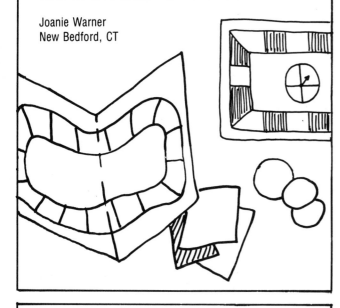

Reading Group Divider

Each year, I let my class choose animals for their reading groups. Then I cut down a big appliance box and make a divider for our reading area. After painting the panels, we not only have an attractive divider but also a handy place for charts, posters, and good work!

Jeanne Mullineaux
Unadilla, NY

Envelope Bingo

Put your bingo board on the front of a string-tie envelope. Pieces can be stored inside for less mess and easy cleanup. I glued wallpaper samples that had a plaid design on both the front and back of the envelope and laminated it for reprogramming.

Lynette Toppmeyer
Clearmont, MO

Napkin Folding

Use directions for fancy napkin folding to make a great reading center or motivate reluctant readers. Pamphlets with directions are available at bookstores. Cookbooks are also a good source.

Linda Rabinowitz
Atlanta, GA

Family Tree

A sturdy tree sprig can serve as a family tree. When studying the family unit, children enjoy hanging photographs of their relatives on the tree.

Lucy Knight
Capital Heights, MD

Instant Trail Games

Make easy, open-ended file folder games with adhesive colored dots and stickers. Choose a theme for each game. Use dots for the trail, and add character stickers that kids love along the trail. Laminate, and provide game cards for various skills.

Debbie Hawkins
Atwood, IL

Start

Take another turn.

Very nice! Go ahead 1.

Color Words

To display color words in kindergarten or first grade, cut clothes from colored paper. Display them on a clothesline with real clothespins.

Fran Petersen
N. Tonawanda, NY

Scavenger Hunt

Here's a fun assignment for students who have completed a reading book. Create a "scavenger hunt" list of questions for students to answer using the completed text. Children enjoy seeing who can be the first to find the answers to all the questions.

Jane Cuba
Redford, MI

1. On which page does a boy get tickets to go to the circus?

Center Management

On the wall next to each of my learning centers, I have pockets with two compartments—one labeled "Assigned" and one labeled "Finished." The children look to see where they are assigned each morning. When they finish seat work, they go to that center. When they finish in the center, they move their name cards to the "Finished" pocket. At a glance, I know to assign them to another center for the next day.

Assigned Finished

Julia Fields
Climax, NC

Brown Bag Centers

Last year I needed containers for my learning center and came up with the idea of using brown paper bags. I selected bags that were free of advertising. I decorated them, put in the activity, and presto, I had containers that cost practically nothing.

Using the bags saved time, money, and much energy. My first graders found the bags easier to work with than boxes. The title above my learning center is: "It's in the Bag." The children enjoy getting a bag and working with the activities.

Dorothy L. Kurkinen
Toledo, WA

Window Shade Vocabulary

To motivate children to learn their vocabulary, try the old window shade trick. Ask a local store that sells and cuts window shades if you can have scraps from shades that were cut off. Thread a piece of yarn through the hollow cardboard tube, and hang it with a thumbtack. Program with sight words, vocabulary, or math problems.

Kimberly Kepp
Rochester, MN

made
sun
good
find

Learning Center Mail

With this mailbox management system, children will love finding out their assignments for the day! Paint inexpensive metal mailboxes with bright colors and place one at each center. Place samples, materials, and instructions inside. When the flag is up, children will know the center is ready to go!

Laurie Comer
Atlanta, GA

Plural Producer

Let your students try being the "brains" inside the box. Find a cardboard box large enough to hold a child in a sitting position. Have children decorate the box to look like a computer. Cut a slot on each side. Label one "IN" and the other "OUT." Write the rules for forming plurals on the outside of the machine. To use, a child sits inside the box with a stack of plural noun cards. Students put singular nouns in the "IN" slot, and the machine returns plural nouns. When a child feels he knows the plural rules, he may try being the brains inside the box.

Pam Huntington
Redington Shores, FL

Shape Box

Turn an empty refrigerator box into a fun shape box! After children paint it, cut the four basic shapes from the box, one per side. Make sure each opening is large and low enough for a five-year-old to climb through. Direct children to crawl in one shape and out another.

Carol Lloyd
Cumberland, MD

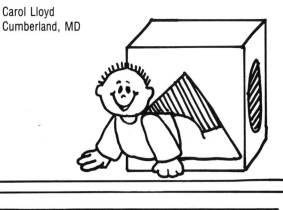

Quick Center

A fantastic idea for a portable and inexpensive center is to cover a 2″ x 24″ x 48″ Styrofoam insulation board with paper. Boards can be purchased at hardware stores in different sizes. Activities can be changed easily when pinned or stapled on. Perfect in rooms with few bulletin boards!

Cathy Chomistek
Indianapolis, IN

Newspaper Patterns

Here is an idea I use in my classroom for centers—a flow chart. I find these are particularly good when the children have to follow step-by-step directions, as in planting a seed. The cook came right out of our local paper. I find the newspaper to be an excellent source of patterns.

Julia Fields
Climax, NC

Recipe for a Good Plant
1. Start.
2. Get a milk carton.
3. Fill it ½ full of dirt.
4. Put in a tomato seed.
5. Add more dirt.
6. Pack it firmly.
7. Water your plant.
8. Set it in the window sill.
9. Choose someone to take your place.
10. Stop.

Actual Size:
20″x13″

State Facts

Learning state names and locations is an important part of elementary social studies. Use folders with maps and numbered states for an easy-to-store identification activity.

Jerry Walls
Phoenix, AZ

Marker Pawns

I never throw away the caps of worn-out magic markers. Instead, I keep them to be used as game pawns or markers. They come in all colors, so it is easy for a child to recognize his own pawn in the game. Best of all, they cost nothing, and I always have some handy if one gets lost.

Helen Burkard
Beckley, WV

Metal Washers

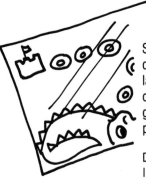

Small metal washers can give a game a new dimension. Glue them on your gameboard and laminate right over the top. Attach a small piece of magnetic tape to the playing pieces. Hang your game on a wall or bulletin board, and your game pieces will stick to the game.

Diana Leibrandt
Imperial, NE

All Keyed Up

I use old discarded keys (from cars, doors, or locks) as pawns for trail games. They are a hit, especially with the boys, who enjoy "driving" around a game. Old games that had become dust collectors are now popular choices.

Nancy Johnson
Greensboro, NC

Picture Pointers

For an attention getter, make an attractive "picture-window" pointer. Cut a section from the center of a tagboard figure. Attach a small piece of paper to the back that a ruler will slip into as a handle. Hold the pointer so that the word you want to emphasize appears in the window.

Mary Lee Dorsey
Littleton, CO

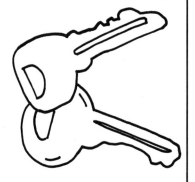

Child-Size Clothesline

Make a mini-clothesline from two, three-pound coffee cans and two large dowels. Cut a hole in the lid of each can and insert a dowel. Stabilize the stick by running a screw up through the bottom of the can and then filling the can with sand or gravel. Decorate if desired, and run string between the two clothesline posts. Great for a variety of skill activities, such as clipping on pictures, words, or numbers written on clothing cut-outs.

Linda Dyer
Simpsonville, SC

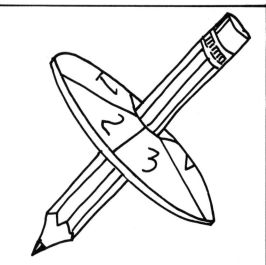

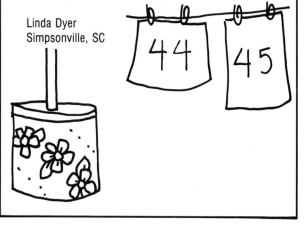

Plastic Lid Spinners

Transform margarine or coffee can lids into game spinners. Punch a hole in the lid's center. Using a permanent marker, divide the lid into sections and label with numbers. Push a pencil through the hole. Students spin and move their markers according to the number touching the tabletop.

Sr. Ann Claire Rhoads
Emmitsburg, MD

File Cabinet Centers

The side of a metal file cabinet is a great place for learning centers. Adhesive magnets can be cut apart and placed on the back of game pieces. A baseball game works very well this way. Make five bats, one for each vowel sound. Make several baseballs with short vowel pictures. Use old workbooks to locate pictures or draw your own. The child places each baseball under the correct bat.

Ann Ballard
Muncie, IN

Alphabet Recognition

I write the letters of the alphabet (uppercase and lowercase) with an indelible marker on dried lima beans. I spray them with clear acrylic. The beans are stored in a covered snack can along with the corresponding letter cards.

One child takes the cards and the other takes the beans. The child with the cards takes a card and says what it is. The other child looks through the beans and finds that letter. They can take turns being in charge of cards and beans.

Lynn Klomfar
Gulfport, FL

Scrabble Spelling

Place the wooden letter squares from a Scrabble game at your spelling center. Students can use the squares to spell the weekly words or to write a sentence using the words. Incorporate math practice by having students add the number values printed on the squares to find the week's "most valuable" word.

Marianne Armstrong
Urbana, IL

Coloring Book File Folders

If you're always searching for new center ideas, take a look at the coloring books and home work-books found in your local grocery or drugstore. They're often full of great, ready-to-use ideas. Buy 2 copies of a book. Program a page, mount it in a file folder, then program the answer key and glue it on the back. Laminate, and provide students with wipe-off markers.

Carolyn Fagg
Cowen, WV

Mail Call

To get my second graders interested in writing letters (and to practice writing skills), I hang a real mailbox on our door. I also have an old mailman's hat, happily donated by my local post office. I begin by writing simple letters to every child, asking them to write back. Each day a new "postman" is picked to wear the hat and deliver the mail. The children are free to answer their letters or write to new people. Expand this activity by writing and delivering letters to children in other classes.

Marie Brown
Bristol, CT

Instant Gameboards

I use extra table space to make permanent gameboards. For math games, I glue squares to a table in a checkerboard pattern and laminate over them. The result is a permanent checkerboard or chessboard. For reading games, I put sticky dots on the table to make a trail. Students can grab some flash cards, a die, and markers for an instant game.

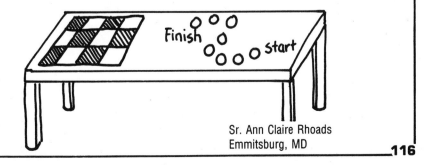

Sr. Ann Claire Rhoads
Emmitsburg, MD

Color Clocks

To help my students learn to tell time, I draw a large clock with the numbers in red. Around the outside of the clock, I write the minutes in blue. Then I attach a short red hand for the hours and a long blue one for the minutes. As I show the children how to write down the time, I use the same color coding, writing the hour in red and the minutes in blue. As the children master telling time, go to a traditional one-color clock. It works!

Geraldine Fossett
Canton, GA

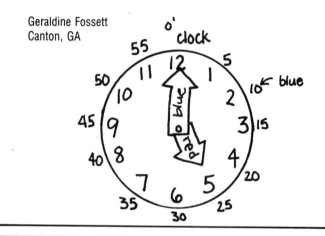

Magnetic Blackboard

Turn your blackboard into a versatile trail game. Draw a simple trail game on the board with colored chalk. Prepare a set of task cards. Provide a die and several refrigerator magnets to use as game markers. No bulky gameboard to store!

Virginia C. Hale
Annapolis, MD

Management Tip For Math Centers

For a simple management system, duplicate pin-on tags shaped like a center theme from heavy paper. Hand out the tags, and pin them on children each day. Assign centers by circling a number, and record completion with an "X."

Leann Fredrickson
Aberdeen, SD

Game Spinners

Make inexpensive game spinners by cutting Styrofoam meat trays into squares. Mark off sections and write in numbers, using a permanent magic marker. Attach a spinner or paper clip with a brad.

Virginia C. Hale
Annapolis, MD

Sturdy Pockets

To make a more durable pocket for one of my centers, I cover the cut-out pocket shape with contact paper or cold laminating film, leaving ½" on the bottom and sides. Then I attach it to the already-laminated center. It makes a sturdy pocket that doesn't tear.

LaDonna Hauser
Wilmington, NC

Riddle Box

I covered a box with plain wrapping paper and decorated it as shown. Fold sheets of paper and write riddles on them at the appropriate grade level. You may wish to include social studies or science questions. Print the answer under the flap. Use the riddle box as a class reading fun time, as an individual activity, or as a game for two.

Fran Petersen
North Tonawanda, NY

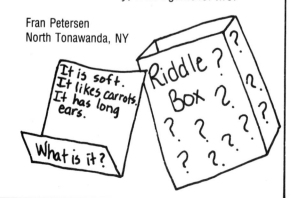

Clinkers

An interesting approach to literature is the discussion of exactly what makes a "bad" book. Children share their ideas, and usually a lively discussion ensues. I then encourage the kids to bring in "clinkers" to share. The books are placed in a basket in the reading corner. Sooner or later we discover that "One man's trash is another man's treasure."

Paula K. Holdren
Prospect, KY

Book Report Movies

I have students summarize books in ten sentences (1-4, beginning; 5-9, climax; 10, ending). Then they illustrate each sentence in one filmstrip frame on adding machine tape. Sentences can be typed onto each frame or typed in running copy to serve as a script. Use cube-shaped tissue boxes to make individual film viewers. Turn a box on its side, so the oval opening will be the screen. Slit above and below it, and insert the story tape. When not in use, store filmstrips in toilet paper tubes, cut to size and labeled with book titles.

Wendy Sondov
Montclair, NJ

Tablecloth Gameboards

Plastic tablecloths paired with bean bags make great manipulative centers. Use a foam-backed cloth (so it won't slip on the floor), and write on it with a permanent marker.

Ann Minarick
Omaha, NE

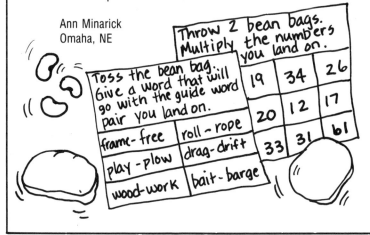

Throw 2 bean bags. Multiply the numbers you land on.

19	34	26
20	12	17
33	31	61

Toss the bean bag. Give a word that will go with the guide word pair you land on.

frame- free	roll - rope
play - plow	drag- drift
wood-work	bait- barge

Message In A Bottle

Passing notes is not against the rules at this center, where messages by students and the teacher are placed in a bottle. Students decorate the surrounding area like water around an island. Anyone writes a bottled message, then students write answers when their work is done.

Sr. Ann Claire Rhoads
Emmitsburg, MD

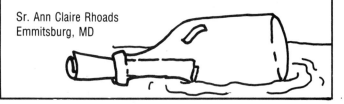

Center Assignments

Make daily center assignments a snap. Label cut-out bees with student names. Cut out a large poster board flower for each reading group. Laminate, and write a center name on each petal. Assign centers by placing bees next to the desired petals.

Ann Barnette
Newnan, GA

LEARNING CENTERS

Listen And Do

Tape-record your art instructions to combine art and listening skills. Place tape recorder, headphones, paper, and crayons at a center. Students listen and draw the items or shapes described.

Pamela Myhowich
Selah, WA

Library Pocket Uses

Tape library card pockets to poster board to make a center, or just tape to the wall under a chalk trough or bulletin board to hold manipulative pieces. Label pockets with numbers, letters, or colors, and have children insert matching strips.

Fran Petersen
N. Tonawanda, NY

Sandpaper Sequencing

To give your students practice in story sequence, purchase two copies of a dime store storybook. Tape a reading of the story, then cut out the pictures. (The two copies are necessary to get all the pictures from the front and back of each page.) On the back of each picture, glue sandpaper so students can place pictures in the correct order on a flannelboard after they have listened to the story tape. Add numbers to the back of each picture for self-checking.

Linda Dyer
Simpsonville, SC

Wipe-Off Fabric

Colorful fabric scraps make useful pieces for learning centers and working bulletin boards. Cover swatches with clear contact paper or laminating film, then cut into shapes for seasons or themes. Use a wax pencil or wipe-off marker to write math facts, spelling words, or special notes to hardworking students!

Julie Robison
Worthington, OH

Pocket Pal Saver

Here's an idea to save wear and tear on envelope centers and to help little hands reach pieces. I glue either a plastic or library card pocket to the inside of the envelope for small cards and pieces. They are less likely to get lost, and my envelopes don't get turned upside down or torn.

Rhonda Thurman-Rice
Catoosa, OK

Counting With The Count

Decorate a wall with the "Sesame Street" count counting his bats! Place the appropriate number of bat cut-outs over number squares 1 to 10. You'll need 55 bats in all!

Terrell Moore
Bowling Green, KY

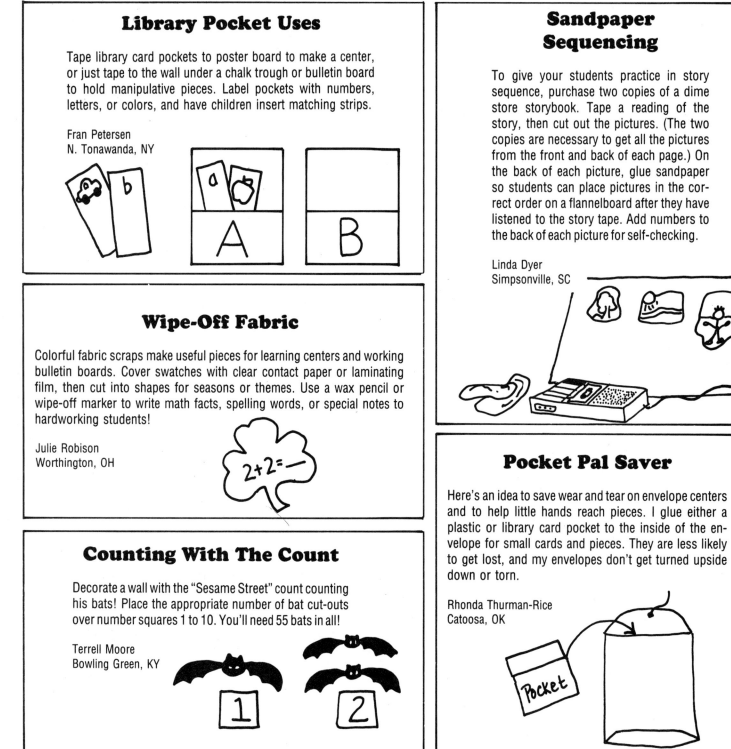

Rack-A-Lot

The plastic display racks discarded by stationery stores are very versatile. Each box on the rack usually is labeled with a number. Use the rack for:
—a bean bag game, adding the numbers where the bean bag lands
— sequencing alphabet pictures or words
— categories and examples

Lorene Hoger
Palos Heights, IL

Burger Box Fragments

Burger boxes make great mini centers. Laminate category labels and attach to the front and insides of each box with two-sided tape. Students place fragments with missing subjects or verbs into the correct section. After sorting, have students turn each fragment into a sentence.

    Doesn't like running
    My best friend
    The slender brown horse
    Has a dog that begs

LaDonna Hauser
Wilmington, NC

Sticker Concentration

To make an inexpensive Concentration game, mount 10 pairs of leftover stickers on laminated, construction paper cards. Store cards in an envelope. Players place sticker cards face-down in rows, then flip two cards at a time to match pairs.

Clarese Rehn
Lake Villa, IL

Pyramid Learning Center

Turn an empty TV or stove carton into a space-saving pyramid of centers. Cut out one side and the bottom of the box. Tape the two free sides together to form a pyramid. Attach different activities to each side.

Glenda Robinson
Augusta, GA

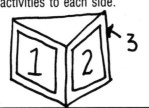

Reading Rabbit's Book Riddles

These reading riddles will build vocabulary and promote good books. Place a stuffed rabbit beside a small slate, and write a riddle on the slate. A paw print at the end means Reading Rabbit signed it! All answers are book titles. Keep each riddle until someone guesses it.

Betty Tipsword
Blacksburg, VA

    1. a feline in a striped chapeau—*The Cat in the Hat*
    2. the eve of a December holiday—*The Night Before Christmas*
    3. white precipitation for 24 hours—*The Snowy Day*
    4. two amphibians—*Frog and Toad*
    5. a small abode in a large forest-*Little House in the Big Woods*

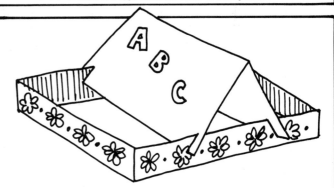

Flannelboard Stand

To make a 2-sided flannelboard, cut the front and back off a wallpaper book and tape the seam together with heavy tape. Cover the 2 sides with felt. Cut 2 slits each on opposite sides of a box to stand the flannelboard up. Decorate the box with contact paper and use the area below boards to store game pieces backed with felt, sandpaper, or used fabric softener sheets.

Delores Camilotto
Fond du Lac, WI

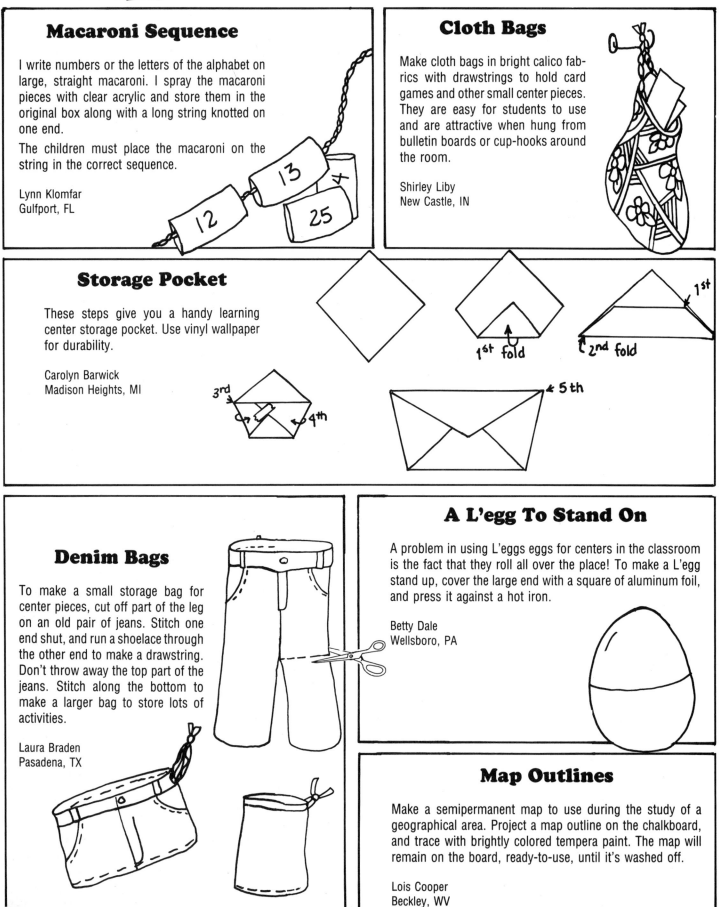

Macaroni Sequence

I write numbers or the letters of the alphabet on large, straight macaroni. I spray the macaroni pieces with clear acrylic and store them in the original box along with a long string knotted on one end.

The children must place the macaroni on the string in the correct sequence.

Lynn Klomfar
Gulfport, FL

Cloth Bags

Make cloth bags in bright calico fabrics with drawstrings to hold card games and other small center pieces. They are easy for students to use and are attractive when hung from bulletin boards or cup-hooks around the room.

Shirley Liby
New Castle, IN

Storage Pocket

These steps give you a handy learning center storage pocket. Use vinyl wallpaper for durability.

Carolyn Barwick
Madison Heights, MI

Denim Bags

To make a small storage bag for center pieces, cut off part of the leg on an old pair of jeans. Stitch one end shut, and run a shoelace through the other end to make a drawstring. Don't throw away the top part of the jeans. Stitch along the bottom to make a larger bag to store lots of activities.

Laura Braden
Pasadena, TX

A L'egg To Stand On

A problem in using L'eggs eggs for centers in the classroom is the fact that they roll all over the place! To make a L'egg stand up, cover the large end with a square of aluminum foil, and press it against a hot iron.

Betty Dale
Wellsboro, PA

Map Outlines

Make a semipermanent map to use during the study of a geographical area. Project a map outline on the chalkboard, and trace with brightly colored tempera paint. The map will remain on the board, ready-to-use, until it's washed off.

Lois Cooper
Beckley, WV

It Makes Cents

Turn sales slips into a challenging and fun math center! Cut off each itemized product list and paste it to a 3″ x 5″ card. Put the total of the sale and amount of money paid on another card. Attach the slip that tells the amount of change to a third card. These cards can be used for easy or challenging activities, including figuring out sales tax. Color-coding by small dots on the back of each card makes it self-checking:

Diana West
Big Horn, WY

Easy Change

Open-ended gameboards or centers that need pictures can be easily changed if both board and pictures are laminated and glued together with rubber cement. The cement holds well until the picture needs to be changed, then peels right off.

Mary Vander Poppen
Seattle, WA

Photo Art

A quick way to illustrate your centers is to use photos of students playing games or using centers. Students enjoy recognizing older friends playing the game they're playing. Kids can even take the photos and make the activity for the class which will follow them.

Alice Gdowski
Lathrup Village, MI

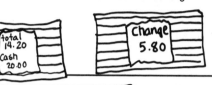

Mini Folders

Make a series of small folders out of white construction paper. On the outside cover, write a color word with a black marker. Inside, draw a happy face in the color indicated on the cover. Children read the word on the cover, then check themselves by opening the folder. Use this same idea for other categories, such as body parts, number words, etc.

Karen Stockstill
Sidney, OH

Zipper Thermometer

To help young students gain a better understanding of temperature, make a zipper thermometer. Glue an 18″ zipper to a piece of cardboard. Mark with the appropriate degrees and mount on a wall. After checking an outdoor thermometer each morning, set your zipper thermometer. Children will enjoy the manipulative aspect of this thermometer.

Marie Brown
Bristol, CT

Envelope Faces

Envelope or paper-bag characters provide a fun way to distribute papers. Round the corners of a manila envelope or paper bag, and cut off the upper layer above the hair line. Draw a colorful character face, and mount it on a bulletin board or a center. Children can easily get a paper from their helpful character.

Jan Karl
Tallmadge, OH

Learning Center Stickers

To identify all of the pieces that go with a center activity, label them with stickers from the same package. Students can locate the activity cards, worksheets, answer key, or game pieces by finding all with the same sticker attached. Some pieces, such as a multipurpose gameboard, may have several stickers on them. These can be filed and reused with another center. Extra stickers can be used as student awards for good work at the center. Students love to collect them!

Jo Ann Adams
Houston, TX

Subscription Cards

Stop throwing away those annoying magazine subscription cards, and start collecting them. Give to children for a fun lesson in writing their names and addresses. Be sure to cross out the backs of the cards so they can't be mailed!

Becky Cebula
Elkton, MD

The Word Tree

Don't throw away that old artificial Christmas tree! Build a word tree. Set up the trunk in a stand and screw in a cuphook for each student. Hang a name tag on each hook. Students make their own vocabulary flash cards and punch a hole in each. When the word is mastered, they hang it on their branch of the tree. Mastered words can go home periodically.

Jill Stine
Dayton, OH

More Than Once!

A four-section, TV dinner tray is too valuable in the classroom to use just one time! Label each section for place value and have students place number cards in the correct section. Use the top three sections for a math fact; the bottom section for the answer card. How about prefixes, roots, and suffixes? Vowel sounds, consonants, blends, and digraphs also work well. Now, can you afford to throw out that TV tray?

Sister William Travers
Williamsport, PA

A Good Listener

To give young children practice in oral reading, place a rug, pictures, and, most importantly, a large stuffed animal in a quiet corner. Above the animal place a sign: "Please read to me. I always listen." This method is very helpful with timid, nervous, or new students.

Linda Mason
Lawrence, MS

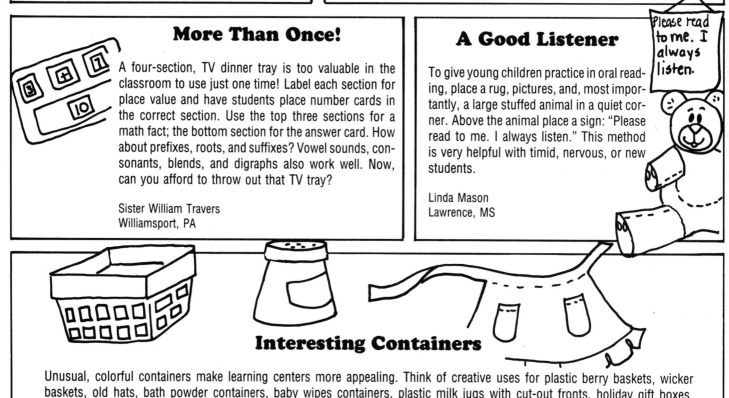

Interesting Containers

Unusual, colorful containers make learning centers more appealing. Think of creative uses for plastic berry baskets, wicker baskets, old hats, bath powder containers, baby wipes containers, plastic milk jugs with cut-out fronts, holiday gift boxes, mesh bags from oranges, cheese boxes covered with contact paper, old purses, aprons with pockets, and powdered drink cans.

Sue Guenther
Waterloo, IA

Tall Tale Box

When studying tall tales, legends, and exaggeration, provide your students with a tall tale box. Students fill the box with their own exaggerated stories or statements, such as: "If I exercise any harder, my feet will fall off." At the end of your study, award an oversized sucker or candy bar to the writer of the "tallest" tall tale.

Rhonda Thurman-Rice
Catoosa, OK

Alliteration Chart

Often, we don't have time to teach all the ways to use words creatively. Alliteration can be reinforced by writing the definition at the top of a sheet of chart paper and listing examples. Students write their own examples of alliteration with felt-tip markers. Or, laminate first for reuse. You'll get a decorative wall chart and students with a better understanding of word use.

Cheryl Smith
Biloxi, MS

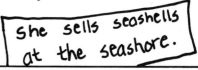

Geometric Puzzles

These puzzles look easy when they are put together. However, they are quite a challenge for your students when cut apart as shown. Try a variety of shapes. Include words of encouragement. Store pieces in an envelope with appropriate instructions.

Nell Gardner
Warrenton, NC

I know you can! *Almost* *Try again*

Almost there! *Hang on!* *Keep on.* *Are you sure now?* *Keep trying!* *Keep on.*

Fit pieces together to make a square.

Paper Bag Centers

VERB *NOUN* *Velcro on back* *Velcro*

Here's a way to make many paper bag centers with only a few bags. Laminate bags and center parts, then add Velcro strips to each. Center pieces can be easily switched.

LaDonna Hauser
Wilmington, NC

Helpful Charts

Provide number lines, alphabet charts, or other helpful guides at appropriate centers to help students who need them. It's no fun to do a center activity if you don't know where to begin!

Sue Guenther
Waterloo, IA

Reusable Gameboards

To extend the use of your centers and gameboards, laminate and program with a permanent magic marker. When you're ready to change the skill, erase the marker using a regular pencil eraser. Activities can be reprogrammed time and time again.

Teresa Badger
Bayboro, NC

$$681$$
$$326$$
$$+ \ \ 99$$
$$1106$$

Song Center

Instead of always providing music for your students to hear, let them write new words to familiar tunes and record them on a cassette tape player. They love listening to each others' songs!

Arnetra Terry
Manson, NC

Hold The Phone

Use a real disconnected telephone for children to dial their names and say the letters aloud. They can also dial simple words or number facts.

Lynn Klomfar
Gulfport, FL

Cuphook Hangers

I recently attended a learning center workshop and made an assortment of posters on display. At school, I attached cuphooks to the bottom of my chalk tray and used metal clips to hang the posters. Former dead space became a colorful hub of activity.

Carol Lapp
Vermilion, OH

Footlocker Game Center

An old footlocker or trunk is perfect for a game center! Paint a checkerboard or gameboard on the top, store games or activities inside, or use it as a game table.

Sr. Annette Fiala
Waterloo, IA

Vinnie, The Vowel Towel

This vowel display was made by gluing felt letters and pictures onto a towel. All year long, it hangs from a dowel in my classroom to remind students of the short vowel sounds.

Eleanore Zurbruegg
Memphis, TN

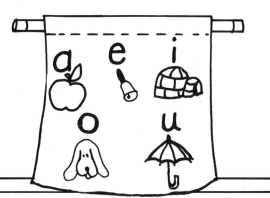

Quick Folder Games

Use cut-and-paste worksheets to make quick folder games and learning centers. Duplicate the worksheets on construction paper. Mount the worksheet, except pieces, on a colored file folder, and laminate. Laminate the cut-and-paste pieces, which become game pieces to store in a press-on pocket.

Lorrie Field
Catoosa, OK

Long-Playing Games

Use old LP records as gameboards. Glue dots or picture trails going around the record toward the middle. Add cards and dice, and you have a compact, easy-to-store game.

Variations:
1. Glue a large picture to the record, and glue a trail on top of the picture.
2. Store them in an old record rack.
3. Make a game on each side.
4. Let the kids make up their own games using old records.

Tilda Sumerel
Spruce Pine, AL

Wallpaper Book Gameboards

Don't throw away wallpaper books after the samples are used! Make sturdy gameboards by cutting off the covers and covering them with vinyl wallpaper. Add pockets to hold cards for reading or math practice. Or paste on felt squares to use as a flannelboard for ABC practice.

Barbara Penn
Niles, MI

Mastering Map Skills

One of the best interest centers I ever had was the simplest! For a unit in map skills, I had the students trace the map shape on large paper using the overhead projector. After all lines and marks are traced, the student finishes the map by adding details and coloring it in. This is good for hand-eye coordination, and it helps students remember the parts of their maps.

Pat Packard
Berea, OH

Battle Stations

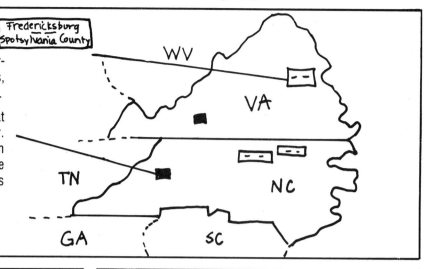

Here is an idea we used in our fifth grade that is particularly adaptable to centers related to wars, capitals, and other factual information taught in upper grades.

Cut pieces of magnetic strips (which can be bought at any hardware store) and glue in place on your center. Staple each fact or answer card. One staple is enough to attract the magnetic strip during use. Children place the matching answer cards on the magnetic strips. This idea can be adapted to use with file folders.

Ann Lee
Norwood, NC

Uniform Letters

This trick will help you make even, uniform letters when labeling centers. Hold a ruler firmly on the page, and write the word. If there are letters with "tails," leave the tails off. Go back after the entire sentence is finished and complete the letters.

Cheryl Helstrom
Pearisburg, VA

Play Money

Use a discarded wallet to store laminated play money. Makes a nifty addition to your math center!

Connie Connely
Catoosa, OK

Quick Centers

I use a magnetic photograph album to organize skill-related worksheets into a center. It's easy for children to use independently. Worksheets can be added or removed quickly, and wipe-off markers are great on the plastic pages. I place answer keys in the back for self-checking.

Sherry Claxton
Charlotte, NC

Pleat-A-Pocket

To make wallpaper pockets more durable, pleat the sides, turn the bottom under, and staple to the center.

Elizabeth Cole
Annapolis, MD

staple sides and bottom →

turn bottom under

Easy Center Storage

Mount centers on window shades. When you're finished with the activities, roll them up and store.

D. Shelton
Memphis, TN

Stretch Your Centers

After laminating learning center materials, use plastic tape to add student directions and answers. The tape can be peeled off and the center used later for another activity.

Sr. Margaret Ann Wooden
Emmitsburg, MD

Hard And Soft Sound Cards

When teaching hard and soft *C*, I paste a *C* made of cotton on a piece of construction paper. I glue or draw the letters *E*, *I*, and *Y* beside it and paste a picture of a soft *C* word in the corner. For forgetful students or those just learning, I show them the *C* is soft like cotton when it is followed by *E*, *I*, or *Y*. I use wood and other hard materials for the hard *C*. This idea works equally well with hard and soft *G*.

Laurie King
Sullivan, OH

Say A-h-h!

I use tongue depressors to help my students read large numbers. After putting down the four guide sticks shown below, the child lines up the numeral sticks in the correct sequence. It's easy to read the number while looking at this visual representation.

Pamela Duke
Lompoc, CA

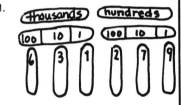

Mystery Sound Box

Cover or decorate any medium-sized box and label it "Mystery Sound Box." Each day, or whenever object is guessed, write a different beginning consonant and attach it to the box. Place a readily available or inexpensive item beginning with that letter in the box.

Students think of objects beginning with the letter that would fit in the box. The first student to guess correctly may keep the object. (Examples: pencil, apple, balloon, lollipop, crayon, stamp.)

Surround the object with tissue paper to prevent rattling. Use with a small skills group, reading group, or the entire class when appropriate. This activity may be used to teach ending consonant sounds, digraphs, or short and long vowels.

Jo Hull
Greensboro, NC

Taped Stories

Start an "exchange program" with a neighboring classroom. Have students tape stories from old basal readers and swap them with another class. The stories can be placed in the listening center so children can enjoy listening to their friends read.

Connie Connely
Tulsa, OK

Extra Pieces

When making learning center pieces, always make two or three extras. Laminate, but don't program them. If a piece is lost, you're prepared with a replacement.

Sue Guenther
Waterloo, IA

Learning Center Backboards

Conserve space by mounting four centers on this single unit. Use ¼" pressboard to cut four 20" x 24" pieces and one 24" x 40" piece. Add 12 hinges to fasten pieces together so that the side pieces can fold flat against the center one. Add a handle for carrying ease.

Michelle Martin
Macon, GA

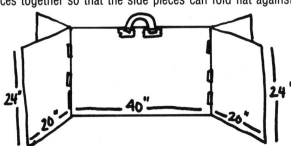

The Ladder Of Success

Use masking tape to make a ladder on the floor to practice letters. On each rung, write a letter. The child climbs the ladder by saying the letters as he climbs. You can also use words or numbers.

Lynn Klomfar
Gulfport, FL

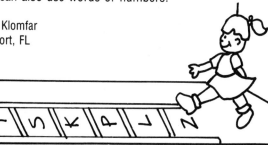

Days Of The Week

I put embroidery hoops to work helping children learn the days of the week. Stretch solid-colored cloth onto 1 large hoop and 7 small ones. Attach a cuphook to the top of each small hoop. Write a day of the week on each small hoop, and decorate it. (I use the 7 dwarfs!) Put a large hoop with the heading up on a wall. The children hang the small hoops in the right order by hooking the cuphook to the tightening screw of the hoop above.

Lynn Klomfar
Gulfport, FL

Fantastic Fireplace

I built a simple fireplace out of wood and covered it with contact paper. It gives a homey touch to the room and goes well with our U.S. history unit. The kids make and bring old cooking utensils when we study how the pioneers cooked. I also use the mantel to display a multitude of holiday objects: Easter baskets, Christmas stockings, Halloween pumpkins, etc. Our fireplace is the focal point of our classroom!

Rebecca Graves
Burlington, NC

Tips For Making Center Pieces

If you want to make game pieces that are self-checking on the back, here's a way to put the answers on before laminating. Trace your game pieces very closely together on a sheet of poster board. Run a straight pin through the center of each piece. Now turn to the back and write your answers exactly where they need to be. The pinhole is so small it will not detract from the appearance. You can then laminate and cut out the completed game pieces without any wasted steps.

Patricia P. Williamson
Winchester, VA

Book Club Circulars

Recycle old book club circulars and advertisements. Salvage colorful characters and seasonal pictures to decorate teacher-made gameboards or file folders. You won't have to draw characters to attract student interest at centers.

Michelle Combs
Bristol, VA

Social Studies Trivia Review

I make studying for social studies tests more interesting and get students involved. Each child contributes five important questions and answers. I make up categories and use the board and pieces from the trivia game. Examples of my categories include important people, dates, places, and definitions.

Mary Larson
Bristol, CT

Instant Easel

This inexpensive easel is super to use in learning centers. Ask a salesperson in a fabric or department store to save the easel-type advertisement that accompanies pattern displays. These are very sturdy for tabletop chart stands either as they are or covered with colorful contact paper. Tape directions written on cards to the easel. The directions can be easily changed when centers are changed.

Sandra Irish
Van Alystyne, TX

Share-A-Book Center

Here's a center that encourages students to develop positive attitudes toward independent reading. On a table in front of this bulletin board is displayed a variety of paperback books. Inside the front cover of each book I place a large self-adhesive label.

When a child finishes his work, he reads one of the books on display and signs his name on the label. He then looks to see who else has already read the book, and he asks one of them to listen to his favorite pages. When the old label is full, I replace it with a new label and write in the name of the last child to read the book.

John Kessler
Davenport, IA

Plastic Garbage Bag Gameboards

Use a white, plastic garbage bag of any size for a gameboard. Permanent markers work great on the plastic. You can wipe the board off if it gets dirty and fold it up for convenient filing. The bag provides storage space for cards, markers, directions, etc.

Mary Lee Dorsey
Littleton, CO

Check Your Mail

Every child loves to get mail! With metal mailboxes painted in pretty, bright colors, I signal when a center is open by raising the mailbox flag. The mail inside gives the instructions for that center. Mailboxes placed at work tables deliver worksheets, morning assignments, or return work.

Linda Ridgley
Palm Bay, FL

Feed The Bear

Make poster board bears as illustrated. Draw in eyes and a nose. Attach a separate piece to form a pocket for the mouth. Make circles about the size of quarters. Print long vowels on one side, short vowels on the other. Store sets together in a plastic bag.

As the teacher says a word or shows a picture, children select the right vowel sound to "feed the bear." Adapt to other skills such as math, digraphs, or blends.

Fran Petersen
North Tonawanda, NY

Pockets Full Of Poems

Cut pockets from fabric and have students decorate them with thread, buttons, yarn, etc. After sewing backs on the pockets, mount them on a bulletin board at your poetry center and fill with students' poems.

Jill Robbins
Ogden, IL

Vocabulary Game

Have students complete a vocabulary matching game. Draw squares inside a file folder, and write vocabulary words with a sentence for each one in the squares. Students locate each word in a dictionary and write the phonetic spelling, part of speech, and definition on a card the same size as a square in the folder. When all squares are covered with cards, students have created a game for a center.

Rhonda Thurman-Rice
Catoosa, OK

Transparency Markers

I use overhead transparency markers instead of wipe-off crayons on laminated games or centers. The crayons are hard to wipe off and leave a residue. My games begin to look dull and dirty after several wipe-offs. The markers wipe off quickly and easily without leaving a film if you use a damp paper towel.

Randie Garrick
Springfield, MO

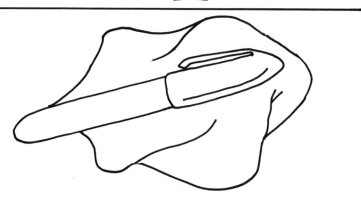

Car Rental Maps

Car rental agencies have provided my entire class with maps to use for math or social studies units. Before using, I have them laminated for durability. My students have enjoyed planning imaginary trips and tracing dictated directions on the maps.

Patricia Shulman
Aurora, CO

Tree Hangings

Insert a tree branch in plaster or in a large Styrofoam block. Decorate the branch each month with vocabulary words, facts, etc. Make it seasonal by using a new shape each time. Examples: September—apples; October—leaves; November—turkeys; December—tree ornaments; January—snowballs; February—hearts; March—shamrocks; April—eggs; May—birds; June—butterflies.

Write answers on the backs of the shapes, or make them double and write the answers on the inside. Hang on branches with yarn, ribbon, string, or twist-ties.

Fran Petersen
North Tonawanda, NY

Pick A Pocket

A shoe holder can be very useful in the classroom:
1. Store game cards in the pockets.
2. Make an alphabetical order center. Put guide words on each pocket and have students place word cards in the correct pockets.
3. Review math facts by putting a number on each pocket. Students place matching problem cards in the correct pockkets.

Gail Hutchinson
Beverly, MA

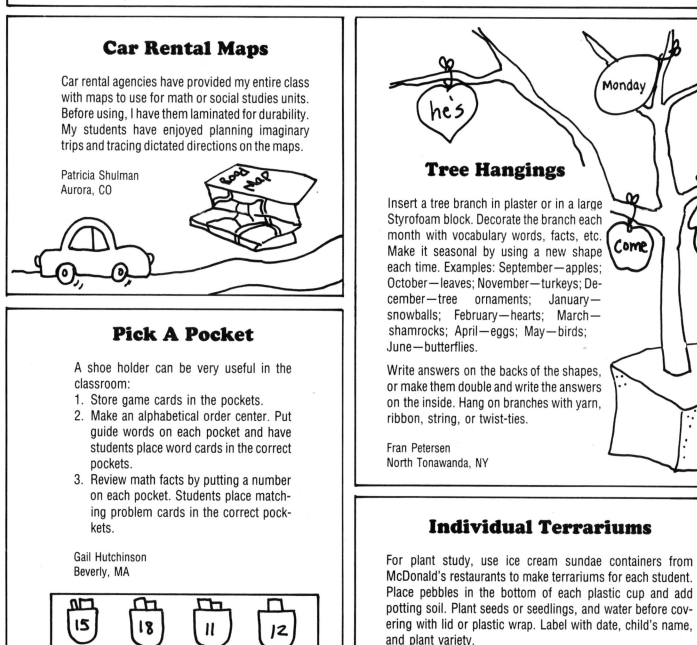

Individual Terrariums

For plant study, use ice cream sundae containers from McDonald's restaurants to make terrariums for each student. Place pebbles in the bottom of each plastic cup and add potting soil. Plant seeds or seedlings, and water before covering with lid or plastic wrap. Label with date, child's name, and plant variety.

Sandra Reynolds
Hixson, TN

Getting Organized

Storage Idea

Discarded lunch boxes are great for storage. Just paint them a bright color or cover with contact paper. Wonderful for games, puzzles, activity cards, etc.

Ann Hudson
Forest, VA

THE MAILBOX Reference

For easy reference to all the ideas in my copies of THE MAILBOX, I cut the pages apart at the center fold of the magazine. After punching holes, I store them in a three-ringed notebook and renumber the pages, adding the issue number before each page number. When I make lesson plans, I can easily refer to the particular issue and page I wish to use.

Suzanne Edmunds
Forest, VA

Holders For Pencils

Containers used for making Popsicles are excellent classroom pencil holders. Individual sections keep various colored pencils, pens, scissors, or paintbrushes organized.

Rebecca Graves
Burlington, NC

To Be Returned

Save time returning papers! I keep a box labeled "To Be Returned" on top of my classroom mailboxes. I put graded papers in the box. As children finish their work, they are eager to return papers to classmates' mailboxes.

Barbara Ihnen
North Manchester, IN

How Many Do You Need?

When you file copies of duplicated worksheets, count and paper clip them, recording the number in pencil on the top sheet. You'll know whether you have enough copies later, especially if students are working at different levels. Be sure to change the number each time you use some.

Debbie Hawkins
Atwood, IL

Record Rack Storage

Envelope games can be stored neatly by standing them upright in a wire record rack. Holds lots!

Patsy Dawson
Celina, OH

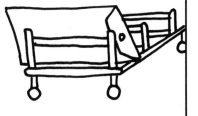

Mailbox Index

To make a handy reference index of your issues of *The Mailbox*, label 3″ x 5″ index cards with basic skills, one skill per card. Go through the pages of *The Mailbox* and write the name of the activity or worksheet, the page, and the date of the issue on the appropriate card. When you get ready to teach, the skills will be at your fingertips.

Darlene Shelton
Memphis, TN

Tackle Box Tote

An old fishing tackle box makes a handy container for school supplies! Use small compartments for stickers or paper clips. The slender sections will hold pencils, markers, or scissors. Store tape and glue in the lower compartment. Carried between home and school, it will help avoid duplicate purchases of expensive supplies.

Paula Holdren
Louisville, KY

Milk Container Organizer

To keep art supplies organized and handy, try using a plastic milk container. Cut out a 5″ square in the carton to hold crayons, glue, and pencils. Place rulers and scissors inside the pour spout. The handle makes it easy to carry.

Elaine Plemons
Calhoun, GA

Materials Index

After years of collecting, do you lose track of all the materials you have? Here's a tip that works! Make an index card for each topic you teach, and list all your resources and their locations. This system will help you in a glance as you're making up lesson plans.

Mary Dinneen
Bristol, CT

Space Savers

If space for centers in your room is limited, your local grocery or variety store may help. Cardboard displays (the ones with all the little cubbyholes) are great space savers and can be used to store file folders, worksheets, activity cards, etc. Most store managers gladly part with these after the merchandise has been sold.

Linda Lofton
Broken Arrow, OK

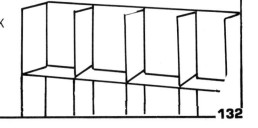

Stackable Storage

Plastic milk crates that come from the school cafeteria or the milk company make great, stackable storage units! They are good for holding books, center activities, and papers your students are ready to turn in.

Suzanne Edmunds
Forest, VA

Reusable Worksheets

When I need to thermofax a worksheet or workbook page for duplication purposes, I laminate the original before making my thermal master. Not only can I make new thermal masters from it, but my children can also use this laminated copy with wipe-off crayons. I use a hole puncher and file these in a notebook.

Wanda Capps
Marshall, NC

Group Planner

Reading group lessons can be planned quickly if you have groups who will be covering the same units at some time during the year. Write lesson plans on 3″ x 5″ index cards, including skills to cover and your own teaching ideas. Each reading group will have five cards per week. Put index cards into a photo album made for 35 mm prints. Further individualize your plans and make notes using a wipe-off marker. You may also want to photocopy each page and place in your plan book. This is a little more work at first, but planning for groups next year will be a breeze!

Jeanne Thomas
Cana, VA

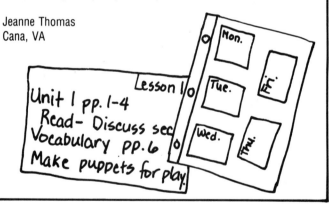

Box Storage

Family-size detergent boxes make great storage containers for skill games. These boxes come with a tape you pull to release three sides of the lid, leaving the lid hinged on the fourth side. Smaller detergent boxes work perfectly for storage of workbooks, magazines, and paper. To make classroom organization easier, place a piece of colored tape on the side of the box, and put an identical piece in the center of the students' work table.

Helen Burkard
Beckley, WV

Word Card Organizer

A memo/letter holder helps me organize my reading groups' vocabulary cards. I paint the dividers to correspond to my reading group colors, then place each group's cards in the appropriate section. Cards stay together and are ready for drill when each group comes to the reading table.

Carol Herzog
Hunting, IN

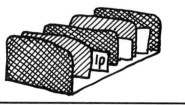

Chair Pocket

To make a storage slipcover for your desk chair, cut fabric about 22″ long and 4″ wider than the chair. Fold it down 5″ from the top, and sew down the sides to make the top of the cover. On the reverse side, fold the bottom end up about 7″, and sew up the sides to make a handy pocket for storing work to be returned to students and other papers.

Linda Bates
Garland, TX

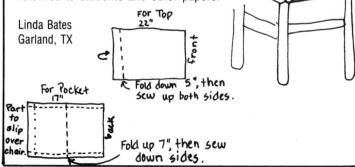

Coat Hook Stand

Build a convenient stand to hold your centers, flash cards, and other materials. Mount a 5′ piece of scrap lumber on a 1′ wide base and attach coat hooks. Place centers in Zip-Loc bags, punch holes in the tops of the bags, and hang on your stand.

Kimberly Kepp
Lake City, MN

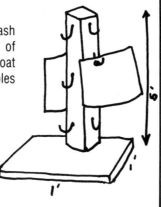

File Folder Storage

Use a dish drainer for convenient storage of file folder activities. Place pencils and wipe-off crayons in the silverware holder for use with the folders in the drainer. Color code folders by subject or level of difficulty for ease in making individual assignments.

Patsy Chevault
Waco, KY

Clothespin Hangers

For a handy place to hang visual aids, maps, charts, etc., tape 2 clothespins to the wall or to the top of the blackboard. Put aids up for one lesson, or leave up for an entire unit!

Linda Johnson
Louisville, KY

Students Help

I file all copies of *THE MAILBOX* in a large notebook along with important clippings and other resources. It's called "Ann's Almanac" and is used by my students almost as much as by me. They look through the assortment and let me know what games and worksheets they want me to copy next.

Ann Hudson
Forest, VA

The Mailbox Notebook

Keep *The Mailbox* worksheets handy and organized. Duplicate and laminate all the worksheet pages for each season. Make a notebook for each skill level, and sort the worksheets accordingly. They are then easy to find and are in good condition. You can also use this notebook to pull together units on several achievement levels to meet students' individual needs.

Kathy Beard
Keystone Heights, FL

Letter Tray Organizers

Use six letter trays to organize dittos and teaching supplies for each day. Label them with the days of the week and one for odds and ends. When I do my lesson plans, I put all filmstrips, tapes, books, and supplies in the tray for that day. Substitutes will love it too!

Karen Johnson
Columbus, OH

Subject Index

To enhance usefulness of *THE MAILBOX* issues, make a subject index. Record page and issue numbers that apply to index headings that correspond to subjects you teach. Subheadings can be made using unit titles for guides. The index can be kept in a card file or small loose-leaf notebook with index tabs. It is helpful to note "bulletin board," "game," etc. by each entry.

Jean O. Youngsteadt
Springfield, MO

Idea Photographs

To keep track of your bulletin boards and centers, photograph them and place the photos in an album. Include an index card next to each picture, listing the storage location of all pieces. Capture other good ideas by carrying your camera to workshops or schools you visit. Place these photos in a separate album for future reference.

Jill Robbins
Ogden, IL

Don't Be Puzzled!

Need a sturdy, flat surface where students can assemble puzzles? Provide a short-legged puzzle table, with molding around the edges to prevent pieces from falling off. Work on classroom puzzles won't be disturbed.

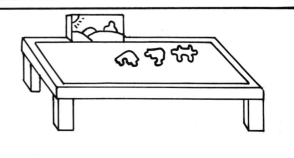

Debbie Wiggins
Myrtle Beach, SC

Work Tubs

Spending too much time distributing work supplies? Color-code a plastic tub or bucket for each table group. Fill each tub with smaller, color-coded containers of crayons, glue, scissors, and more. Assign each table captain the responsibility of placing his tub on his table each morning. Saves time and confusion!

Pamela Myhowich
Yakima, WA

Buddy Reading

Encourage silent and oral reading while your students clean and reorganize the library shelves. About once every nine weeks, clear the shelves and pass out 10-15 books per child. Have children spend a set time reading the varied books, then pair off to share or read books together. This activity is a change from the routine, plus it gives you a chance to clean shelves and replace the books in order.

Pat B. Redgrave
Kissimmee, FL

Margarine Container Storage

To store things for my learning centers, I have found that the small margarine containers are just the right size. I punch two holes in the side of the container and run pretty yarn through the holes. I hang the container on a working bulletin board to store cut-out pieces.

Donna Bridges
West Plains, MO

Can It!

Use frosting or chip cans with plastic lids to store crayons, markers, or all those little things that need keeping. They last well and fit into desks easily.

Mrs. Guy Beale, Jr.
Forest, VA

File Holder

A dish drainer that fits inside the kitchen sink is a great storage spot. Letter-sized file folders fit perfectly. The holder at one end works well for pencils, pens, tape, spinners, game markers, or anything else needed to accompany the file folder games stored in it.

Bonnie Jo Kyles
Ennis, MT

Mousetrap Organizers

A mousetrap makes a small but efficient organizer for centers, papers, etc. Remove the top piece from a regular mousetrap. Decorate the trap and use it to clip together task cards, worksheets, flash cards, and game pieces.

Beverly Bippes
Madison, NE

Clipping Ideas

Store idea clippings in a notebook, and keep it handy for future reference. Let students help by pasting in clippings and by selecting the worksheets or activities they would like you to try!

Carrie Davis
Atlanta, GA

Sticker File

Use a plastic file with small drawers (the kind used in workshops for nails and screws) to keep stickers neatly sorted for holidays, skills, etc. Also good for pawns and dice.

Fran Petersen
N. Tonawanda, NY

Cuphook Display

A good way to display envelope games is to punch a hole in the flap and hang them on cuphooks. The cuphooks can be screwed into bulletin board borders, corkboards, bookcases, chalkboard frames, or any wood frames.

Mrs. M. Curran
Manistique, MI

Fishnet Display

If display space is minimal in your classroom, make more by hanging a decorative fishnet across a corner. It's easy for students to hang their work up with paper clips or clothespins.

Lynn Klomfar
Gulfport, FL

Real-Life Readers

Place free pamphlets in decorated cereal boxes to give your students a variety of real-life reading materials. Pamphlets can be obtained by writing many institutions: travel agencies, government consumer agencies, and armed forces recruiting offices, to name a few.

Jane Meyer
Frankfort, KY

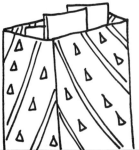

Picket Fence

I've used rolls and rolls of tape, trying in vain to hang items on the cement block walls of my classroom. My solution to the problem was a ten-foot picket fence, which I hung on my wall with concrete nails. I strung wire across the fence, then used clothespins to hang items from it. This made an attractive wall decoration that held even heavy poster paper easily.

Louise Alexander
Cordele, GA

Getting Organized

Classroom Storage

Here are some quick-to-make or easy-to-find storage ideas for organizing game pieces, posters and charts, learning center materials, and student collections:

–plastic shoe boxes
–plastic sweater boxes
–deluxe magazine file boxes
  (available from school or office supply stores)
–Pringles snack cans stacked on their sides
–plastic hanging shoe bags

–partitioned liquor boxes covered with contact paper
–cardboard tubes from gift wrap
–plastic egg cartons
–large margarine tubs
–empty milk cartons stacked on their sides

The Mailbox Staff

Hanging Gameboards

Tagboard games can be stored easily if you punch holes along one side and insert clip-type shower curtain hooks. Hang them on hooks under the chalkboard, on shelf bracket ends, or on extra coat hooks.

Julia Ford
Davisburg, MI

Center Bucket

Store all those loose center pieces in an indestructible center bucket. Cover a large (3½-4 lb.) peanut butter bucket with brightly colored paper, and use it to store game pieces. Also good for collecting papers or storing answer keys.

Carolyn Fagg
Cowen, WV

Learning Center File

After several years of using preprinted centers, I found myself wondering if I had already used a particular center with my present class. I developed a filing system to keep track of centers on 3″ x 5″ cards. I listed the title, skill, and alternate skills on one card for each center and filed cards under subject headings. Every time I used a center, I dated its card. This file is also helpful in finding a center on a needed skill.

Tammie Jacobs
Longmont, CO

Accordion Files

An accordion desk file from an office supply store is an excellent space saver! Store assignments at a center, or use it to collect finished work. Instead of carrying stacks of papers, take the collapsible file to your favorite paper-grading spot.

Linda Huffman
Shalimar, FL

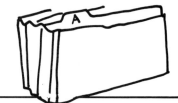

Teacher's Catchall

Do you find yourself without the supplies you need for making games at home? Grab an old lunch box, tackle box, or sewing box, and drop in scissors, crayons, felt pens, pencils, tape, and other materials you may need. Take it home with you each day so you'll have everything you need at your fingertips.

Pamela Myhowich
Yakima, WA

Student Folders

Sheets from old wallpaper books make great student folders. Sew two sheets together on three sides to make a folder just the right size for school papers.

Sharleen Kelly Berg
Jefferson, SD

Film Canisters

Here are a couple of good uses for those canisters that 35mm film comes in. They are ideal for putting paste in so each child can have his own. The child uses his finger to apply the paste, the top can be replaced on the canister, and the paste doesn't dry out. The cans are also good for storing dice and game markers. Kids can pick up a game and a canister with all the pieces needed. It's a neat storage idea!

Carolyn Duncan
Adel, GA

Clothes Rack Display

With table space being so limited in my classroom, I had a problem displaying file folder games, poster board games, and other activities. So, I bought a wooden, collapsible clothes rack and some of the plastic laundry hangers that hang and clip like a clothespin. Now I can hang my activities on both sides of the rack, the activities are at eye level for the children, and they are easy for the children to manage alone. The best part is that the rack folds flat for storage!

Lynne Willis
Augusta, GA

Center Storage Tips

For storing learning centers in a minimum of space, use extendable skirt/pant hangers. Poster board centers can be attached to these hangers to be kept neat. Clip on a Zip-Loc bag containing loose center pieces if necessary.

Sandi Nolte
Lynchburg, VA

Masking Tape Hanger

You can use masking tape to hang papers on a cinder block wall. Attach a long strip of tape along the wall, then push straight pins down through the student's papers and the tape. The tape strip can be used over and over for several months.

Sandy Latham
Atlanta, GA

Scissor Keeper

Here's a way to keep the children's scissors neat and untangled on the shelf. Take a wide, flat can, like a peanut can, and cover it around the outside with colorful contact paper. Place the can bottom side up, so that the open end is down. Take a bottle opener and punch out holes around the entire closed end. Scissors can now be placed in these holes in a neat and orderly fashion.

D'Leigh Harvell
Atlanta, GA

Cereal Box Files

Save medium-sized cereal boxes for file holders. Cut down the middle of one side, fold resulting flaps in, and staple. Cover the box with contact paper for a container the ideal size to hold center folders and worksheets.

Sharon John
Loring, MT

Portable Art Center

Keep all of your art supplies centrally located on an art cart that can be moved around as needed to various work areas in the classroom. Students learn to return supplies to the art cart. Appoint one student to be in charge of keeping it tidy.

Margaret & John Kessler
Davenport, IA

Wallpaper Envelopes

Follow these steps to make durable wallpaper envelopes to hold game pieces, flash cards, etc.:
1. Cut wallpaper twice as wide as you want the envelope.
2. Fold sides in to the center and tape down.
3. Cut 2″ off top corners to make a flap.
4. Cut 1″ off bottom.
5. Trim unneeded flap from top and bottom. Fold over bottom and tape.

Elizabeth Cole
Annapolis, MD

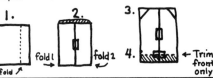

Worksheet Storage Bags

When you put out a series of worksheets for students, try putting each set in a plastic food storage bag. The bags cost about a penny each and can be written on with a permanent magic marker. File extra sheets, the ditto master, and the answer key along with each set.

Jane Cuba
Redford, MI

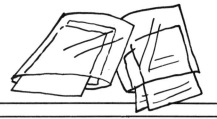

Colored Paper Clips

A package of colored paper clips brightens up my classroom each day. I use them with file folder games. Just clip them to the folder for no more lost pieces! They also make handy reward tokens, gameboard pieces, and color-coding markers.

Margie Bohler
Rolla, MO

Ditto On Ditto

Have you spent hours drawing ruled lines on a ditto master so that you can write straight? Lines that won't be seen on the final copy?

Here's a timesaving way to put lines on the top sheets of dittos. Make lines on one ditto so they go through and print on the machine. Now, instead of running paper through, simply put other clean ditto masters through the machine and print the lines on them. Stock up on these lined dittos, and it will save you hours of time plus assure you of straight-lined copy.

Colleen Doherty
Clifton Park, NY

Diaper Boxes

Economy-size Pampers boxes make great storage containers. Cover with contact paper and use to store file folders. Not only are these boxes sturdy, but they also have convenient carrying handles.

Jean Davis
Commerce, GA

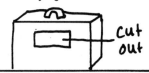

Reproducibles Record

Make a copy of the table of contents of each reproducible worksheet book that you plan to use with your class. Keep copies in a folder and make a notation on the list each time you distribute a worksheet to students. You can also indicate favorite reproducible pages with the dates you plan to use them. There won't be any guessing later about which ones you have used.

Debbie Hawkins
Atwood, IL

Colored Chalk Emphasis

Use colored chalk on your chalkboard to point out capitalization and punctuation. Trace over the letters and marks that need emphasis.

Connie Connely
Catoosa, OK

Coffee Canister Delight

When requesting supplies from home, add canisters from General Foods International Coffees to your list. Cover with contact paper to make them attractive. These small containers with plastic lids are perfect for game pieces, school supplies, learning centers, or students' miscellaneous items.

Patricia Shulman
Englewood, CO

Skill Unit Booklets

When working on a particular unit, combine all those loose worksheets into one compact booklet. Add a cover for students to decorate, if desired. Children will be better able to see their progress while completing the booklets, and you'll find them easier to monitor than individual loose sheets.

Jill Stine
Dayton, OH

Trash Can For Books

My students were so bad about leaving and losing their books that I started putting the misplaced books in a standard-sized trash can, which I decorated. Students either paid 25¢ to get a book out or gave up one recess period. The money was used at the end of the year for a class party. It really helped my students become more responsible for their belongings.

Debbie Wiggins
Myrtle Beach, SC

Storage Bags

Games, card sets, etc. are easily stored using Zip-Loc storage bags (gallon size). I tape the top edge to a hanger so that they can be hung on a rod for easy access. To be sure that the bags are safe should a student put one over his head, I punch holes down the sides in several places.

Carol McWilliams
Minneapolis, MN

Game Pieces Can

I had a problem keeping pawns, dice, pennies, and wipe-off markers together to use with games. Pieces often damaged press-on pockets and were not secure there. My solution was to decorate a large, powdered-drink-mix can with colorful contact paper and label it "Game Can." All kinds of game supplies are stored in it. When students finish with pieces, they replace them in the can.

Amelia K. Burns
Willoughby, OH

Make Kids Feel Special

Child Of The Week

A very special activity I instituted in my classroom is the "Child of the Week." Each child is assigned a week when he can share information about himself.

At home with the help of his parents, the child prepares a poster for display. He includes information about hobbies, family, pets, etc. After each child has had a turn, my teacher's aide and I become "People of the Week."

Marla Budd
Dresden, OH

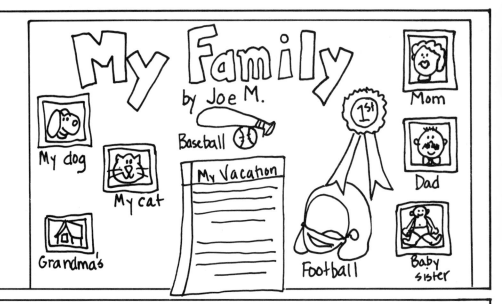

Record-Keeping Pets

Trace a large pet shape from a coloring book and draw lines to divide it into many sections. When a student completes a book report, he writes a title in one of the sections and colors it. Children take pride in recording their progress and have a complete book report history at the end of the year.

Barbara Hosek
Valencia, CA

Lunch With The Teacher

Invite a student to a pleasant lunch. Once a week or every ten days, make lunch for a student in your class. Give him choices for a sandwich and a dessert, and have him provide his own drink. Find a nice, quiet spot, and enjoy your time together on a one-to-one basis. Be sure to allow time during the year for lunch with each student in your class.

Diane Jones
Levittown, PA

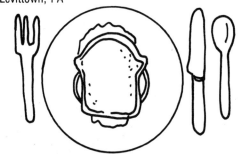

Sticker Badges

Increase the recognition value of a simple sticker award by making it into a student badge. Craft stores often sell stiff, inexpensive ribbon which is ideal for this.

Jane Cuba
Redford, MI

Creative Stickers

Save clear contact paper or laminating film scraps to create your own stickers! Add remarks with colorful permanent markers and give to students as rewards.

Mary Lee Dorsey
Littleton, CO

Reading Certificates

This reading award with a different twist will encourage students to read more and more books. For each student, cut a prepared certificate or award into 6-10 strips. Number the backs of the strips to help reassemble later. Place the strips in an envelope for each child. Students earn one strip for each book read and glue strips in order onto their own construction paper shape mounted on a bulletin board. Students will enjoy earning strips and seeing their awards take shape!

Carol Carpenter
Boston, MA

The Golden Egg

A golden egg motivates students to be as good as gold! Paint a plastic egg gold. Each day before children arrive, choose a recipient and place it in his desk. I judge conduct, attitude, and effort of the previous day to determine who receives the egg. That student gets to carry it all day.

Darlene Shelton
Memphis, TN

Cut Pass

Use a "cut pass" as an incentive for good work or extra effort. The cut pass is good for cutting in line once when going to music, library, lunch, etc. The students really work to earn a chance to stand by their friends in line.

Phyllis Roland
Henryville, IN

Write About Us!

Writing about a classmate makes each hand-writing lesson a special one for the whole class. At the beginning of the year, I put each child's name in a big envelope. Each Friday, we draw out one name and write a paragraph about the special student of the day. We interview the child to find out birthday, pets, favorites, and other information. The student of the day takes his paragraph to the principal to receive special recognition and a sticker.

Phyllis Davis
Lexington, KY

Postcard Name Tags

Bridging the gap between home and school is easier when children receive postcards from their new teacher. Before school begins, the teacher prepares and sends a postcard name tag, decorated with simple symbols or stickers, to each student. Be sure to have some extra postcards on hand for students who do not wear their tags to school. Receiving these postcards allows the student to experience the joy of receiving mail of his own; to learn his room number, his teacher's name, and other pertinent information; and to have a feeling of belonging!

Harriet Kinghorn
Grand Forks, ND

VIP Nail Keg

Feature a student each week on a Very Important Person nail keg display! Tack baby pictures, birth certificates, and good papers onto an old keg. It doesn't take up valuable bulletin board space!

D. Shelton
Memphis, TN

Make Kids Feel Special

Welcome Wagon

A welcome wagon is just the thing to ease a new student into the group. Cover a box with colored paper and fill with items to make the days easier. A class schedule, student list, crayons, new pencils, stickers, puzzles, and examples of class work might be included. Place the box near the student's desk and let an old-timer be host or hostess to accompany the student for a day.

Paula Holdren
Louisville, KY

Tape Recorded Greetings

When my aide was absent, the class sent a weekly tape to update her on what had been happening. The students loved talking into the microphone and produced a lasting record of their activities. This would be a nice way to keep in touch with students who are ill!

Karen Heichel
Lancaster, PA

Peanut Rewards

Good work is worth real peanuts here! Post a huge elephant outline and attach a bag of shelled peanuts. Display good work on the elephant, inviting students whose work has been posted to take a peanut as a pat on the back!

Denise Hunt
Lawrence, KS

Special Reward

Improve the quality of homework papers with a special reward. Occasionally laminate a well-done paper and return it to the owner to keep.

Isobel Livingstone
Rahway, NJ

Featured Story

Choose a student's creative writing paper to feature for one week. Mount his story on colored paper, and display where others may read and autograph it. When the week is over, laminate for a treasured poster. Each student gets a poster during the year.

Judy W. Jones
Circleville, OH

Stumped??

Here's a real conversation piece for your classroom. Bring a sawed-off stump into your room. It's a great seat for one or a special spot for students to stand on for reports or speeches.

Jodie Hodge
Great Falls, SC

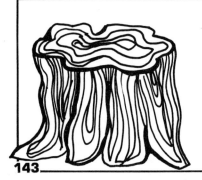

Reward & Motivate

Several teachers who attended The Education Center workshop were staying at my home and were talking about submitting center ideas. My nephew, Chuck Mather, wanted to share this idea his kindergarten teacher uses.

She gives each student a paper ice cream cone. When they say memory work, she gives a paper scoop of ice cream. When they get six scoops, they are eligible for a small prize, a longer recess, or some other special privilege.

Mrs. M. Stuart
Haddon Township, NJ

B.Y.O.B. Day

Have a B.Y.O.B. (Bring Your Own Banana) Day! After a week when the class has worked especially hard, provide ice cream and toppings and help children make banana splits as their reward.

Connie Connely
Tulsa, OK

Library Leopard

To encourage library reading, give each student a leopard without spots. After the child reads a book, she adds a spot to her leopard. This makes a nice take-home award for eager readers!

Deretha Schmittlein
Slippery Rock, PA

Get Well Puzzle

To cheer a sick student who is absent several days, my class sends a get well puzzle. After printing a short message on poster board, my students sign their names. Then we cut the poster board into puzzle pieces, place them in a Zip-Loc plastic bag, and send the puzzle home to the sick child.

Sylvia McFeaters
Slippery Rock, PA

100 Gang

Urge students to study their spelling with the creation of the "100 Gang." To belong to the club, a student must score 100% on the weekly spelling test. He is rewarded with a certificate that can be turned in during the next week in place of one daily spelling assignment. Great incentive!

Tanya Wilder
Broken Arrow, OK

Free Drink

A reward my students like to earn for good work is a free-drink pass. During a specified time, students with passes may take a short break on their own. Students really enjoy this idea and work hard to earn a pass.

Karen Bellis
Stover, MO

Using Leftover Stickers

I've found a good way to use old reward stickers. I put leftover stickers in a decorated shoe box. When a student turns in a perfect paper, I write "E = St" (Excellent = Sticker) on his paper, indicating that he may choose a sticker from the box to put on his paper. The children enjoy this even more than when I place stickers on their papers.

Claudia Wilcox
Vernon, CT

Make Kids Feel Special

R.A.T. Pack

These rats are pointing out students for recognition. R.A.T. stands for Reward Activity Time, a special time for students who have shown improved efforts in scholastics, behavior, or other areas. They're invited to remain inside during one recess for R.A.T. Pack, when they get a certificate, refreshments, and time to play a quick game. This uninterrupted time with the teacher really motivates students.

Anne Flaherty
South Windham, ME

Math Facts Are Lifesavers

Good math skills can be lifesavers! Post a 3' x 4' strip of gift wrap that is illustrated with lifesavers on a bulletin board. Attach a lifesaver cut-out for each student. For every perfect math paper, place a star on the individual's lifesaver. 10 stars might earn a real pack of Lifesavers candy or an achievement certificate!

Jill Stine
Dayton, OH

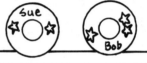

Book Reward

I have many outdated books I have accumulated. I put my children's names on a chart and place a star by their name for good work and behavior. Five stars earns them one of my old books. Not only does it help me clean house, it provides reading motivation through book ownership.

Arnetra Townes
Manson, NC

Apple Of Our Eye

Each week, post biographical information about one person in the class—items like photos, examples of hobbies, vacation or sports T-shirts, magazine pictures, etc. The personality of the week is also my helper for that week, taking lunch count, attendance, helping with errands, etc. This way, the "apple of our eye" for the week gets a little extra attention.

Gail Martin
Sugarland, TX

We Miss You

Here are several special remembrances for a student who is hospitalized or out for a long time:
1. Give each student a balloon. Have him blow it up and write his name or a cheerful phrase on it. Tie these together and deliver.
2. Enlarge an outline of a favorite cartoon character, trace, and cut two copies. Have students color and sign it, then stuff it with paper and staple.
3. Design a large paper flower with students' names on the petals. Place it in a dirt-filled flowerpot.

Paula K. Holdren
Prospect, KY

Teacher's Pet

Each student in my class gets to be teacher's pet several times a year. On his day, he takes the roll to the office, runs all errands, hands out all papers, and eats lunch at a special table. He gets to invite four friends to eat at his table also. They love this special day.

Ann Hudson
Forest, VA

Take The Pepsi Challenge!

For a motivational technique, "Take the Pepsi Challenge!" Each student has a Pepsi cup. When Friday's spelling test is returned, he writes words he missed on a card and places it in his cup. When we have our review test, students are retested on those same words. Anyone who has a perfect score on all the unit tests and keeps his cup empty wins a Pepsi. Give a Pepsi also for perfect scores on the review test.

Linda Johnson
Louisville, KY

Reading Album

Even kindergartners can experience a sense of authorship with this activity. Provide a photo album with clear magnetic pages. Each child has a week to fill the album with any pictures he chooses. Then on Friday, he "reads" the book to the class. The album is then passed on to the next author.

Lynn Klomfar
Gulfport, FL

Money Stamps

My children have a difficult time learning money skills, so my aide and I put money stamps on their papers. The children really enjoy figuring the monetary value of their work and seeing who can get the highest amount for the best paper.

Margery Grier Schaening
Haslett, MI

Select A Sticker

Tack up a sheet of sticker rewards in a prominent, convenient spot in the classroom. During the day, as you wish to reward a student for good behavior, call out his name. The student selects his own reward from the sheet to wear proudly.

M. Corso
Bristol, CT

Put A Feather In Your Cap

Reinforce positive behavior by adding feathers to Indian headbands. Duplicate an Indian cut-out for each child to color and decorate. Write his name on the headband, and display it. For each reward earned, add a cut-out feather. Have each student make a headband to wear, and add the same number of feathers that are on his cut-out. They wear the headdresses for a day that ends with a powwow party.

Nancy Platt
Rock Hill, SC

Make Kids Feel Special

Celebrity Luncheon

Our principal cares about children and seeks ways to make them feel important and needed.

Each Monday an important citizen of the community is invited to have lunch at school with the principal and four students in the school's conference room. The children honored by an invitation are usually selected by their base teachers. Each receives a personal note from the principal.

The honored guest is asked to discuss his/her occupation and contributions to the local community. Children have the opportunity to ask questions and learn about others. Each luncheon is ended with a dramatic autograph signing session, when snapshots are taken for the school's celebrity scrapbook.

This method of recognition means a great deal to the children, and much happiness is exhibited as the honored child shares his experience with the class.

Isabel B. Rand
Hightstown, NJ

Silhouette Puzzles

Using a filmstrip projector, trace a child's silhouette on a piece of light-colored paper. Cut it into puzzle pieces, one for each class member (including the teacher). Distribute the pieces and ask each student to write a positive statement about the chosen student. That student then assembles and glues the pieces of his own personal puzzle onto a piece of contrasting paper. A great way to recognize a student in a special way!

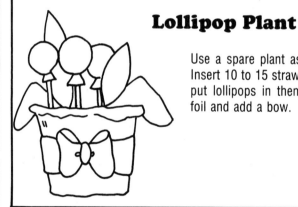

Melissa Noonkester
Christiansburg, VA

Lollipop Plant

Use a spare plant as a gift for a sick child. Insert 10 to 15 straws around the plant, then put lollipops in them. Wrap with aluminum foil and add a bow.

Connie Connely
Catoosa, OK

Reading Folders

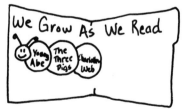

To motivate and reward good reading habits, give each child a file folder decorated with a small worm. Each time a child finishes a book, he prints the book's title on a cut-out worm segment and pastes it in his folder. As their book worms grow, so will their interest in books!

Debra Alvarez
Ft. Bragg, NC

Spelling Badges

I make spelling badges for those students having a perfect score or showing improvement on weekly tests.

Use plastic name card holders such as those used at conventions to create your own badges. See the illustration of badges made with stickers.

Sister Mary Myra, S.N.D.
Fort Wayne, IN

Super Student

Each day I choose two super students based on good behavior or good work. My students decorate two super student badges, which are inserted in plastic name tag covers with pins on the back. Super students get to line up first and choose someone to line up with them. Children love it when other students ask, "What is a super student?"

Caroline Carter
Leesburg, FL

Local Authors

Give your students a chance to make some youngsters feel extra special. Pair up each student in your class with a student from one of your school's primary classes. Older students interview their young partners. The collected information is used to write a picture book about the child. After editing, illustrating, and making covers for their books, students read them to their partners. Books are placed in the library in a "Local Authors" display. Later, the young students are allowed to take their books home.

Kathy Ray
Leavenworth, KS

Smelly Stickers

You can make any sticker a smelly sticker! Add a dab of cologne to the sticker and scratch!

Connie Connely
Catoosa, OK

Class Flag

Promote a feeling of class unity by designing a class flag. This can be a community design or a series of squares with individual designs based on a theme such as Our Favorite Things.

Susan Chisari
Orlando, FL

Water Spelling

I have found a way to reinforce spelling skills and clean the chalkboard at the same time. I select three children who have worked at their seats the hardest. Each student is given a small tub of water and an oval sponge. After dipping and squeezing the sponge in water, the children practice spelling and writing their words with water. Soon our chalkboard is clean!

Connie Connely
Tulsa, OK

Special Privileges

Make this chart and a deck of cards to reward students for completion of work or good behavior. Write special privileges on cards, and turn them facedown. Students draw cards to determine their rewards, then clip their name cards to the reward slits on the chart. Add excitement to the draw by making bonus cards allowing them to have the privilege of their choice.

June Brantley
Warner Robins, GA

Teacher's Helper	First in line all day!	15 min. extra computer time	Arts & Crafts Activity
Jim	Al	—	—
—	—	Sally	—
—	—	—	—

Make Kids Feel Special

Student Of The Day

Instead of having individual jobs for the students, such as line leader, paper passer, etc. I combine all jobs for one day. Every day one student is chosen to be the student of the day. During the month of February, because we honor two presidents, the student of the day becomes the president of the day and is allowed to make one law of his choosing at the teacher's discretion: 5 extra minutes recess, no math, extra math, free time, etc.

Kay D. Ulrich
Lavina, MT

Framed Writing

To motivate my students to do their best in cursive writing, I bought a 9″ x 12″ picture frame at a garage sale. Each week, I pick a story that is well written to place in the frame. Everyone wants to do his best in order to have a story framed and hung in the classroom.

Ann Sargent
Champaign, IL

Cheery Messages

Place a blank sentence strip on each child's desk. Then cover with clear contact paper. Each day, write a nice comment with a wipe-off marker.

Linda Rabinowitz
Atlanta, GA

Bunny Awards

Children love to wear these bunnies over a shirt button. The button becomes the bunny nose. Cut the bunny out of felt or construction paper, and add details with felt pens.

Marjorie Linhares
Portsmouth, RI

Sticker Folders

Cash in on the craze to collect stickers with incentive folders. Have students make their own sticker folders. Cut tagboard into 6″ x 12″ pieces. Cover one side with a solid color or small-print contact paper, or laminate. Fold the tagboard in half so it opens like a book. Students decorate the cover and add stickers earned for good work inside. Displaying folders, attractively hung in a row, keeps all stickers together so they won't get lost or stolen.

Barbara Partell
Buffalo, NY

Class Awards Day

Have each student decide what award or honor he feels he should receive on class awards day. Children choose their awards and give reasons for their choices to the teacher. The teacher presents awards to children in a class ceremony. You can learn a lot about individual students from this activity.

Rebecca Webster Graves
Burlington, NC

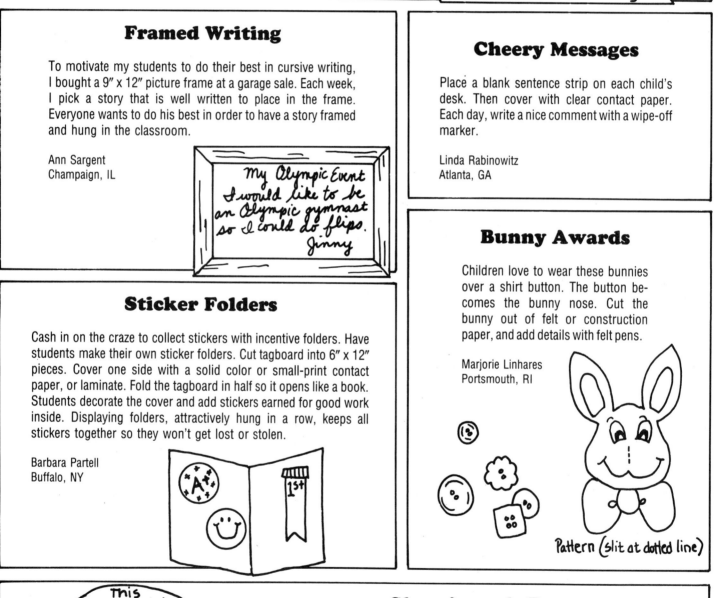

What's In A Name?

I try to make every child feel important by holding a class study of names, derivations, and meanings. I begin by having the children write what they think their names mean; then we compare their original ideas with results after they've researched. I found that diaper companies will provide name lists for the asking.

Patricia Shulman
Englewood, CO

School Pictures

When school pictures arrive, make copies of the black-and-white sets that are usually placed on cumulative folders. Laminate and mount copies on students' booklets, writing papers, desks, and helper charts. Children love the extra touch!

Patsy Capps
Winter Haven, FL

Self-Concept

Encourage good self-concepts and language development with life-size "student bodies." Trace each child's body on brown wrapping paper. Cut out and label with the child's name. Each child in turn says something good about his classmates. Positive statements are written on the cutouts. Add smiles!

Terri Noboa
Miami, FL

Friendship Beads

If friendship beads on a safety pin are "in" at your school, use the idea as a motivator for hard work! Laminate a large, cardboard safety pin and post. Each time students receive good grades or read books, give them a paper bead to write their names on and slide onto the pin. Reward with a prize when students earn a designated number of beads.

Anne Ogdon
Kankakee, IL

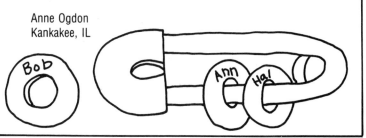

Hopping Helpers

When I need a child to do a task, run an errand, or answer a question, I have the students draw from the magic, black, top hat. Take a coffee can and cover it with black construction paper, and put a brim on top. Fill the hat with a rabbit for each of the students. The students become excited when their names are drawn for an activity.

Margo Maust
Harrisonburg, VA

Top Bananas

To earn a banana, a student places a perfect paper on an award board decorated with a monkey. There are no monkeyshines at the end of the week when students who have earned bananas make chocolate-covered bananas, banana splits, or other treats.

Mary Jo Bailin
Toledo, OH

Make Kids Feel Special

Teacher-For-The-Day

Getting students to finish their home-readers can be a test of a teacher's creativity. To alleviate this problem, keep a ladybug chart for each student. After a child completes a home-reader, record it on his chart. When all the spots are filled, that student becomes "teacher-for-the-day." Special privileges could include helping correct papers, eating with the teacher, running errands, etc.

Sheri Diller
Waynesboro, PA

Handshakes And Hugs

For an end-of-the-week highlight, make Friday "H and H Day." As your students line up to go home, give them the choice of a hug or a handshake from you. It's a surefire way to go home smiling!

Pamela Myhowich
Yakima, WA

Red Carpet Kids

Each day I select a student to be the Red Carpet Kid for the day, based on classroom and playground behavior. The Red Carpet Kid gets special attention on his day and sits on a red carpet square placed on his seat. Keep a record to make sure everyone has a turn once every month.

Dianne Labor
Rapid City, SD

I Can!

At the beginning of each month, I post 6 skills or activities that children can work on in their free time or at home. Skills are listed on a shape for the month, and a record is kept as each child completes each skill. A shape necklace is given when all skills are completed. At the end of each month, I take a picture of all the children who have earned the shape. I save these photos and use them as prizes for end-of-the-year games.

Virginia Neubold
Harrisburg, VA

Say a nursery rhyme for the class.

Write your full name.

Garden Plots

Here's a project that's sure to motivate youngsters. Cover a long table or windowsill with butcher paper, and divide it equally among students. Each child claims a "garden plot" by drawing his emblem on it. Place a good supply of small, soil-filled milk cartons on the table, along with Popsicle sticks for plows, shovels, and markers. Each time a child completes a contract, receives a perfect score, etc., he earns the right to plant a new crop and places it in his plot to tend. Some suitable plants for small containers include parsley, dill, beans, lettuce, and marigolds.

Jill Robbins
Ogden, IL

Handwriting Helper

During my penmanship lessons, I enlist the aid of a small, stuffed Big Bird. Big Bird sits on my arm and watches for good penmanship habits. When he locates the most improved or neatest writing, Big Bird lands on that student's desk to remain for the rest of the day. My children work more carefully now that Big Bird is watching!

Sandy Anderson
Montevideo, MN

Super Reader Rewards

Here's a reward idea I use in my first-grade classroom that is very successful. I cut reading group symbols (butterflies, mushrooms, etc.) out of construction paper and write "Super Reader" on each. After laminating, I punch two holes in each and pull a string through to make a necklace. Students who read without an error get to wear a reward for the day.

Jayne Haenel
Medford, WI

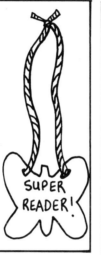

SUPER READER!

Popcorn Praise

Popcorn is a nutritious treat for children and can be used to help celebrate a special event or to make dreary, uneventful days special. Cut out the letters that spell "popcorn." Each day that the class has an outstanding achievement, tape one letter in a prominent place in the classroom. When the letters spell out "popcorn," celebrate by popping some popcorn and eating it as you view a movie together.

Kathy N. Winchester
Shirley, MA

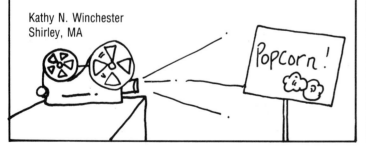

Popcorn!

Wishing Well

Children can "wish for" stickers or treats with the good conduct tickets they earn from a class wishing well. Place tickets in a large, wooden, wishing-well planter, and have children who earn them draw tickets from the well each day. If they have earned four tickets by the end of the week, they choose a prize.

Jeanette Freeman
Bryan, TX

Good Behavior Marbles

When a student exhibits good behavior, call out that child's name and drop a marble in a jar on your desk. The sound of the marble dropping in the jar reminds the rest of the class to do their best. Add an extra incentive by holding a popcorn party when the jar is full.

Gail Felker
Park City, IL

Your Award Day

Once a week, pass out blank awards, and let each child give himself an award! Have the student select either the skill that he has done well or a good quality that he has shown. Sign the awards, and display them on a bulletin board. Students improve self-awareness, and teachers gain insight into each child's feelings about himself and his work. A variation is for students to give awards to each other.

Mary Anne Haffner
Waynesboro, PA

Neat Nest Award

Children will try harder to keep their desks neat when they have a chance to win the weekly Neat Nest Award. Make a cut-out birdhouse from heavy tagboard, and laminate. Choose a different student each week to receive the award. The award can be attached to the student's desk for a week of recognition that's worth chirping about!

Connie Hamlin
Sweeny, TX

Make Kids Feel Special

Spelling Ribbons

To reward excellent spelling test grades, I make personalized spelling ribbons from colorful wallpaper samples. Once my students have earned 7 ribbons, they turn them in and receive a free 100 on our final weekly test. They also are allowed to choose a free-time activity to do while the rest of the class takes the quiz.

Kathy Peterson
Alpha, IL

Fold over and staple

Good Statement Bags

Select five students and give each a paper sack labeled with their names. Give all your students 5 strips of paper, and have them write a positive statement about each of the chosen five on a strip. Collect the strips in the paper sacks, and allow the five children to read the statements in their sack. Choose five different students the next time, until all children have participated.

Linda Shofner
Shepherdsville, KY

Billy is my best friend.

Little Ladies And Gentlemen

Save all that unwanted cologne, perfume, or hand lotion for school. Reward students with perfumed dabs for being courteous ladies and gentlemen or for doing good work.

Rhonda Thurman-Rice
Tulsa, OK

Silent Messages

Children often do not receive enough positive reinforcement during the school day. I like to send silent messages to tell my students they are doing great or that I love having them in my class. They try even harder after receiving a special note from the teacher.

Laura Bartlett
Normal, IL

Star Strategy

To add a note of positive encouragement to your corrections on creative writing papers, star the sentence, phrase, or word which you like best. This "star strategy" works well on handwriting practice papers, too. Look for the letter which is formed best of all.

Isobel L. Livingstone
Rahway, NJ

Reading Motivator

To spark my students' interest in reading, I encourage them to keep a book handy on their desks at all times. Then, when I see someone reading in their spare time, I sneak up behind them and drop a small treat (a sticker or pretzel fish) right in their book and whisper, "I love to see you read." It certainly motivates my children to read more often!

Marian Bronero
Waldwick, NJ

Autographed Bags

Make a special memento for students who move during the school year. Since the student often doesn't come prepared to carry home all of his belongings, I keep a supply of large grocery bags in my classroom. When the student's last day arrives, I write a note on the bag, let all of the students autograph it, and add our school address. We promise to write to our friend as soon as he sends a new address.

Barbara Gordon
Spring, TX

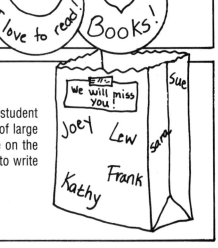

Flowery Words

Surprise each student with a large zinnia or other flower in a bottle for parts of speech practice. Place a word card naming the flower by each bottle. The next day discuss adjectives, and have each child write a word to describe his flower on another card. The third day, children write the possessive forms of their names and place the cards in front of the noun and adjective.

Suzanne Edmunds
Forest, VA

Super Spellers

Every time a student has a perfect spelling test, place the child's name on a paper badge and staple it to a special bulletin board. After a designated time span, students who have badges up on the board may trade them in for a small reward or treat for each badge. Really encourages super spelling!

Kathy Kuehn
Amery, WI

Sticker Books

If you give stickers as rewards, your children will love to keep their collections in these classroom sticker books. For each child, laminate a 9″ x 12″ sheet of construction paper. Cut in half lengthwise. Have each child place the two halves together, fold them in half, and staple the sheets at the fold to make an 8-page album. Each child writes his name on the cover with a permanent marker.

Kay M. Sweat
Ft. Stewart, GA

Job Board

Reinforce self-responsibility and give all students a chance to be teacher's helper. On a board, list daily jobs. Laminate name tags that are to be drawn at the beginning of each week and place them in a container. After drawing, write names beside the jobs. Children not chosen for a job have first choice for the next week. Students select the jobs they want and show enthusiasm for their responsibilities.

Harriett Carruthers
Charleston Heights, SC

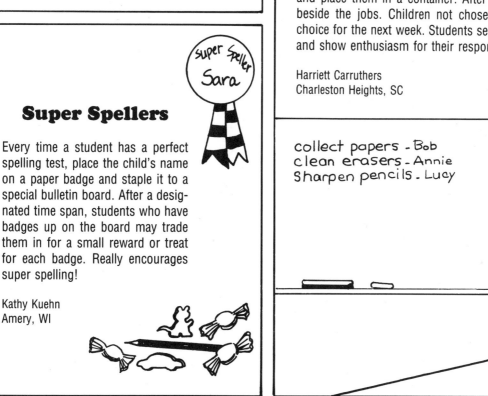

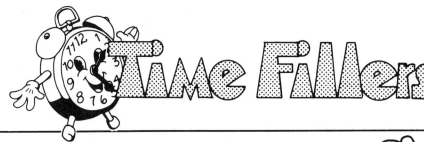

Time Fillers

Humpty Dumpty

This fellow on the wall provides children with a choice of familiar rhymes and songs. Cut out a large, oaktag Humpty Dumpty, and make a slit across the top of his belt. Insert 3″ x 5″ cards, each labeled with a song, poem, or fingerplay. To fill in a few extra minutes, a child chooses a card, and the whole class joins in.

Diane Billman
Dayton, OH

Hula Hoop Time

Teaching time with a hula hoop is a fun way to involve the entire class. Tape black cut-out numbers around the rim of the hoop like a clock. Have class members take turns saying times and indicating the time using their arms. Tape an hour or minute label on each arm.

Marie Van Diver
Carrollton, KY

Free-Time Doodles

Be prepared for students who complete their work early. Hang a large, blank sheet of paper on the wall, and let them create. Whenever the doodle sheet is complete, place it in the hallway for others to see.

Pamela Myhowich
Yakima, WA

Reusable Worksheets

Get more use from your language arts worksheets! After students have followed the directions, give them additional instructions. Tell them to underline compound words with a purple marker, draw a box around all pronouns, circle all contractions, circle short "e" words with a yellow marker, and underline suffixes with blue.

Diane Murray
Troy, MI

Movement Streamers

Cut 5-feet strips of colorful crepe paper for streamers. When you need a quick movement break, give one streamer to each child, and play a lively record. Children whirl the streamers to the rhythm of the music.

Marjorie Linhares
Portsmouth, RI

Children's Story Time

Every day after lunch my second graders have a 10-to 15-minute story time. They enjoy reading a book for the class more than listening to me read one. I enjoy the chance to give my voice a break. I have set up a schedule allowing everyone who is interested to read the story of their choice. They select a book ahead of time and practice reading it so they are not surprised by unfamiliar words on their day to read. It encourages outside reading and enhances oral language.

Judy Kramer
Houston, TX

Seek And Find

Place spelling words across, backwards, and diagonally in a "seek and find" puzzle about every other week. This gives students a break from routine spelling work, but still gives them a word review.

Phyllis Roland
Henryville, IN

Sound Jackets

Use butcher paper and magic markers to mark these sound jackets. Trace and cut the jackets on the fold. Cut out the neck, and write a letter on each jacket. Students stand together while the rest of the class sounds out the word. This idea can also be used with any sequencing skill.

Connie Connely
Tulsa, OK

The Everyday Game

Set up this class game so it's ready to play whenever you have a few spare minutes. Prepare about 50 question cards for basic skills or information that needs frequent practice and reinforcement. Place in numbered pockets on the board. Choose a child to spin the wheel, read the questions, and give the answers. If the child answers correctly, he gets to line up first. Others listen carefully because they may get the same question another day. Add new questions often.

Reba S. Walden
Granite Falls, NC

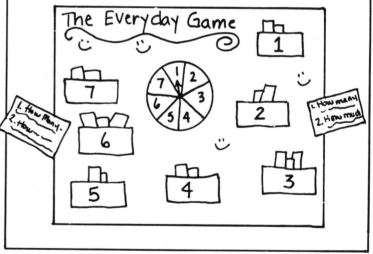

Silly Seat Work

Use this activity for a change of pace in the classroom, to perk up seat work, and to encourage careful reading. Give each child a sheet of activities with directions to follow. Two important directions are that all work should be done silently and in order as listed. Include a math or language worksheet, spelling word search, alphabetizing activity, or science words to define. Between the activities, add special directions (such as take a jelly bean from the teacher's desk, take a restroom break and get 3 swallows of water, or duck walk to the filing cabinet and look in the third drawer for a treat). Place a star beside special activities. Children love doing this seat work and strive to do their best when work is fun!

Janet Capps
Lynchburg, VA

Chain Rhyme

Either the teacher or a student begins a poem with two rhyming lines. Go around the room, with each child using the last word to continue the next two lines of the poem. Kids think as they have fun.

Rebecca Webster Graves
Burlington, NC

Purple Math

Glue extra math worksheets or old workbook pages on 100 individual sheets of purple construction paper. (Optional: Write answers on backs of purple sheets.) Number the pages 1-100, and put them in a box. Duplicate a sheet showing 100 numbered boxes for a progress chart for each student. During spare time students may go to the purple math box and choose any worksheet they want. They copy and work problems on their papers, check their answers, and color in the correct boxes on their progress charts. (Worksheets may be given to the teacher for checking instead.) At the end of the year, students completing all 100 sheets (or whoever completes the most) can receive an award or prize.

Cheryl Luckie
Fitzgerald, GA

Special Of The Day

Each day, I write a puzzle, riddle, problem, or a question requiring research skills on a laminated piece of poster board. When students arrive, they begin to solve the "special of the day" while I take the lunch count.

Kaylene Carr
McKinney, TX

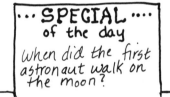

Creative Tasting

Ask students to bring in their favorite dry cereals and bowls. Have children create new cereals by mixing two or more kinds and think of names for them. Serve new cereals to a panel of tasters who rate them.

Pamela Biery
Aschaffenburg, Germany

Library Book Box

Each month, I decorate a large box for a particular theme or topic of study—holiday, current event, famous person, etc. I fill the box with ten or more appropriate books written at different reading levels for children to read during free time. By selecting some poetry, nonfiction, fiction, and magazines, my students are introduced to new and different reading material.

Jo Farrimond
Broken Arrow, OK

Color-Coded Fun

Be prepared for those students who finish assignments early or need extra practice. Place extra worksheets or tasks in colored folders. When a child completes his work, hand him a colored disk that matches the folder you want him to use. This does not interrupt the others, and the student is directed to an appropriate activity without embarrassment.

Laura Bartlett
Normal, IL

Suspense Quieters

On the blackboard, write a new riddle, joke, or secret message in any type of code each morning. Children hurry to their desks as soon as they arrive to figure out the coded message and do whatever the message reveals.

Tomia Fingerle
Ocala, FL

Using Cardboard Tubes

Make a kazoo by fastening a piece of waxed paper over the end of a cardboard tube with a rubber band. If the children blow too hard as they hum, a hole punched with a paper puncher near the mouthpiece end will relieve excess air pressure. Kazoos can be decorated with notes and other music symbols. They can be played for an exciting accompaniment to a marching record as children march around the room for an indoor rainy day activity.

Also use the tubes for "telescopes." Cover the tubes with construction paper, and decorate them with stick-on stars. Peering through a telescope is a good way to focus attention on review items on the blackboard or bulletin board.

Jean O. Youngsteadt
Springfield, MO

Cross The River

Develop young children's jumping skills with a game which can be played indoors or out. Place 2 yardsticks a few inches apart to make the "river." After each child has had a chance to jump across, widen the distance between the yardsticks. Allow children to stay in line, even if they miss, to guarantee lots of practice.

Lynda Modell
Simi Valley, CA

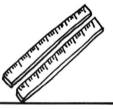

A Classy Story

I write the first line of a story on chart paper and put it on a wall or on a table. Students take turns adding one line at a time. This is a great activity for students who arrive early or finish work quickly. Add a title, and read the story to the class when it's finished.

Rebecca Webster Graves
Burlington, NC

Magnetic Tape

My students enjoy drawing or cutting small pictures and attaching a little piece of magnetic tape to the backs. They put these on the metal part of their desks or take them home to put on the fridge. Children will learn about magnets by exploring on their own, examining the contents of their desks, and testing objects in the room to see if they are magnetic.

Connie Luginsland
Waverly, KS

How Many?

Write a "how many" question on the board each morning. How many desks are in the room? How many children are wearing sandals? When the children have an extra minute, they tally the answer and write it in a designated place.

Linda Rabinowitz
Atlanta, GA

Secret Satchel

Pack a real suitcase with learning games that students can do independently. After a child completes all of his work, he receives a key that entitles him to open the satchel and choose a game to enjoy.

Hope Speranza
Edison, NJ

Time Fillers

All Mixed Up

Students of any age will enjoy this alphabetical order game. On one side of the chalkboard, list all your students' first names. On the other side, list all the last names. The students take a piece of paper and list all the first names in ABC order. Then they start at the top, and beside the first names, they list all the last names in ABC order. The boys and girls are really tickled at finding their new, mixed-up names.

Lynne Willis
Augusta, GA

Gray Hester
Jake Lundy
Rose Michel
Virginia Owen

Rose   Hester
Jake   Michel
Gray   Lundy
Virginia Owen

Free Bookmarkers

Encourage reading with inexpensive bookmarkers. Save the newspaper comics sections and place at a reading center with a pair of scissors. In their free time, students go to the center and cut out individual strips. Place them in a box labeled "Free Bookmarkers. Take one and use it!"

Rebecca J. Caldwell
Hancock, MD

Alphabits

To practice alphabetical order with your students, use cereal Alphabits. When the child has his letters in the correct order, he may eat his "lesson"!

Chris Davidson
Mobile, AL

I'm Thinking Of...

Sharpen number-combination skills by playing "I'm thinking of . . ." Give students a number, having in mind a specific combination which totals that number. Children guess until they give the correct answer.

Lynn Klomfar
Gulfport, FL

Bus Ride Busy-ness

To keep thirty squirmy youngsters quiet on the bus ride back from a field trip, provide them with a word search (or other puzzle) on information they learned on the trip. This not only holds down the noise, but it also immediately reinforces the purpose of the trip.

Ruth Catalano
Peoria, AZ

TO MAKE CLOTH, WE TAKE A FIBER, AND BY CARDING, WE GET THE STRANDS NEATLY IN A LINE WITH EACH OTHER. THEN WE USE A SPINDLE TO TWIST THE FIBER INTO A YARN. WE CAN USE ALL KINDS OF ANIMAL HAIR TO MAKE CLOTH. THE MOST COMMON IS WOOL. BUT WE CAN ALSO USE GOAT, POODLE, OR SOME OF THE UNUSUAL SHEEP VARIETIES AVAILABLE. THE UNCLEAN WOOL IS CALLED GREASE WOOL AND IS VERY SMELLY. WEAVING IS DONE ON A LOOM. THE FIRST THREAD ON THE LOOM IS CALLED THE WARP.

MAKING CLOTH

W	E	A	V	I	N	G	B	E
O	L	X	R	S	O	N	G	S
O	D	Z	G	B	Y	I	L	A
L	O	O	M	W	O	D	G	E
L	O	I	A	Y	A	R	N	R
N	D	R	I	M	T	A	O	G
S	P	E	E	H	S	C	V	U
S	P	I	N	D	L	E	H	D

159

Practice With Pudding

For handwriting practice or learning to write names, put fingerpaint or pudding all over a table. Provide a spray bottle for cleanup, and you'll have lots of help.

Cathy Whittle
Nashville, TN

Thumbs Up

Make a stack of picture cards to correspond to a pack of word cards. Hold up a picture card and place a word card underneath it, exposing the two for only an instant. If the word and picture match, the children put thumbs up. If not, children put thumbs down.

Nancy Simmons
Whittier, CA

Secret Challenge

Add spice to each day with a secret challenge. In the morning, I write the name of a person or topic on a piece of paper and place it in a large envelope labelled "Secret Challenge." I post a clue about the challenge on the board. Before class begins, I give five students who are sitting quietly a chance to guess the word or name in the envelope. If a student answers correctly, I ring a bell and award a small prize. If the challenge is not correctly identified by the end of the day, I add another clue to the board. Clues are added daily until a correct guess is made.

Sr. Margaret Ann
Emmitsburg, MD

1. lived many years ago
2. born in Kentucky
3. 16th president of U.S.

Self-Description

For a creative writing activity with a twist, have each student write a self-description. Collect and choose one to read aloud. Students try to guess the identity of the writer. Use a stopwatch to time each reading. The student whose identity is guessed in the shortest time is the winner.

Sharon Bramlett
Clyde, NC

Creating Activities From *The Mailbox*

Looking for a new challenge for students who have finished their seat work? Distribute old copies of *The Mailbox* and let them make their own learning activities. Promotes creativity, learning, and decision making. Students will enjoy playing each other's games, too.

Verena Harp
Pineville, LA

Picture Starters

Picture starters are great for stimulating the imagination.

Karen Jahnke
Lena, WI

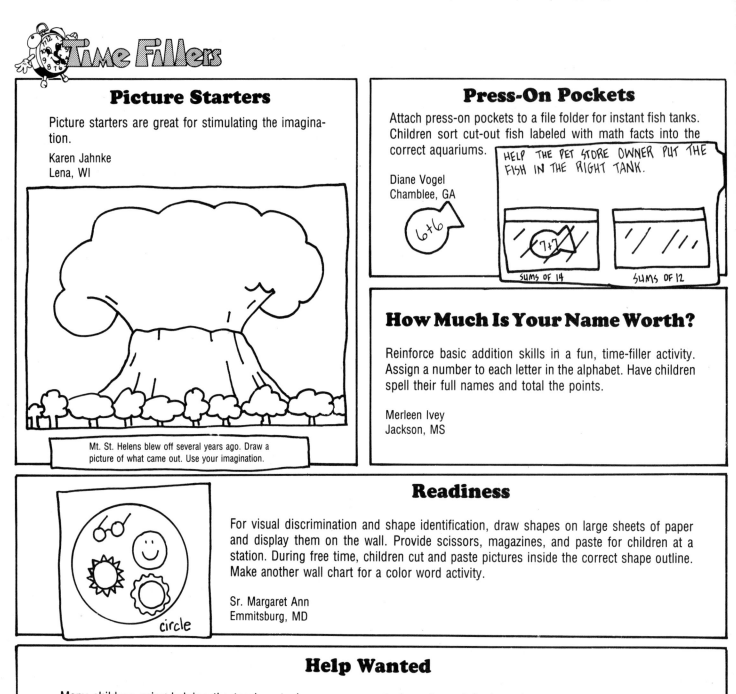

Mt. St. Helens blew off several years ago. Draw a picture of what came out. Use your imagination.

Press-On Pockets

Attach press-on pockets to a file folder for instant fish tanks. Children sort cut-out fish labeled with math facts into the correct aquariums.

Diane Vogel
Chamblee, GA

HELP THE PET STORE OWNER PUT THE FISH IN THE RIGHT TANK.

6+6

7+7

SUMS OF 14   SUMS OF 12

How Much Is Your Name Worth?

Reinforce basic addition skills in a fun, time-filler activity. Assign a number to each letter in the alphabet. Have children spell their full names and total the points.

Merleen Ivey
Jackson, MS

Readiness

For visual discrimination and shape identification, draw shapes on large sheets of paper and display them on the wall. Provide scissors, magazines, and paste for children at a station. During free time, children cut and paste pictures inside the correct shape outline. Make another wall chart for a color word activity.

Sr. Margaret Ann
Emmitsburg, MD

circle

Help Wanted

Many children enjoy helping the teacher staple papers, erase task cards, sort flash cards, or count worksheets. After guiding students through these tasks once, they can usually complete jobs without supervision. Set up a "help wanted" desk for students who have completed their work. Clip a direction card to the task (sort, count, erase), so the helper can proceed without instructions.

Jane Cuba
Redford, MI

COUNT

SORT

Frisbee Contest

Frisbee throwing guarantees graphing practice and fun. We had a contest. Children had to measure how far their Frisbees went with a meter stick and graph it on a chart. The winner got a Frisbee!

Mary Dinneen
Bristol, CT

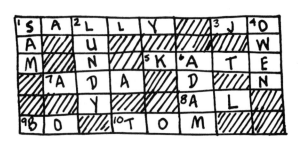

Class Crosswords

Make up a name crossword puzzle about your class, using your students' first names. Have each student supply a clue about himself. For example, "I was born in Detroit and have 2 older sisters."

Melissa Noonkester
Christiansburg, VA

Color-Shape Partners

Color-shape name tags are great for visual discrimination and developing social and verbal skills. Make sets of name tags in several colorful shapes. During the day at various times, call for children to find a partner with a matching color and shape. Then children introduce their partners to the rest of the class.

Bess Anne McKnight
Jonesboro, AR

Current News

Use the homeroom time before class begins to share current news items. After students place newspaper clippings on a newsboard, have them explain to the class why the articles interested them.

Debbie Wiggins
Myrtle Beach, SC

Map Study

Post cardinal directions on the room walls (north, south, east, west). I give children oral instructions using Simon Says. Examples:
Simon says, "Face east."
Simon says, "Take 2 steps north."
"Point your left hand south."

Janis Tysko
Athens, OH

Fact For The Day

This activity keeps students on their toes and requires them to retain information while learning lots of neat facts. In the morning, I put up an interesting fact in a special, visible location. Students read it in anticipation of the question I will ask that afternoon. I ask a question that requires a "yes" or "no" answer. Children must turn their answers in. Laminate fact cards, and glue a permanent clip or clothespin to the blackboard or wall to make daily fact changes easy.

Debbie Wiggins
Myrtle Beach, SC

Puzzle Power

To reduce homeroom chaos, my students may work at an ongoing puzzle table as they arrive. On rainy days, we have a puzzle contest between groups of 6 to 8 children. Each group is given a puzzle with the same number of pieces. The group to assemble their puzzle first wins a prize.

Sr. Margaret Ann
Emmitsburg, MD

Bubble Fun

Do this activity outdoors on a day that isn't windy. Mix ½ c. of liquid detergent with 2 qts. of water in a 9" x 13" pan. Have students make a string loop 30 inches long by threading it through two straws and knotting the ends. Let a child hold the straws apart to form a rectangle, place the frame in soapy water, and lift it out slowly to make a soap film window stretched across the rectangle. The child holds the frame just below his waist at arm's length and pulls upward. As a bubble forms, the child brings the straws together to close it off.

Mary Lou Jenkins
Dallas, TX

Fishing For An Activity

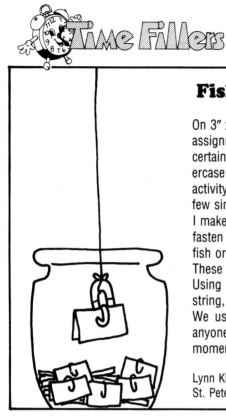

On 3" x 5" cards, I print or draw easy seat work assignments. Examples: finish pattern, color a certain number of items, write uppercase or lowercase letters, read a certain book, do an art activity, go on a scavenger hunt, or even do a few simple P.E. stunts.

I make about 20 of these cards, fold in half, and fasten each with a paper clip. Each one has a fish or other sea creature drawn on the outside. These cards are kept in a real fishbowl.

Using a toy fishing pole with a magnet on the string, the children go "fishing" for an activity. We usually use this during free play or when anyone finishes his work and has a few spare moments.

Lynn Klomfar
St. Petersburg, FL

Quick Ring Toss

Make a super, quick, ring toss by turning a chair upside down over a wastepaper can. Tape numbers to legs and use rubber canning jar seals for rings.

Lynn Klomfar
Gulfport, FL

Extra Practice

Get extra math or spelling practice without asking! Post problems or word lists by the water fountain or sink and see the results while children stand in line! Or, post facts on the rungs of a poster board ladder. Children try to "climb to the top" by giving correct answers.

Brenda Tanner
Leesburg, VA

Joke Box

I cut jokes (suitable for school) from old school publications, the newspaper, or worn-out joke books I'm ready to discard. I keep them in a joke box. To end each day on a happy note, I select one student to reach in, pick a joke, and read it to the class. Sometimes when tempers have flared and everyone has finally made up, I let students select a joke, and everyone walks away with a smile.

Jill Robbins
Ogden, IL

Riddles Make Readers

Here's a fun way to encourage reluctant readers to read for pleasure. Display a sign-up chart and a large selection of riddle and joke books. Students select a riddle from a book and sign up to read it to the class. Each day, four or five children may read their riddles to the group and call on their classmates to guess the answers. The chart will fill up in no time!

Jane Cuba
Redford, MI

Rap Session

Each morning before we begin our day, my class holds a "rap session." The children have the opportunity to share anything interesting about themselves, their family, recent news, hobbies, and other general information. It's a great way to start the day and learn about each other.

Darlene Shelton
Memphis, TN

Doodle Book

Give each child a doodle book of 20 blank pages. At the top of pages, children glue or write titles or captions. If they finish class work early, they may doodle in their books.

Linda Rabinowitz
Atlanta, GA

Musical Phonics

This is a favorite of my students for those extra minutes we find during our day. A child picks out his favorite musical instrument and stands in front of the group. I say a series of words, and every time he hears one that begins with an "s," or whatever phonics skill I want to reinforce, he bangs his drum, shakes his tambourine, taps the triangle, etc. After several turns, he chooses another child to come up front.

Nancy Johnson
Greensboro, NC

THE SAND AT THE SEA
A SNAIL AND A STARFISH

Got A Minute?

What do you do with students who always finish 5-10 minutes early? Send them to the "Got A Minute?" box. On index cards or 3" x 5" manila folders, put short brainteasers, puzzles, word searches, etc. Place the games in a recipe box. Students with a few spare minutes go to the box, pull a card, and do the activity. Store answer keys in a separate file box placed in another area of the room to prevent traffic build-up at the "Got A Minute?" box.

Karen Spunaugle
Tulsa, OK

Palm Reading

Motivate your students for creative writing with palm reading. Write a word with paint, on the palm of each student, and have them write a story about their words.

Meg Hendrick
Abilene, TX

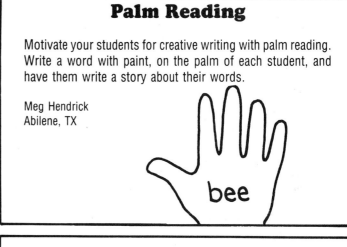

bee

Classroom Book Mural

Display a large piece of paper labeled "Good Books We've Read" on a classroom door. During free time, students write the names and authors of favorite books they've read and add original illustrations. This mural uses otherwise wasted space and often shows the best artwork of the year!

P. Dickerson
Cutchogue, NY

GOOD BOOKS WE HAVE READ!
GO BANANAS! by C.I. Monts
BIG FOOT!

What's In A Name?

When there are a few minutes to spare with nothing to do, have your children spell their full names and see how many words they can make using the letters. Award a colorful sticker to the student with the most words.

Merleen Ivey
Jackson, MS

JULIE KAY DIVELY

DIVE	DAY	JAIL	LAID
DIE	AYE	JELL	ILL
LIVE	EEL	DELVE	KILL
LAKE	KEEL	DEVIL	KID
JADE	LIED	DIAL	LAD
ADE	DIED	EYE	LADLE
AID	DUEL	KEY	LADY
LEAD	YEA	DUE	ALE	YE
LAY	YELL	DULL	KALE	LIKE
LID	LIVELY	JIVE	JELLY	LED

Time Fillers

Time Out

You deserve a break today! Take a class break at least once a day for 15 minutes. Write, "Time out for _____," on the board and fill in the blank. I usually choose a reading, writing, or listening break. Everyone stops immediately and begins the new activity.

Barbara R. Blackburn
Boiling Springs, NC

Time out for reading.

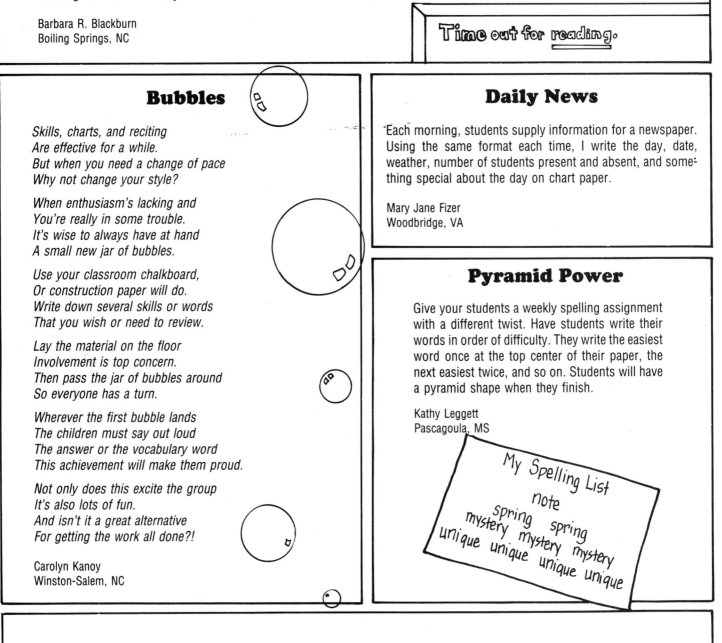

Bubbles

Skills, charts, and reciting
Are effective for a while.
But when you need a change of pace
Why not change your style?

When enthusiasm's lacking and
You're really in some trouble.
It's wise to always have at hand
A small new jar of bubbles.

Use your classroom chalkboard,
Or construction paper will do.
Write down several skills or words
That you wish or need to review.

Lay the material on the floor
Involvement is top concern.
Then pass the jar of bubbles around
So everyone has a turn.

Wherever the first bubble lands
The children must say out loud
The answer or the vocabulary word
This achievement will make them proud.

Not only does this excite the group
It's also lots of fun.
And isn't it a great alternative
For getting the work all done?!

Carolyn Kanoy
Winston-Salem, NC

Daily News

Each morning, students supply information for a newspaper. Using the same format each time, I write the day, date, weather, number of students present and absent, and something special about the day on chart paper.

Mary Jane Fizer
Woodbridge, VA

Pyramid Power

Give your students a weekly spelling assignment with a different twist. Have students write their words in order of difficulty. They write the easiest word once at the top center of their paper, the next easiest twice, and so on. Students will have a pyramid shape when they finish.

Kathy Leggett
Pascagoula, MS

My Spelling List
note
spring   spring
mystery mystery mystery
unique unique unique unique

Be An Explorer

An explorers' area is challenging for students who always complete work early. Post a list of activities, including research, drawing maps, making worksheets or games, writing letters, and making birthday cards. Tie activities to areas of class study or fun. Keep a set of folders in this area so students can store completed work. Pull activities to use with the class.

Kathy Gallman
Charlotte, NC

Musical Words

A word skill game we play is musical words. I place in a box or bag about ten or fifteen easy sight words. The children sit in a circle, and we start passing the box around while a record plays. Whoever has the container when I stop the music must pick out a paper and read the word. If he can't, he is out. We continue on until there is only one person left. The winner must be able to read at least five of the words.

I usually use very easy words that all the children know, so I seldom have any losers. They get the biggest kick that I didn't stump them!

Lynn Klomfar
Gulfport, FL

Making Sentences

As a free-time activity, I have a game that the children really enjoy because they get to use the one-minute timer.

In a large envelope, I place several business envelopes. On each is written a simple sentence. (I include some with simple words that the children can read, and some others with more difficult, new words.) Inside the envelopes are the sentences cut into individual words.

The child chooses an envelope, starts the timer, dumps out the individual words, and tries to recreate the sentence on the outside of the envelope. The child must correctly read the sentence before the timer is stopped.

The children love to try to beat the timer, and it becomes a challenge to see who can go the fastest!

Lynn Klomfar
Gulfport, FL

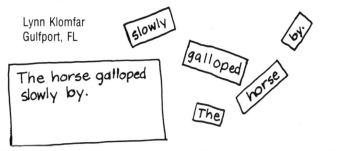

Shape Party

To culminate a unit on shapes, I have a shape party with my first graders. We all get to eat different shapes! Try some of the foods from our shape menu:

circles: M&M's, Ritz crackers, Oreo cookies
squares: Cheese Nips, Saltine crackers, Wheat Thins
rectangles: sugar wafers, graham crackers, ice cream sandwiches
triangles: Doritos corn chips, sandwich halves cut diagonally

Martha Ann Davis
Greenwood, SC

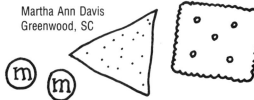

Free Reading Materials

I have one large box which contains many smaller boxes. The smaller boxes are cereal or detergent boxes that have been covered with contact paper, then labeled. Each of these smaller boxes contains free pamphlets on a certain topic. The free pamphlets can be obtained by visiting or writing state tourist agencies, travel agents, university departments, armed forces recruitment offices, car dealers, or government consumer information guides. Once you start looking for this type of material, you will find it in a wide variety of places. "In The Box" provides hours of reading enjoyment for my students.

Tanya Wilder
Broken Arrow, OK

Student Activity Sheets

Fast workers can keep busy by designing their own activity sheets. I select some of the best papers for duplication. Work must be readable, the questions must pertain to a current topic of study, and answers must be included.

Sheila Bivens
Denver, CO

Sounds & Things

Place an assortment of small objects in a box. Include small cards with letters written on them. Students match the letter to the object with that beginning sound.

Jo Hull
Greensboro, NC

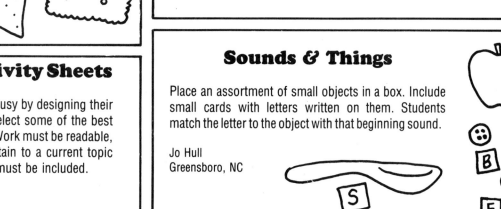

idea Catchall

Transparency Counting

Teaching counting to 1,000 is simplified by using number grid transparencies. By placing the transparencies on the overhead projector, with the hundreds on top of the base hundred chart, the children can see that the ones and the tens remain the same. Ten transparencies are needed to teach counting to 1,000.

Diana Vacura
Dodge Center, MN

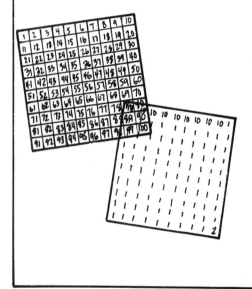

Story Starters & Creative Writing

Here are some story starters that I have found to be good motivators even for the most reluctant writer.

We had just finished lunch in the cafeteria when we heard an earth-shaking noise that sounded like . . .

I have always wanted to be a hero. Quite unexpectedly my dream came true when . . .

I've always told the truth, except one day when I made up a whopper of a tale about . . .

As long as I live, I will never again . . .

My mother expects me to act grown-up, but she says I'm too young to . . .

Last week I got a letter telling me that I won 1,000 crocodiles! I had to . . .

If I owned a zoo, it wouldn't be just an ordinary zoo. I'd have . . .

Being last can be a very good thing when . . .

My friend and I had a quarrel that ended happily because . . .

I wish I had never answered the door the night we were making popcorn . . .

Jacqueline Armin
Albany, NY

Dots Made Easy

To make dots for matching number games cheaply and easily, use a new pencil eraser and a stamp pad.

Joyce Timm
Bangor, WI

Lima Markers

For inexpensive, take-home game markers, color large, dried lima beans with permanent markers. If desired, spray with clear varnish. The beans are easy to carry home, and I don't worry if they're not returned because of their low cost.

Margaret Leyen
Iowa Falls, IA

Shhhhh . . .

Ask your favorite carpeting store to save samples from discontinued styles and colors. These fit nicely on children's desks.

They are very handy (and quiet!) when children are using puzzles or other noisy items. They also keep things from rolling off flat desktops.

Fran Petersen
North Tonawanda, NJ

Long Division Aid

Graph paper can be a lifesaver when introducing long division. Let students work their problems on the paper, putting one number in each square. This keeps numbers properly aligned and helps students remember the various steps in the division process.

Cheryl Koenemund
Wolcott, CT

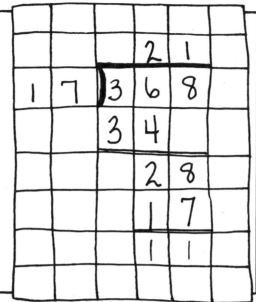

Shelving Library Books

Our librarian was swamped with library books to shelve until reading groups learned how to do the job. Students learn the Dewey Decimal System, and the librarian checks to see if they have found the correct spot before the book is placed on the shelf.

Ann Hudson
Forest, VA

More Ideas For Pringles Cans

—Stack them on their sides to use as mailboxes.
—Decorate with wallpaper and store things in the can.
—Print a different number on each of several cans. Students put the appropriate number of objects in the cans.

Karen J. Jahnke
Gillett, WI

Good Ending, Good Beginning

End a long week of school on Friday afternoon with a fun creative writing exercise. Then on Mondays, let volunteers read their stories to the class as an entertaining way to begin a new week. Some topics you may want to try:

Traveling with a Rock and Roll Band
My Wonder Drug Cures . . .
The Day I Lost My Freedom
If I Had Eyes In the Back of My Head
How to be a Boring Teacher
I Found a Thousand Dollars

Debbie Wiggins
Myrtle Beach, SC

Chalk Talk

Paint shoe box lids with slate paint for miniboards. Students write answers to the teacher's questions on these makeshift slates. (They may not talk during chalk talk.) Slates erase easily with an old sock.

Judy Stevens
Birmingham, AL

Games To Take Home

Get more use out of your math and language games! Attach library pockets and cards to the envelope or the back of each game. The kids in my class check the games out overnight to take home. One of my helpers counts game markers and dice in the mornings. Since the kids know that things will be checked in, they are very careful. In three years, I've lost only 1 die and 1 game marker.

Jill Robbins
Ogden, IL

Plain Laminated Paper

Plan ahead by laminating blank sheets of 9″ x 12″ and 12″ x 18″ oaktag. Use the laminated sheets in the following ways:
1. When you need a pattern for students to trace, cut the item to be traced from a sheet of laminated paper. Makes a durable pattern that lasts through lots of tracing.
2. Need a sturdy folder? Fold a piece of laminated 12″ x 18″ paper in half.
3. For a quick classroom sign, write on a piece of laminated paper with a permanent marker.

Mary Dinneen
Bristol, CT

Mailing Cartons

Turn a mailing carton, such as those from The Education Center, into a wall-mounted holder for poster-sized learning activities. Carefully open the carton where it is taped in the middle. Fasten one closing flap to the side flaps with brads. Leave the other side unfastened, and cover the entire carton with wallpaper. Fasten to the wall with picture hangers.

Rebecca O'Dell
Leivasy, WV

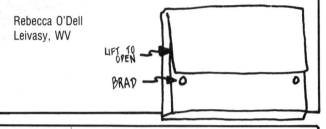

Screen Dividers

Window screens hinged together make foldable, easy-to-store area dividers. Cover by attaching fabric or vinyl with Velcro strips. The screens double as attractive display panels.

LaDonna Hauser
Wilmington, NC

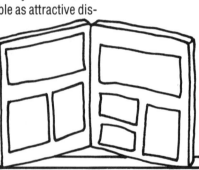

Gum Recipe

This sticky recipe allows you to make stamps or stickers from any cut-out picture.

Sticker Glue:
  ¼ packet unflavored gelatin
  1 T. cold water
  3 T. boiling water
  ½ t. white peppermint extract
  2 drops boric acid solution (made from 1 tsp. boric acid in 1 pt. water)

Sprinkle gelatin in cold water to soften. Pour into boiling water; stir until dissolved. Add remaining ingredients and mix. Brush thinly on the back of any paper and let dry. The entire batch must be used at once since it will gel. Lick and stick on student papers, or give as student rewards.

Bonnie Pinkerton
Bowling Green, KY

Teachers Are Special, Too!

Recognize the special efforts and interests of teachers! Post the photo of a different teacher weekly, and have the teacher write a brief description of interests and hobbies. Fellow teachers may list complimentary statements on paper slips and post beside the photo. Faculty members will get better acquainted and discover common interests.

Cindi Novella
Glen Burnie, MD

Individual Instructional Boards

Laminate pieces of poster board that each child may use for reading and math activities. Children write with crayons and wipe the poster board clean with a tissue. Note that some types of crayons leave more residue than others.

Janis Tysko
Athens, OH

Good Manners Place Mats

Here's one student's suggestion for remembering good table manners! List rules on a mat-shaped piece of paper. Add pictures, and laminate. Good to use at home and at school.

Mary Glavin
Gorham, ME

Field Trip Tip

Here's a way to get rid of one field trip hassle. Instead of having the kids keep their own sack lunches or stowing them in a big cardboard box, use a large, rectangular clothes basket. It's easier to carry and pack than a cardboard box.

Kathy M. Peterson
Alpha, IL

Add-A-Bead Award

Teachers can make their own add-a-bead necklaces for an eye-catching way to motivate hard work. Beads are made by sticking 2 gummed circles together on a string. A bead is earned for each class accomplishment (perfect attendance, perfect test scores). The class might earn a minute of game time for each bead, or a popcorn party for every 10 beads as a thank-you gift from teacher!

Merleen Ivey
Jackson, MS

Mini-Folders

To make small activities with a maximum of 5 answers, I make mini-folders. I simply cut the file folders in half. These are great for short games, handwriting practice or spelling centers.

Mary Anne Haffner
Waynesboro, PA

Flair Pens

Fine-line Flair pens work well on overlays and are cheaper than Vis-a-Vis pens. They wipe off easily with a paper towel and a spray of water from an old Windex bottle.

Betty Huffman
Zanesville, OH

Social Studies Reinforcement

Reinforce social studies concepts by reviewing topics just before the day ends. Take a few minutes to jot special points on the board. This holds students' attention while waiting for the bell and keeps information fresh on their minds for parents who ask what they've learned in school.

Dr. Robert Clarke
Scranton, PA

Computer Photo Frames

Help nonreaders follow directions for computer programs by providing a reminder on a reusable frame. Place an acetate photo frame with a stand on or near the computer. Slip a drawing of a friendly computer into the frame. Then print the correct sequence of keyboard responses directly on the acetate with a wipe off pen. Change for different programs with a quick wipe of a damp cloth.

Delores Pease
Hardin, MT

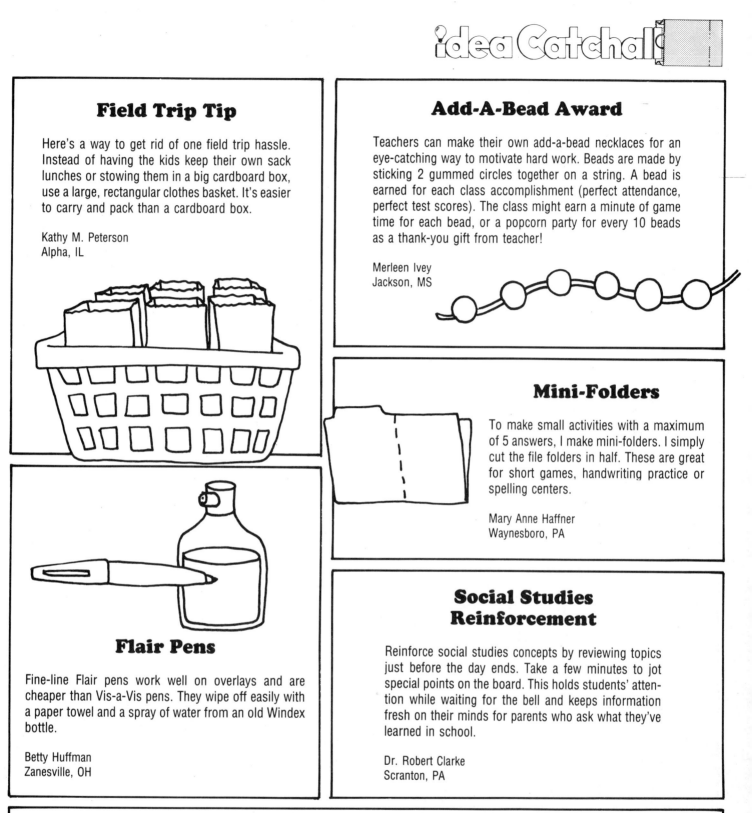

idea Catchall

Field Trip Helpers

If you're planning a field trip, try these tips:

1. Prior to your trip, work with your class to establish money values for good behavior: 5¢ for good bus behavior, 10¢ for good behavior during the tour. A week before the trip, have students donate old toys or books for a classroom store. On the day of the trip, give each child a name tag. With money stamps, stamp name tags throughout the day to reward good behavior. When you're back home, let students "cash in" their tags to buy items from the store.

2. Make a contract outlining behavior rules with your class prior to the trip and give each child a name tag as shown. During the trip, use a hole puncher on the tag to indicate good or poor behavior. Students exchange their tags later for small rewards or stickers.

Connie Connely
Catoosa, OK

Stamp Pad Scents

Get out your stamp pad for some surprise incentives! I use a couple of drops of scented oil or candle scents on my stamp pad. They last a long time on little hands or papers. Children are thrilled with the many scents available: strawberry, blueberry, pine, apple, watermelon, and more.

Georgena Netto
Watertown, NY

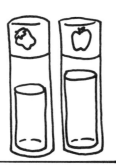

"Out-The-Door" Questions

As my students leave my room each day, I give them something to think about. I put a box of questions by the door. Each child chooses a question and whispers the answer in my ear. My children look forward to picking a question, and it gives me a special moment with each child every day. Students who don't know the answers are anxious to find out and tell me the next day.

Donna L. Kelley
Palatine, IL

Can't Afford Kleenex?

Take a clean shortening can and cover the outside in contact paper. In the center of the lid, cut a circle about the size of a quarter. Take scissors and cut the tube in the middle of a roll of bathroom tissue from top to bottom. Remove the cardboard. Take the end of the roll of paper that was attached to the cardboard tube and pull straight up. Drop the entire roll in your can, and thread the paper through the hole in the lid. Now put the lid on the can. Pull out the amount of tissue needed for those little noses.

Geraldine Fossett
Canton, GA

Blue Jean Pillows

Transform old blue jeans into durable, reading corner pillows. Cut off the legs right below the crotch seam. Turn pants inside out and sew up the leg openings. Turn back to the right side, and sew across the waistband using a size 16 or 18 machine needle. Then unzip the pants and fill with fiberfill or Styrofoam packing chips. Zip back up and hand-stitch a few stitches under the zipper tab to secure. Pillows can be washed and dried. Back pockets can hold reading task cards too!

Marianne Armstrong
Urbana, IL

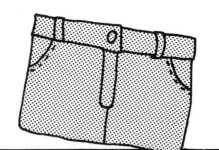

Mountains And Valleys

I use this handy idea to help my students remember how many days are in each month. I tell the children to make a fist showing their knuckles.

All the mountains have 31 days, and the valleys have 30 or less.

Clarice Greiner
Grimes, IA

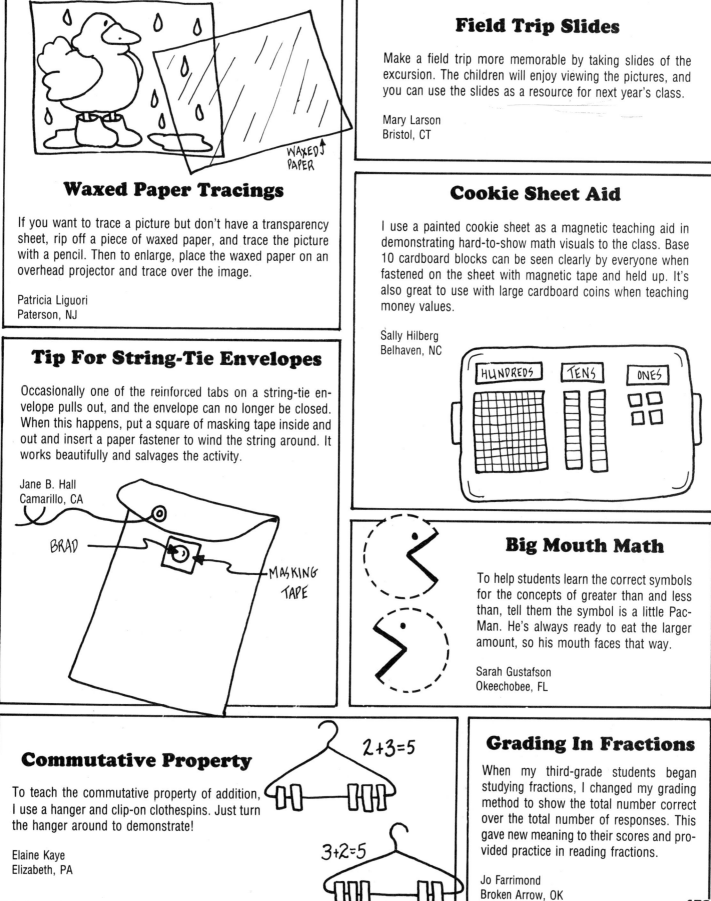

Waxed Paper Tracings

If you want to trace a picture but don't have a transparency sheet, rip off a piece of waxed paper, and trace the picture with a pencil. Then to enlarge, place the waxed paper on an overhead projector and trace over the image.

Patricia Liguori
Paterson, NJ

Tip For String-Tie Envelopes

Occasionally one of the reinforced tabs on a string-tie envelope pulls out, and the envelope can no longer be closed. When this happens, put a square of masking tape inside and out and insert a paper fastener to wind the string around. It works beautifully and salvages the activity.

Jane B. Hall
Camarillo, CA

Commutative Property

To teach the commutative property of addition, I use a hanger and clip-on clothespins. Just turn the hanger around to demonstrate!

Elaine Kaye
Elizabeth, PA

Field Trip Slides

Make a field trip more memorable by taking slides of the excursion. The children will enjoy viewing the pictures, and you can use the slides as a resource for next year's class.

Mary Larson
Bristol, CT

Cookie Sheet Aid

I use a painted cookie sheet as a magnetic teaching aid in demonstrating hard-to-show math visuals to the class. Base 10 cardboard blocks can be seen clearly by everyone when fastened on the sheet with magnetic tape and held up. It's also great to use with large cardboard coins when teaching money values.

Sally Hilberg
Belhaven, NC

Big Mouth Math

To help students learn the correct symbols for the concepts of greater than and less than, tell them the symbol is a little Pac-Man. He's always ready to eat the larger amount, so his mouth faces that way.

Sarah Gustafson
Okeechobee, FL

Grading In Fractions

When my third-grade students began studying fractions, I changed my grading method to show the total number correct over the total number of responses. This gave new meaning to their scores and provided practice in reading fractions.

Jo Farrimond
Broken Arrow, OK

Today's Menu

Reading and writing are on this school menu. Make a pocket chart and sentence strips with food words written on them. Assign one or two students to put the correct food strips on the chart each morning for the class to read and copy.

Connie Connely
Tulsa, OK

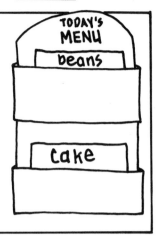

Double-Faced Tape

Children love to wear all kinds of badges, but the straight pins that hold them on poke the child, tear the badge, come off, and present a safety hazard. Double-faced carpet tape is the answer! Cut tape into ¾" squares, and adhere one side to the badge and the other to the child's shirt. It's safe and easy, and everyone is happy!

Sandy Anderson
Montevideo, MN

Painted Chalkboards

Poster paint applied to a chalkboard washes off easily, but won't erase if written on top of with chalk. (Test a corner before doing this to your whole board!) Paint on:
—Lines for penmanship practice
—Rockets and number facts with missing addends
—Baskets labeled with vowels
(Students write correct words on the baskets.)

Glenda Sternin
N. Tonawanda, NY

Wipe-Off Tiles

For a different surface for mark-off activities, try pieces of ceramic tile obtained from businesses which make bath or kitchen tile. A nonpermanent marker will wipe off with a wet paper towel.

Denise Cox
Greenville, NC

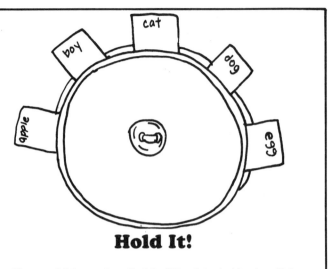

Hold It!

Young children often find it difficult to hold a handful of playing cards. These card holders are simple to make and really do the job! Place two plastic lids, flat sides together. Place a button in the center on each side, and sew the entire unit together with strong string or dental floss. Children simply slip cards between the two lids and hold the card holder.

Jane Cuba
Redford, MI

Super Smoothies

Treat your class to nutritious smoothies! Have members of the class bring in a canned or frozen fruit; a soft food, such as ice cream, yogurt, or pudding; and a liquid, such as lemonade, fruit juice, or milk. Mix one ingredient from each category together in a blender. Pour smoothie into cups. Sip with straws, or eat with spoons. You'll blend reading recipes and following directions with every smoothie.

Rhonda Thurman-Rice
Catoosa, OK

Homework Notes

Use "homework notes" to keep in touch with parents and add interest to sharing time. Send cute notes home telling what type of item each child is to bring back. Then give each child a thank you note if he successfully completes the assignment.

Linda Ball
Normal, IL

Curriculum Themes

I use a weekly thematic approach to my first-grade curriculum. We have The Big Apple Week, Celebrate Ladybug Week, etc. During the week, worksheets are illustrated with the themes, at least one center focuses on our special subject, and our bulletin board announces our topic to all. The thematic approach brightens up our routine and makes learning memorable!

Melissa Tumbleson
Corcoran, CA

Cheese Pretzels

Following these directions creates a big batch of pretzels to share. This recipe gives all of the children a hand in the preparation and encourages sharing and reading.

1 pkg. yeast	4-5 c. flour
1 tbsp. sugar	1 egg
1½ c. warm water	
4 c. sharp cheese, grated	

Dissolve yeast and sugar in warm water. Combine flour and cheese. Knead for 5-10 minutes. Make into shapes—pretzels, letters, or numbers. Brush with beaten egg. Bake at 425° for 15-18 minutes. ENJOY!

Ruth Haynes
Potomac, MD

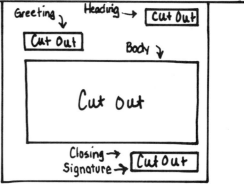

Friendly Letter Stencil

This stencil will be helpful for a social letter unit. Have each student make one to place over his paper as he writes. Duplicating the stencil on colored construction paper makes it more durable.

Julie Hagedorn
Sioux Falls, SD

Preserve Your Posters

Are you sick of peeling the tape off the backs of your posters until you soon have no posters left? Here is a cheap and simple solution for preserving your posters. On the back of each poster, stick down large pieces of masking tape. Then whenever you put up your poster, all you need to do is place curls of tape right on top of the tape strips. This keeps your posters looking as good as new!

Kathy M. Peterson
Alpha, IL

Cardboard Tubes

Save sturdy cardboard tubes and loan them to your students for transporting their large drawings to and from school. I tell my students that architects and engineers often carry their work in such protective tubes.

Lois Huffman
Lafayette, IN

Egg Carton Ice Trays

Did you know that plastic egg cartons make great ice trays? Just fill the carton with water and freeze. Then throw the carton away after removing the ice.

Connie Connely
Catoosa, OK

Throwaway Items

Turn throwaway items into attractive classroom aids. Here are several ideas that I use in my classroom:

- To keep word or number cards organized, fasten two plastic lids together, rims to the outside, with a paper fastener. Lids must be the same size. Holds cards for alphabetical order and sequencing drills.
- Cut egg cartons apart and use individual cups to hold tempera paint.
- Cover plastic hamburger containers with furry material to make attractive puppets, storage containers, or decorations.
- Use clothespins as behavior modification devices. Each student clips his clothespin to his clothing and tries to keep it all day by not misbehaving. Those who don't lose their clothespins receive a small reward.
- Write math facts or sight words on small wood scraps for a different kind of flash card. Lumberyards provide them free of charge.
- Old cookie sheets can find lots of uses in the classroom. Fingerpaint on a sheet, and lay a piece of paper on the finished design. Smooth over with your hand, then remove the paper and hang to dry. Or spray paint a cookie sheet, and use it as a magnetic board.

Joyce Wittenhagen
St. Cloud, MN

Pictures, Pictures!

Colorful and interesting magazine pictures provide creative opportunities galore:

1. Mount a picture on a large piece of butcher paper. Add an interesting caption and post in the room. Students write comments or observations about the picture on the paper and sign their names.
2. Fill a decorative box with interesting pictures mounted on index cards. Children use these ideas for creative writing, oral discussions, role-playing, and creative dramatics.
3. Mount unusual pictures on oaktag. Students will enjoy adding original captions to the pictures.

Beverly Bippes
Madison, NE

Game Boxes

Reinforce corners of game boxes and lids with postal strapping tape (the type containing strings). No more split corners and lost pieces!

Kathy Barrow
Orange Park, FL

Tooth Saver

Use film cans as containers for precious baby teeth that fall out at school. Decorate with smiley face stickers or a tooth drawing. Label the lid with the student's name and room number to identify the "lost" tooth.

Kay Dunbar
Rock Hill, SC

Reading Flowers

This garden of reading flowers will grow as students complete book reports. For each child, attach a large flower to the ceiling with a streamer that reaches the floor. Students add leaves or smaller flowers for each book report they write. The parts added are determined by the book's length, and they can also be given point values.

0- 50 pages	= 1 leaf
51-100 pages	= 2 leaves
101-200 pages	= 3 leaves
over 200 pages	= 1 flower

Dee Klein
Gillette, WY

State Study Latchhook

Students get hooked on this class project. Use an overhead projector to copy the outline, rivers, and major highways of your state on latchhook canvas. My class hooked the state green, rivers blue, and highways red to fill the design. We presented it to our state senator in the capitol, and it hangs in his office.

Beverly Strayer
Red Lion, PA

Typewriter Fun

Do you have a typewriter in your classroom? If you do, you are very lucky. My class has found it to be a very good learning aid. The children look forward to the day when the parent volunteer comes. She supervises their use of the typewriter. The children enjoy practicing their spelling words by typing them. They also enjoy typing a "telegram" to a pen pal.

Mrs. Kay Scott
Hightstown, NJ

Black Slate Mates

Make erasable black slates for children to use during reading or math circle time. Cut heavy corrugated cardboard into 6" x 9" pieces. Cover one side with black contact paper. Put masking tape around edges. Attach a plastic sandwich bag to each slate to hold chalk and a little piece of an old towel for erasing. Children love to write and show answers, then quickly erase!

Debbie Engles
North Linthicum, MD

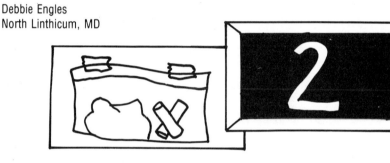

Checking Spelling Sentences

When checking spelling sentences, only put checks by sentences that are written correctly. Return papers to students and have them rewrite the incorrect sentences on another sheet. If sentences are rewritten correctly, adjust the spelling grade.

Ann Hudson
Forest, VA

Portable Chalkboards

Remember the convenience of individual slate boards? Now you can make durable, portable chalkboards. Spray or paint discarded cafeteria trays with chalkboard paint from a school products company.

Rocky Shelton
Memphis, TN

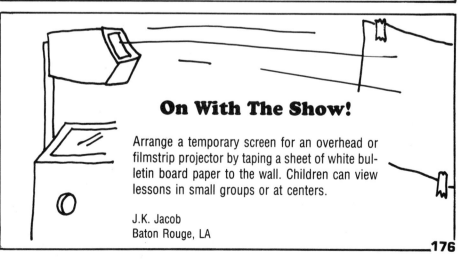

On With The Show!

Arrange a temporary screen for an overhead or filmstrip projector by taping a sheet of white bulletin board paper to the wall. Children can view lessons in small groups or at centers.

J.K. Jacob
Baton Rouge, LA

idea Catchall

Magnet Magic

When experimenting with iron filings, place a bar magnet under an aluminum cookie sheet lined with newsprint. Shake filings from a shaker-type spice bottle. Filings are easily collected to use again.

Jane Cuba
Redford, MI

Practice Slates

I make wipe-off slates for my students with empty 8" x 10" cardboard holders once used for lace or braiding. Obtain holders from a fabric store, draw lines for handwriting practice, and laminate. Students can also use these laminated slates for math practice.

Gwen Denton
Van Alstyne, TX

Popcorn Sale

If you're looking for a way to earn money for the class treasury, try a popcorn sale. Each student brings a large bag of popped popcorn to school from home. Sort it into small popcorn bags and sell to other classes. Be sure to advertise beforehand!

Sheri Grigsby
Colville, WA

Wet Chalk

Brighten up your blackboard with colored chalk! Soak one end of a piece of chalk in water. Use wet chalk to draw graphs, pictures, or circles to explain fractional parts. Allow chalk to dry. You can now erase over graphs or pictures without erasing them. To adapt this for a spring art activity for the entire class, draw the outline of a flower, bird, or insect with wet chalk, and let children add features when dry.

Ann Sargent
Champaign, IL

Clean Paperbacks

Want to keep your paperbacks clean, handy, and visible, but still get good use out of them? Place individual books in large Zip-Loc plastic bags and hang on a pegboard. When the students carry them home overnight, you can expect them to come back in good shape!

Jeanne Jackson
Houston, TX

Help For Ditto Errors

Here's a way to cover up mistakes on ditto masters. A piece of scotch tape, cut to the size of the error and taped over the error on the back of the ditto, will cover your mistake. When the ditto is run off, the mistake won't be noticed. This method is especially good to use for larger mistakes or those made when you either start or finish making a ditto, and it's much better than starting all over again!

Kathy M. Peterson
Alpha, IL

Bubbles

It's easy and inexpensive to make your own bubble solution. Combine equal parts of liquid detergent and water. Add a few drops of glycerine to make the bubbles more colorful. Children can use a pair of scissors as bubble wands. Use at the end of a unit as a class incentive.

Lynda Modell
Simi Valley, CA

Map Work

Do your students have trouble remembering map locations? Set up an overhead projector and let them trace outlines on a large piece of paper. Then students fill in details and colors. This helps students remember because they've drawn the maps themselves!

Paula Reid
Dayton, OH

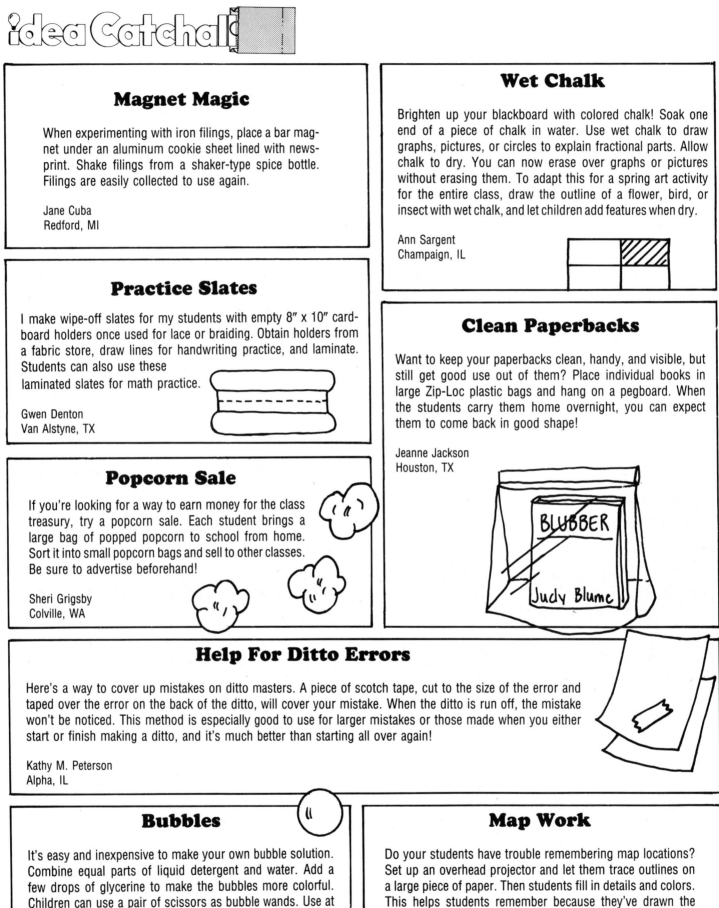

Mood Meter

How are your students feeling about themselves and school? Make a mood meter so students can indicate how the day is going. Have children clip a clothespin to their name tags along the color spectrum from red hot to moody blue so you can keep track of the classroom temperature.

Melissa Matusevich
Blacksburg, VA

red	SUPER
orange	Great
yellow	Good
green	OK
blue	Not So Hot
indigo	Bad
violet	Terrible

Lynn

Sue

Comparing Clocks

To familiarize young students with the different types of clocks, display several, including a digital, around the room. Let them compare and contrast the digital to the standard clock.

Brenda Tanner
Leesburg, VA

Message Clothesline

Each day children check this personalized clothespin lineup for messages to take home, papers to redo, or assignments for absentees. Label and laminate name tags, then attach to plastic clothespins. Hang clothespins from a line along the bulletin board, or hook them on a row of straight pins.

Trish Frazier
Broken Bow, OK

Jan   Tom

Quick Correction

For a quick way to correct errors on a ditto master, I use typewriter correction fluid. I place a small amount on the carbon side over the error and let it dry. Then I go back and type in the correction.

Paige Lubra
Fernley, NV

Tape Chalk Holder

Wrap chalk with masking tape to help protect "drying" fingertips and to avoid breaking when chalk is dropped. The tape can be peeled back like a crayon as you use it.

Ann Sargent
Champaign, IL

Display Space

Running out of display space? Tie one end of a piece of yarn to a jumbo paper clip and the other end to a metal clothespin. Slip the paper clip end between the metal strips and the panels in your ceiling. The clothespin end will hang down. Clip work up using the clothespin.

Sandra Gray
Gaithersburg, MD

Plastic Overhead Transparencies

Don't throw away the plastic bags that contain your book club orders! Cut them in half to make two inexpensive overhead transparencies. Write on the transparencies with a laundry pen or wipe-off marker.

Becky Gibson
Auburn, AL

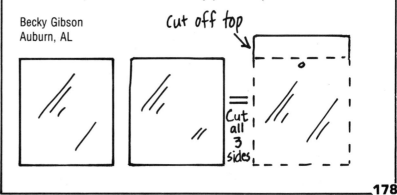

Cut off top

Cut all 3 sides

Finger Math

To facilitate the learning of the nine table, have children use their hands as follows: Place both palms down on desk. To find 9 times any number, count that many fingers over from the left pinky. When you reach that finger, fold it under. The fingers to the left of the folded finger are the tens; to the right are the ones.

Melissa Noonkester
Blacksburg, VA

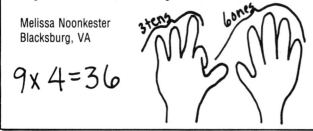

$9 \times 4 = 36$

The Mystery Box

How does a shoe box encourage sharing, listening, and self-confidence? Transform a shoe box into The Mystery Box by wrapping the box and lid with colorful paper. Select a student to take the box home. The child brings the box back the next day with an item inside to share. He gives the class three clues to guess the contents. To keep track of who has had the box, tape a checklist to the bottom of the box.

Pamela Myhowich
Yakima, WA

Fancy Flash Cards

Fascinate your students with eye-catching skill flash cards. Cut appealing pictures from gift wrap and glue on the backs of flash cards. Laminate the cards to make them sturdy. The children love the extra special appearance given to ho-hum flash cards.

Margo Maust
Harrisonburg, VA

Carpet Square Wipe-Offs

Small pieces of jute-backed carpet make excellent erasers for wipe-off cards and laminated gameboards. Your local carpet dealer will be happy to donate samples. They last for years and may be stacked in a box with your wax markers.

Lois Phillips
Brookfield, MO

Old Worksheets

Don't let old worksheets just pile up in your room! Here are some practical suggestions for using old duplicating masters:

1. To build a supply of pictures for game construction, cut pictures from old worksheets and file in a box according to beginning sounds.
2. Store old worksheets in a box or crate. Use for review, or let children get one when they finish class work.
3. Send old worksheets home over the summer for practice.
4. To cut lesson-planning time, file a copy of each worksheet according to the skill it covers. When it's time to teach that skill, one glance in your files lets you know what worksheets are available.

Luanne Burrier
Zanesville, OH

Sand Pail For Flowers

A child's sand pail makes an attractive, unbreakable, inexpensive container for flowers. Use as is, or put a can inside to hold the flowers and water. You may want to have more than one for variety.

Isobel L. Livingstone
Rahway, NJ

Earmarked Sentences

When explaining quotation marks to children, point out that they look like pairs of ears. Show little pairs of ears enclosing what is said or heard.

JoAnn S. Nixon
Dalton, GA

Old Calendars

Use discarded calendar pictures to make eye-catching folders for absentees or "travelers." The pictures also make nice, giant get well cards, with enough room for everyone to sign. Cut the illustrations up for puzzles and save the numeral squares for math games. Don't let a single old calendar go to waste!

Claudia Wilcox
Vernon, CT

Flower Container

Put a small can in an empty, cube-shaped tissue box. You'll have an attractive, unbreakable flower container!

Isobel Livingstone
Rahway, NJ

Masking Tape Tip

Use this helpful trick to remove backing from contact paper or similar coverings. Choose a corner, and position two pieces of masking tape (sticky sides together), one on each side of the paper. Rip the tape apart, and the paper and backing separate at the same time.

Roberta Brankman
Hoosick Falls, NY

Library Book Keys

Here's a great reading incentive to encourage your classroom readers. Students write the book titles they've read on construction-paper keys. The number of prongs indicates whether the book was easy, medium, or difficult (as determined by the teacher). Keys are collected on pipe cleaner key rings hung on pegboard. Be sure to emphasize that an easy book for one student may be judged as a medium book for someone else.

Helen Reinertson
Estherville, IA

Portable Slates

Plastic coffee can lids and 1-pound margarine tub lids make great portable slates! Children write answers with crayons, hold their slates up to be checked, then wipe them off with a tissue.

Jane Sewall
Denver, CO

Field Trip Poem

To make a field trip more memorable, my class writes an original poem about their excursion, using all of the children's names. After completing it, we send a copy to the field trip site.

Mary Larson
Bristol, CT

Tooth Envelopes

Loose teeth that come out at school can be sent home safely by storing in coin envelopes. Make envelopes attractive by writing the poem "But Then," by Aileen Fisher, on one side and drawing a smiling clown on the other.

Dorothy Miller
LaMoille, IL

Image Lifts

Add visual interest to your overhead sheets by pairing them with image lifts.

1. Cut out a colorful magazine picture. Most slick magazine paper is appropriate for this purpose. Check suitability by rubbing a small spot on the page with a wet cloth. If color rubs off, the paper will work well.
2. Laminate only the front of your picture.
3. Soak in warm, soapy water for 1 hour.
4. Remove from water, and squeegee the remaining pulp off of the back.
5. If necessary, repeat steps 3 and 4. Dry.
6. You should now have an image that will project. Laminate the back of your picture or laminate directly to an acetate sheet. This method will work with contact paper and with both cool and heat laminating film. (Do not heat the acetate sheet.)

Ann Fausnight
Canton, OH

Comics In The Classroom

Comics are good for more than laughs! Here are some ways my class uses them.

1. Reading enjoyment and practice
2. Sunday funnies wrapping paper
3. Sunday comics background on bulletin board
4. Enlarged comic characters for centers, boards, or motivation
5. Teaching sequencing
6. Vocabulary development and word meaning in context
7. Reviewing contractions (the child circles contractions found in comics)

Capitalize on student interest and put the comics to work in your classroom.

Kathy Peterson
Alpha, IL

Comprehension Items

Motivate students to read more carefully by attaching comprehension questions to story-related items. If the story is about tools, write questions on construction paper tools. For an animal story, insert question strips in an animal puppet's mouth. When reading fairy tales involving gold coins, attach questions to foil-covered chocolate coins. There's always something unique to use with every story!

Beth Holder
Kinston, NC

X-Ray Transparencies

To make a transparency for the overhead projector, I obtain washed X-ray film from the hospital. I cut it to the size I need, then write on it with a permanent marker. This is much sturdier than clear acetate.

Delores Camilotto
Lafayette, IN

Comic Worksheets

Clip school-centered comic strips from the daily newspaper, and use them to decorate teacher-made worksheets or parent newsletters. Black-and-white cartoons duplicate easily.

Connie Connely
Catoosa, OK

Soft Flash Cards

Don't throw away those used fabric softener strips. Use permanent marker to write letters or words on them. These adhere nicely to a flannelboard, last indefinitely, store easily, and smell good!

Pauline Lawson
Fuquay-Varina, NC

Pop Bottle Planters

Don't throw away those 2-liter plastic pop bottles with the black bottoms! After the bottle is empty, squeeze all the air from the bottle to allow the bottom to drop off. This separate piece has 3 drainage holes, perfect for a classroom plant pot. It also makes a good container to hold sets of small objects.

Pamela Duke
Lompoc, CA

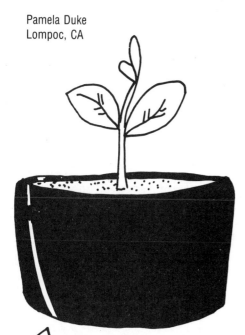

Away With Purple...

School children today see too much purple on their daily ditto sheets. To combat this, I make an extra effort to use colored duplicator paper and red, green, and blue ditto masters. In addition to the burst of color, I try to add accents whenever possible. Making children's papers more attractive and appealing is an incentive to make them want to work.

Patricia D. Shulman
Englewood, CO

Prescription For Reading

Throughout the year, I encourage my second-graders to do outside reading with this teacher's prescription for fun. Write the directions on a card, and tape a roll of Smarty candy to it.

Katherine Kwoczalla
Marion, IN

Cereal Material

Here's a new source of interesting material to use for student notebook covers or creative writing booklets—cereal box fronts! Laminate for extra durability.

Jill Purdy
W. Linn, OR

Smiley Faces

When working on activities concerning emotions, self-esteem, careers, or drug and alcohol use, encourage students to share personal ideas with each other. Use large smiley faces of different colors that have been laminated and divided in various ways. After the activity, give each student one half of a face. They must find the person with the missing half and share their thoughts on the subject.

Kim Smith-Nagee
Seagrove, NC

Rebus Writing

Rebus stories are a good way to get primary children to start writing. Using picture words enables them to use words they may have difficulty spelling.

Gail Hutchinson
Beverly, MA

Lamination Shortcut

Avoid problems in cutting out small items that have been laminated on one side only. Place the item on the film as usual. Now place a piece of scrap paper (such as newspaper) directly over the item. With scissors, cut around the item as closely as possible. The scrap paper backing will peel right off!

Karen Stockstill
Sidney, OH

Snack Mats

Use vinyl wallpaper samples for snack-time place mats. Also use them as working mats for clay, painting, and cut and paste activities. Wipe with a damp cloth for easy cleanup.

Jo Farrimond
Broken Arrow, OK

Ideas From Karen

Karen Kubouchick of Faith Community Christian School in Bethel Park, PA, shares several ideas that have been successful in her classroom.

1. For open house, place a photograph of each student near his work or at his desk with a self-description.
2. Have your children make "talking murals" as a new way to share books. Paint a large picture and cut out holes for faces to look through. Students become part of the story event as they dramatize it.
3. On rainy days, students can play Antonym Antics while standing at their desks. Call out a direction such as "Cry." The students do the opposite action. Any student who doesn't perform the opposite is out.
4. To perk up handwriting practice, have children use carbon paper. One copy goes to you to find mistakes, and the students keep the other.

Karen Kubouchick
Bethel Park, PA

Counterfeit Coins

I am a teacher of students with learning disabilities. When working with money, I find it very helpful to make my own play money so students can count it.

I purchase tags from any office supply store and stamp them with rubber stamps. Not only can these coins be used for teaching money, but they can be used as tokens if a teacher uses a behavior management system in the classroom.

Lorraine McCarty
Versailles, KY

Wallpaper Pockets

Use vinyl wallpaper to make durable storage pockets for game pieces. Sew the pockets on a sewing machine, and add a strap to keep flaps tucked in. Easy to make, easy to write on, easy to clean!

Donna Bjorklund
Shakopee, MN

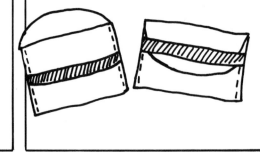

Puppet Show Table

Turn an ordinary worktable into an instant puppet stage. Lay a square or rectangular table on its side, and place student puppeteers behind it. Great for all of your class puppet shows.

Barbara Sellberg
Bristol, CT

It's Friday

Fridays are special days in my room! On Wednesdays, I tell the kids what Friday is—maybe "Blue Friday" or "Sweater Friday." Some examples could be: hat day, mix-up day, cowboy day, sports day, backwards day, tennis shoe day, dress up day, T-shirt day, shorts day (great when it's warm), and of course any color day!

Susan Nutzman
Falls City, NE

Submitting Ideas For Publication

To save time and ensure the return of materials submitted for publication, purchase inexpensive return address labels printed with your name, school, and home address. Attach one to each page of submitted materials.

Lorrie Field
Catoosa, OK

Laminated Book Covers

Cold laminating film serves as an excellent protection for soft-cover books or workbooks. We have covered hundreds of our books with the film. It definitely prolongs their life!

Sister Diane
Fond du Lac, WI

The Buddy System

Here are two practical ways to help young children develop motor control and eye-hand coordination. Let four-, five-, and six-year-olds tie each other's shoes and fasten each other's jackets.

Lucy J. Knight
Washington, DC

Spelling Bonus Word

At the end of each weekly spelling test, I give a mystery bonus word discussed that week in another subject. If students miss it but answer all the test words correctly, they make 100. If they spell the bonus word correctly and get all spelling words correct, they earn 100+. If a student misses a word but gets the bonus correct, he may replace the misspelled word with the bonus and still get 100.

Claudia Nisbett
Greenville, MS

End of the Year

Dictionary Of Students

To teach dictionary skills each year I have my class create their own "Dictionary of Students." After we discuss alphabetizing, guide words, and entry words, each student writes his name as an entry word, followed by a definition of himself. As a class, we assemble entries in alphabetical order. I add school pictures to pages and make copies for everyone in the class. Children add a cover for a special year-end keepsake.

Fran O'Rourke
Everett, WA

ELDRIDGE, SHAUN (el' drij, shon) n.: 1. has two sisters, a mom, and a dad 2. likes to play basketball 3. has goldish hair and brown eyes 4. likes to go to the beach 5. likes to play soccer 6. likes roller skating

SIMPSON, JENNIFER (simp' sən, jen i fər) n.: 1. likes to play tennis 2. likes to do art 3. has a sister and a mom and dad 4. lives in a big house 5. has a birthday in January 6. has brown eyes

Photographic Memory

When kids get restless at the end of the year, try this old memory game to calm them down. Display a collection of varied items on a table. Children file past, return to their seats, and list every item they can remember.

The Mailbox Staff

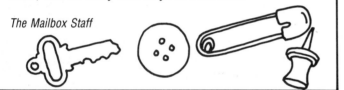

A Special Thought

Every year I take time in May to write each student in my class a personal letter. I try to remember special incidents we shared that year, to offer thanks for help around the classroom, and to praise and encourage progress. It takes quite a bit of thought on my part, but the enthusiastic response from students is well worth it! I've heard that these become treasured keepsakes.

Paula Holdren
Louisville, KY

Poem Bug

Our poem bugs encourage poetry appreciation all year with an attractive display. We learn a short poem each week that relates to a unit of study or the season. We recite together each day. On Friday, children recite individually and color in a spot on their poem bug cut-out. At the end of the year, we have a "poem party" for parents and friends. Students are proud to show all of the poems they know!

Judy W. Jones
Circleville, OH

School Flowers

Pick an official school flower with a school-wide vote. After researching a favorite flower, each child writes a campaign speech and designs an original poster. Present speeches to other classes, and have children vote for their favorite. Provide empty milk cartons, soil, and seeds for students to demonstrate how to plant and care for the school flower. Students enjoy instructing younger children in planting methods, and each child in the school has a plant to nurture during the summer.

Kathy Horsley
Marshall, IL

Headache Pillows

For an interesting end-of-the-year gift for your school office staff, how about a headache pillow? As a group project, have the children draw pictures using fabric crayons. Iron their pictures onto white fabric, then sew and stuff as pillows. Attach tags which say, "Use when headache occurs!"

Connie Connely
Catoosa, OK

June Auction

Clean out your closets and motivate your students with a June auction. Students accumulate points in class to spend at the auction. Give points for doing class chores, finishing work, doing extra work, completing centers, etc. Keep track of these points. In June, give each child a card showing his or her total points. Clean out your cupboards for old magazines, plants, games, lost-and-found items, etc. Auction these off to the highest bidder, deducting that number of points from the child's card as an item is purchased. Include a mystery item—a snakeskin in a paper bag—for added excitement.

Teresa Wilkinson
Hope, B.C. Canada

Basal Teacher's Guides

Before throwing out old reading kits or basal teacher's guides, cut out pages, glue them on cardboard, and laminate. Students can take them home and use as task cards. Their parents can use the instructions written for the teacher to work with the students at home.

Connie Connely
Catoosa, OK

No Cleanup Complaints

Looking for a way to motivate your students to clean up? Dab damp Handiwipes with peppermint or another flavoring. Place scented wipes in empty butter or Cool Whip containers at work tables. These make cleaning up a sweet-smelling treat!

Pamela Myhowich
Yakima, WA

Swap Day

On swap day, each student brings a used book, game, or toy that he or she wishes to trade. It is exciting to witness the barter.

Suzanne Edmunds
Forest, VA

End-of-the-Year Raffle

If you're running out of ideas for special rewards for students, try raffling off one large prize instead. Each time a child completes a contract, write his name on a raffle ticket and place it in a fishbowl. At the end of the year, one ticket is drawn and the prize awarded to the lucky winner. Remind students that the more tickets they earn, the greater their chances of winning.

Susan Stryczek
Buffalo, NY

Treasure Hunt

Have a treasure hunt to get your classroom cleaned that last day of school! Divide students into teams of 3 to 4 members each. Write clues on paper and hide them around the room, making several clues for each group. Each clue should direct finders to the next clue. The last clue could send students to the cafeteria for an ice cream treat!

Nancy Greeley
Hopkins, MO

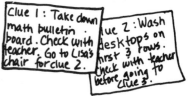

Thank-You Place Mats

Thank homeroom mothers for their help during the past year with special place mats. Trace 1″ block letters on construction paper. Each student decorates a letter with a design and signs his name. When complete, the mats are laminated and presented to the homeroom mothers to take home.

Diane Fox
Seffner, FL

Thanks For The Memories

Reserve a bulletin board at the end of the year for students to have the last word. Children may write and post notes to the teacher or to each other, describe their memories of the class year, or list things for which they want to be remembered. At the beginning of the year, use this empty board for students to write what they hope the year will bring.

Betty Vaughan
Lynchburg, VA

 ## Leftovers

If the school year ends and you're faced with restless students and a lot of half-used markers, pens, and stickers too good to throw out, try this. Put clean paper on a bulletin board and the leftover supplies in a box. When students finish their work, they may use the supplies to decorate the board. This results in a unique board, students who've worked hard, and a good end to leftover materials.

Diana West
Big Horn, WY

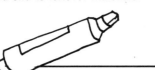

Autograph Books

Every June, I make each of my students a personal autograph book. The cover is decorated with the student's picture, followed by a personal letter from me. The rest of the book includes blank autograph pages for faculty, classmates, and other school friends. My students are always very happy with their booklets and look forward to collecting their favorite autographs.

Ruth Ann Humphrey
Columbus, OH

"Hi, Friends"

At the end of the school year, have your students write letters to welcome future class members. They can tell them what to look forward to during the upcoming school year. Have some write two letters, so you'll be sure to have enough. In the fall, address a letter to each child on your new class list and post them on a bulletin board for a personal welcome to your classroom.

Janice Dowd
Buffalo, NY

A T-shirt Thank-You

When your students want to say thanks to a student teacher or aide, how about giving a "thank-you T-shirt." Purchase a T-shirt printed with your school name, or add the name to a shirt with a permanent marker. Include the teacher's name and the school year. Then let students write their names on the shirt with markers. Makes a truly personal and unique gift.

Judy Rhodes
Broadway, VA

Year In Review

At the end of each calendar year, many magazines do a "year in review" that is great. This year my third-grade class made a beautiful mural depicting the most interesting events during the past year. We took several class periods discussing the year. When creating the mural, we were very conscious of the proper sequencing of events and had a marvelous project we could share with the whole school.

Brenda McGee
Burlington, NC